The
Typewriter
Revolution

The Typewriter Revolution

A Typist's Companion for the 21st Century

Richard Polt

THE COUNTRYMAN PRESS · WOODSTOCK, VT.

DEDICATION

To Remington Noiseless Portable Model Seven #H49561

and to the typosphere

The Countryman Press
www.countrymanpress.com

A division of W. W. Norton & Company, Inc., 500 Fifth Avenue, New York, NY 10110
www.wwnorton.com

For information about special discounts for bulk purchases, please contact W. W. Norton Special Sales at specialsales@wwnorton.com or 800-233-4830.

Printed in China

The Typewriter Revolution
978-1-58157-311-4 (pbk.)

10 9 8 7 6 5 4 3 2 1

Table of Contents

THE TYPEWRITER
MANIFESTO

We assert our right to resist the Paradigm,
to rebel against the Information Regime,
to escape the Data Stream.

We strike a blow for self-reliance,
  privacy,
    and coherence
      against
dependency,
  surveillance,
   and disintegration.

We affirm the written word
  and written thought
      against
multimedia,
  multitasking,
   and the meme.

We choose the real over representation,
the physical over the digital,
the durable over the unsustainable,
the self-sufficient over the efficient.

THE REVOLUTION WILL BE TYPEWRITTEN

Introduction

In a high school English class in Arizona, a student takes his favorite Royal down from the shelf and gets to work.

A young woman on the Venice Beach boardwalk types impromptu short stories for strangers on her Smith-Corona.

At a digital detox party in San Francisco, an Olympia helps victims of electronic overdose remember the material world.

An artist in Brooklyn keeps typing until a balloon carries his page off into the sky.

From Australia to Estonia, people gather for public type-ins.

The typewriter revolution is clicking.

The typewriter has crawled back from its near-death experience, thanks to the people who use and love this machine. Who are these twenty-first-century typists? They come from all ages and groups; they speak different languages and practice many professions. But something ties them together: the love of typewriters and the will to swim against the tide. Call them the typewriter insurgency—the vanguard of the typewritten revolution.

Billimarie Robinson

In the age of instant global information, using a typewriter is an act of rebellion. Against what? In the name of what? Ultimately, that's for you to type—the insurgency has no leader and no dogma. A typewriter has endless possibilities, like language itself. You might type a brainstorm, a journal, a letter, a story, a poem, a travelogue, a zine—or use your machine to make pictures or music.

But whatever we create on our typewriters, whenever we turn to them, we're choosing something that violates the digital Paradigm—something durable, intimate, focused, and self-sufficient. When our typescripts intersect with the digital world, they aren't defined by it. We rebel against the totalitarianism of the Information Regime.

This book explores the ramifications of this rebellion.

For one, consider the question of efficiency. If you typewrite in public, you're going to get some curious questions, some reminiscences, and perhaps some puzzlement from those who won't understand why you'd want to do something so *inefficiently.* It's a fair question, and it makes you realize that typewriters today don't mean what they meant before the personal computer came along.

Typewriters used to be part of a system of efficiency. When they were first developed, they were a tool for speed and standardization. They made writing look uniform, and they churned out documents and carbon copies. "To Save Time is to Lengthen Life," proclaimed the Remington Typewriter Company. Typewriters served progress, clacking away in government and commercial institutions. The typical typist was no creative writer, but a secretary skilled at transcribing the words dictated by her boss. Typewriter inventors were techies who hoped to make a mint from the march of civilization. If they were around today, they sure wouldn't be sitting at a typewriter—they'd be developing apps.

Now, the typewriter is out of the system. True, most big offices still keep an electric typewriter sitting in some corner; once in a while it gets trotted out to fill out a form, type a label, or address an envelope. But for most purposes, in an increasingly paperless environment, computers are more efficient: They let you edit and share your writing far more easily, and of course they can do much more than write. Typewriters have been left in the dust.

So what's going on in that dust? The dust is a place where, dismissed from the realm of the efficient, machines can seek new identities. It's a place where the typewriter can take a rest, catch its breath, and find a way to be itself—not just a means to an end, but a thing with its own individuality, integrity, and beauty. It's a place where we can try doing things in a new way, a place for thinking in terms other than efficiency. The dust may be fertile soil.

But why turn our backs on efficiency?

Consider where its cult has gotten us. All our efficient devices have freed up a lot of time—supposedly. But we use up that extra time doing more of the same. Matt Chojnacki, who sells and fixes typewriters in Toronto, puts it simply: "The problem is that every time we save time, we find other stuff to muddle into, and we end up spending less time on stuff that's more important."

We make things so efficiently that they're all disposable; none of them endure, none can belong to us for long before they end up on the scrap heap.

We process information so efficiently that we don't dwell on thoughts and words anymore—we flit incoherently from one set of distractions to the next.

We've exploited the earth so efficiently that it's baking in our fumes.

For a planet desperate for conservation, for a mind starved for concentration, inefficiency starts to look like nourishment and life. Maybe to save time is not to lengthen life, after all. Maybe the more efficiently you speed through life, the quicker you reach your death.

Everyone who has ever seen a
typewriter displayed for
sale in a thrift store will
have observed small
children happily
thumping away at the
keyboard. They do
not thump at
apparatus whose
keybuttons produce
no mechanical
effect; nor will they
later, as adults, think of
such dead keybutton boards as being in any important way
different from disposable cigarette lighters. The latter
will always be empty artifacts, never interesting play-
things; certainly not friends--only means to an end.

. . . [It is] very easy for me to imagine people in the
future who have no fond connection whatsoever with the
past. After all, everything is being driven by the same
forces--forces unlike anything seen in history, such that
there is only cold laughter directed at anything built or
created more than two days ago. This has profound potential consequences for a large number of human spheres, but
some of the most serious are bound to be those relating
to reading, publishing, spelling, written language, and
that terrible word that sums up and reduces so much that
is wonderful to such a freeze-dried, sterile concept:
"information."

--Fred Woodworth

It's not efficient to cook a meal from scratch.

It's not efficient to ride a bike down a country path.

It's not efficient to learn an instrument instead of downloading a song, or to sketch a landscape instead of pointing your smartphone at it.

Why do we do inefficient things? Because sometimes we don't want life to be seamless—we want to feel resistance, we want to take our time, we want to savor the experience. When what you're doing isn't just a means to an end, you're in no hurry to get it done.

For the typewriter revolution, writing is one of those intrinsically valuable experiences.

Sure, sometimes we still want efficiency, and most of us insurgents are ready to do things the quick way when we need to. Most of us are willing to take advantage of computers, and we recognize the potential that they've unlocked. The enemy isn't computers themselves; it's an all-embracing, exclusive computing mentality. The Paradigm denounces and mocks any way of doing things that takes more time and focus. It won't tolerate your concentrating on a single task, but wants to grab your attention and shift it to the next development, the next message, the next possibility. It assumes that better means faster. By those standards, a typewriter is nothing but a very bad computer.

But a typewriter isn't a bad computer. Computers can do countless things typewriters can't. But a typewriter still has a computer beat when you want a self-contained, secure, lasting, physical writing machine. Turn to a typewriter and you'll find yourself focusing on writing—the reason the machine exists. You'll find the impatience and anxiety of your computing mind ebbing away. You'll gradually stop wanting to be interrupted. You'll concentrate on the page.

I expect your next question is: What did I use to write this book?

A MacBook, for the most part. Yes, a computer is the right tool for assembling a complex text whose elements need frequent reshuffling and rewriting, with plenty of online research and communication. But my most important ideas here were first developed on typewriters, and come from my experience of typewriting. These two kinds of writing, which are also two kinds of thinking, can find harmony, each playing its appropriate role in your life.

Comrades Unite!
The Glorious
Revolution
Will Be
Typewritten!

Join The
Revolution
@
Typosphere
dot net

The insurgency doesn't ask us to
smash our digital devices. Instead,
it helps us to keep them in perspective and invites us to question our
assumptions about progress.
It may seem like the
only way to look to the
future is to generate
and gobble up brand
new information, joining
in the chaos of updates,
posts, and tweets. But most
of that noise is an empty echo,
and the busiest participants are
just running in place. No, it's in the
quiet places and idle moments that the
seeds of something truly new are being
planted. When we typists use our "things of the past," we're opening up
a space where we can take our time and make messages that will last.
When we write our stories by typewriter, we're typing the future.

My own typewriter story begins when, as a boy in the sixties and seventies, I became fascinated by the Smith-Corona electric that my father
used to type his academic papers, and the large-type Woodstock that my
grandparents bought in the Depression and my mother now used to prepare
mimeographed handouts for her students. There was an irresistible magic
in these machines, something like the allure of a piano. When I took typing
lessons in junior high, my father bought me my own machine at a garage
sale: a Remington Noiseless Model Seven, a sleek and shiny Deco sculpture
that I prized as I used it into high school, college, and graduate school.

The eighties were ending by the time I adopted a personal computer:
a Macintosh SE with a massive built-in twenty-megabyte hard disk. The
Remington went into the closet and I lugged the Mac with me to Europe and
Asia, eventually writing a dissertation with it on the philosophy of Martin

Heidegger. Not for one moment do I regret having missed the opportunity to write hundreds of picky footnotes on a typewriter!

In 1993 I sent my first e-mail, using a terminal at Xavier University, and I embraced the Internet along with so many others in that decade. But in 1994 my dormant curiosity about typewriters was jolted awake by Paul Lippman's *American Typewriters: A Collector's Encyclopedia.* From the moment I set eyes on the New Model Crandall on this book's cover—a Victorian machine with a curved two-row keyboard, inlaid with mother-of-pearl, which types with a spinning cylinder—I became a passionate seeker of antique typewriters. In 1995 I started The Classic Typewriter Page, a website meant to connect me to like-minded eccentrics around the world. It worked. The site has garnered well over a million hits, and every day it brings me into conversation with other collectors, loyal typewriter users, or people who've found an old machine in the attic.

At first, my passion focused on the rare and bizarre inventions of the nineteenth century, which are fascinating but usually sit on the shelf instead of being used. Then I learned more about twentieth-century typewriters, especially the midcentury portables that Cleveland collector Will Davis explored in depth on his website. As I accumulated these fine, functional writing machines, I found myself wanting to use them. When I took the opportunity to do so—by typing up comments about my students' philosophy papers or drafting a section of a book—it was a refreshing experience, a break from the lures of e-mail and eBay. Meanwhile, I continued to build up a sizeable collection (now pushing three hundred machines), and in 2006 I got the opportunity to edit *ETCetera*, the magazine of the Early Typewriter Collectors' Association.

I'd been hearing for a while about people who were "typecasting" by uploading images of typed pages to their blogs. In 2010 I followed the impulse to start my own typecast blog. I found that the "typosphere" was a welcoming place, where we bloggers enjoyed using our beloved machines and sharing news about them. As I accumulated a stack of typewritten reflections, transmitted worldwide from my favorite typewriters, I came full circle to the magic experiences of typing in my childhood, now enriched with far greater knowledge. With the encouragement of the typosphere and a group called the Typewriter Brigade, I also managed to fulfill a longtime fantasy: I met the challenge of National Novel Writing Month by eking out a fifty-thousand-word story in thirty days. I did it on typewriters, of course— including my good old Remington Noiseless—and felt that my fetish had finally achieved its purpose. Predictably enough, the novel was also *about* typewriters: My hero escapes from his modern life, moves to a small town, and starts writing by typewriter, eventually discovering a repair shop, an old inventor, and a network of typing individualists.

Experiences like this convinced me that typewriting had something to offer the twenty-first century. We typospherians also realized, to our delight and amazement, that we were part of a broader cultural movement that was embracing typewriters. And as the bad news about our digital obsessions accumulated—including their corrosive effects on our privacy, sanity, and relationships—typewriting felt increasingly like an act of resistance. In a moment of defiance, I typed up The Typewriter Manifesto—a document that quickly made the rounds of the typosphere and got retyped, adapted, posted online and on paper, and translated into languages from Serbian to Swedish.

It's in the spirit of that manifesto that I conceived of this book. *The Typewriter Revolution* defiantly resists technological conformity, the totalitarian information-processing world view, and the destructive assumption that all human activity should be judged by the test of efficiency. These threats are real, and a typewriter is a weapon against them.

But using a typewriter isn't just an act of resistance—it's also fun. If the fun disappears, the insurgency will die. Our most successful agents know how to preserve the enjoyment of typing and keep a sense of humor about what they do. You can best spread the rebellion by typing with imagination and pleasure.

This book is meant to help make that kind of typing possible. It wants to be a portable companion, a lasting inspiration, a durable friend—much like your typewriter. Tuck it into your typewriter case, your coat pocket, or your glove compartment. Check it when you find a typewriter for sale or when you're dreaming up what to type. Use it as a field guide to typewriting in the twenty-first century—and a field manual for a combatant in the revolution.

If you have any doubts that typewriters are alive, Chapter One should open your eyes and provide inspiration. It presents some of the most visible and exciting ways in which type-writers are playing a fresh role in culture and counterculture today. Through type-ins and type-outs, street poetry, digital detox, and other initiatives, people around the world are exploring the potential of writing machines. But how did typewriters get here? What did they once mean? Chapter Two glances back at the lively history of typewriting in the nineteenth and twentieth centuries and provides some advice for those interested in starting a collection of historic typewriters.

Chapter Three is a buyer's guide to finding the right typewriter to join the insurgency. It gives you a rundown of the most popular standards, portables, ultraportables, and electrics, as well as some offbeat choices. Here's everything you need to know about typeface, pitch, keyboards, and other technical features as you choose your machine.

Once you have a typewriter, you'll want to know its ins and outs and understand how to keep it running. In Chapter Four, you'll get to "learn it as a brother." Essential tools, techniques, and tricks will help you understand and care for this machine that's going to be part of your life for decades.

So what do people write on typewriters today? Why? How? Chapter Five delves into some of the infinite potential of a writing machine. You'll explore typewriting in many genres and places, for many audiences and purposes.

In Chapter Six you'll enter the typosphere: a place in the digital world, but not of it—a zone between the typewriter and the computer. Here you'll learn about typewritten blogs, typewriters that can communicate with computers, and other ways in which text and ideas can be exchanged between the digital and typewritten worlds.

A typewriter is not just a way to make text, but a fascinating object in itself. One way to bring out the fascination is to modify and enhance your machine. Chapter Seven looks at contemporary techniques and examples of hot rod typewriters.

Just as there's no limit to what typewriters can write about, there's no end to the ways they can be incorporated into other pursuits. In Chapter Eight you'll discover some cultural crossroads where typewriters are meeting everything from music to film, bikes to tattoos.

Finally, Chapter Nine looks forward to the typewritten future. The typewriter revolution is not nostalgic; it points a way forward, creating a space for concentration and self-reliance in the information age. This final chapter imagines some possibilities for typewriters and typewriting in years to come.

Between chapters, I expand on the Typewriter Manifesto and look more closely at the perils of the all-digital mindset in order to understand why our time has come.

Just as a typewriter isn't a bad computer, a book isn't a bad website. That's why I won't be littering it with Web addresses, which may soon be obsolete; you already know how to find things online when you need to. (I do give my online sources due credit in the "Sources" section.) This book isn't a substitute for the Internet. No, it's a book to crack open for the hundredth time and review the varieties of Olympia portables by the light of the sunset over the lake as you and your typewriter rest on the porch of the cabin; to consult when you need to install a new ribbon or improve your alignment; to get inspiration when you're organizing a type-in in your hometown; to remember that there are others like you when you've pulled to the side of the road and grabbed your Skyriter to get your thoughts down on paper; or to show prospective recruits some of the potential of the insurgency.

Enjoy this book, enjoy your typing, and remember:

The revolution will be typewritten!

1. The Insurgency

On December 18, 2010, a band of renegades assembled at Bridgewater's Pub in Philadelphia. Their purpose: to commit public acts of typewriting.

Mike McGettigan, typewriter fan and bike shop owner, came up with the idea.

> Casting an eye over the cast-iron casings of the classic typers scattered around my home, I wondered—who else was doing the same? I thought how grim the usual Laptopistan café scene is, where the brightest bulb in the room is the Apple logo, and considered what a gang of typewriters would sound like instead of that chitinous clicking completely lacking in bells. A lovely pub manager agreed to share that hallucination, and presto—a Type-IN.

The concept was a typewriter jam session, a meeting of like-minded souls who weren't afraid to advertise their avocation. McGettigan contacted record stores, English programs, stationers, coffee shops, and the media. His press release claimed that "typewriters are following vinyl records out of the grave that digitalization is digging for everything analog." And the type-in helped to make it so: The event was a success, featuring a typing contest, some typewriter swapping, and lager-lubricated camaraderie.

Word of the Philadelphia type-in spread fast through the typosphere—the network of mechanographophile bloggers. We realized that our love for these antiquated machines didn't have to be pursued in solitude anymore, or shared through digital screens. Type-ins started happening in Phoenix, Tacoma, and Los Angeles. They jumped national borders and sprouted up in Switzerland, Australia, Holland, and Estonia.

When I organized a typewriter collectors' meeting in Cincinnati the next summer, it was natural to include a type-in at a local coffee shop. We showed up with our machines in tow and set up some for the public, including a big Smith-Corona that I'd spray-painted Day-Glo pink. Repairman and *Typewriter Exchange* editor Mike Brown dispensed technical tips as I took assiduous notes on my Groma Kolibri.

While Mike McGettigan coined the word independently, the term "type-in" was first used in a 1967 Smith-Corona ad that shows a teen girl and boy sitting back to back on typewriter cases, with electric Smith-Coronas on their laps. "It's the in thing with teenagers who want to swing college. Not the sit-in. Or the be-in. The type-in. . . . it's the natural choice of today's bright, young studyboppers."

Curious customers sat down gingerly at the public typewriters and gave them a spin, using the custom stationery I'd created for the event. Put a computer in front of people and they'll probably gravitate to their usual sources of messages, updates, and entertainment. Put a typewriter in front of people and they'll want to write from within. The typewriter doesn't push "content" at them; it draws words from them.

Afterwards, I posted photos and typescripts on my blog, so that typospherians around the world could peek in. Since then, I've enjoyed several type-ins, including gatherings at London pubs and a big event at California Typewriter, a repair shop in Berkeley.

So what do you do at a type-in? Get to know each other, talk about anything and everything (including the machines, naturally), type reports to share with the typosphere, have a speed contest, do a round-robin storytelling exercise, try out each other's machines, hoist a pint, laugh. You might want to bring some stationery, envelopes, stamps, and copies of a text to be copied in the speed contest.

The type-in is still an evolving concept—make it up as you go along. But its essential element is publicness. By typing together outside your homes, you say: *We're typists, we're here, and we're not afraid.* Jennifer Rich, co-owner of Oblation Papers & Press in Portland, Oregon, held her first type-in in June, 2013. "We support public typing," she says, and she rejects any idea that the typewriter is a weaker medium: "It's really a powerful machine you can put in the hands of anyone who loves words and correspondence."

That's the bold, unapologetic spirit of the typewriter revolution. This chapter introduces some of the events and personalities that are driving the movement.

THE NEW TYPISTS

Tom Furrier took the movement to the streets; in Arlington, Massachusetts, he organized the first type-*out*. Typists gathered on the sidewalk, sharing the clatter of typebars and ringing of bells with the world.

Furrier has more of a stake in this development than most of us do: He is a professional typewriter repairman. There are more of them than you'd think, and many are being rewarded for holding on this long to their craft. People are walking through the doors of their inky, oily shops and asking: Can you bring this typewriter back to life? Furrier has his hands happily full.

Bino Gan, who retired at the end of 2013, didn't close Typewriters 'n' Things, in Greenwich Village, for lack of customers. In his final months he reported, "Now everybody is looking for manuals, and I don't have any. I get calls from people asking me all day if I have them to sell, or do I fix them, or do I still have ribbons."

As the long-time typewriter technicians retire, some new shops are stepping in to fill the gap. On London's funky Sclater Street, a shop called Type hangs Underwoods over its front door. Richard Clark reports that his customers include screenwriters, poets, technophobes, students, illustrators, collectors, and "people who have inherited machines." He compares his customers to photographers who are fascinated with film, or musicians who want to "savour the analogue richness as opposed to digital copies." Typewriters, he says, combine romance with mechanical reproduction.

In Toronto, Jamie and Matt Chojnacki are the twentysomethings behind Old Fort Typewriter. Matt, who's mechanically minded, taught himself typewriter repair by disassembling an Underwood into its thousands of parts. Jamie grew up with eccentric parents who typed everything on an ancient Royal. Now she manages Old Fort's social media and also works as a florist. She's found plenty of crossover business: Brides who want flowers also want to send typewritten wedding invitations, and they want typewriters that complement the bridal party to serve as guest books.

The Chojnackis have found a small but real market of Torontonians who want to rent or buy typewriters, who need them fixed, and who love to use and talk about them. Their customers value the physical connection to their machines, the delight of hearing the bell and returning the carriage, and the way the typewriters bring out self-expression.

Jamie and Matt believe this is not just a flash in the pan. The great typewriters are "ridiculously well made," their appeal is perennial, and there's plenty of room for growth, as people increasingly appreciate typewriters not only as writing machines but as "functional art" with "both emotive and rational qualities." When they started the business, says Jamie, "We never thought anybody would come. But—wow—we have a backlog." It's "a testament to just how aesthetic and romantic typewriters are, how they are a prominent fixture in modern times, and how they won't be going away any time soon."

Naturally, some of the patrons of typewriter shops are seniors who never embraced computers, or middle-aged people feeling nostalgic for the experiences of their youth. But what about people under thirty, who may never have had experience with typewriters at all? They've grown up in a world where text is malleable and electric, where it can be duplicated and transmitted almost instantly, along with every variety of sight and sound. Could these young people also be interested in typewriters?

The answer is yes. In fact, the younger generations are major drivers of the typewriter renaissance. The customers walking into Tom Furrier's shop are often in their teens or twenties. They may be looking for their first typewriter; they may be asking for medical assistance for a machine they found in Grandma's attic or received as a gift from parents or a boyfriend or girlfriend. Entering a typewriter shop is an almost religious act for them. Furrier says, "They are fascinated by the sensory feedback they get. The feel, the sound, seeing the printed image, immediately amazes them. The number one reason younger people tell me they like typewriters is that they can type with no distractions. No Internet or e-mail or googling to distract them. They're just typing, creating."

Maybe these young people aren't buying into the digital world precisely because they grew up surrounded by that world. Greg Fudacz, who sells refurbished typewriters under the name The Antikey Chop, puts it this way: "Every generation tends to fight the establishment, and the establishment right now is social media and the Internet. Typewriters are the exact opposite."

That's why you'll find some teenagers at the forefront of the insurgency. In Michigan, Jeff Hendrie became the talk of his high school by using typewriters for every assignment, and even bringing his favorites to school. His teachers were impressed, but critics (such as his mom) complained: "They make too much noise"; "They're not professional"; "They're too dirty"; "They're out of date"; "It's not acceptable to use them anymore." Some of his peers also gave him a hard time. But Jeff was unfazed:

> Hey, if they don't like me using typewriters, and if they want
> to make fun of me, or discourage me from using them, or

complain about me being so old-fashioned, then too bad. It's either accept me for who I am or hit the road. I *will* use my typewriters as they were meant to be used, and I will not give up on them, ever. Computers, they give up easily, but my 1914 Woodstock, and almost all other typewriters, they all give up *only* when their owners give up on themselves, or on them. We *are* the typewriter, and the typewriter is *us*.

Jeff sums up the meaning of typewriters in four words: "passion, care, dedication, individualism."

FROM STEAMPUNKS TO BURNING MEN

One subculture that has rediscovered typewriters is the steampunk community. With its origins in alt-history fiction of the 1980s and '90s, steampunk envisions a world of Victorian technology taken to extremes, with dirigible battles and steam-powered computers. Sometimes steampunk takes the desultory form of gluing a few gears onto your topcoat or wearing goggles, but the more dedicated steampunks have created elaborate, working machines that hybridize old and new.

That's where typewriters come in. Steampunks rarely adopt them unaltered, instead incorporating elements of typewriters or entire machines into computing contraptions. We'll take a closer look at some of these constructions in Chapter Six; for now, let's just say that they can be beautiful and fantastic. Of course, the steampunk aesthetic can be a target for

Steve La Riccia, *Wozniak's Conundrum*

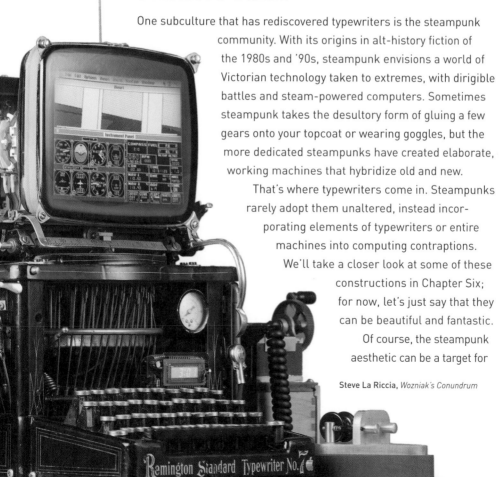

parody, as in this scene from a 2012 episode of *2 Broke Girls* where Max the waitress approaches a mustachioed, behatted individual writing on a big, black Royal No. 10:

Max: Wow! Bummer, dude. You have a time machine and somehow it got programmed to this crap diner?

Steampunk Guy: I must admit, I am quite taken with steampunk.

Max: Oh, steampunk! Right, I remember that trend. It happened for, like, ten seconds back in 2000-and-are-you-kidding-me? Dude, seriously, you're sitting in a public place tap-tap-tapping on an oldie typewriter? What are you? In The League of Extraordinarily Pretentious Gentlemen?

Steampunk Guy: Aren't you being a little aggressive?

Max: Yup. That's how people are here in the present where we live. But don't get me wrong, I'd like to go back in time, too. Maybe stop 9/11 or that creep who had sex on my shoe, but I can't.

Steampunk Guy: Present? Where's that uniform from? Like, 1998?

Max: Oh, stop, or I'm gonna have to shoot you with a Smith & Wesson I'm currently packing in my bloomers.

Well, at least Steampunk Guy attempted a retort.

Steampunk surely can be silly—but why not indulge in some imaginative fun? And with its appreciation of the mechanical, its pursuit of the art of tinkering, steampunk is part of a broader hunger for technology that we can understand and control.

One vital manifestation of that trend is the maker movement. The maker ethos is one of sharing and innovation: open-source plans, collaboration, borrowing, transformation. This approach has struck a chord. Maker Faires attract tens of thousands of visitors. In over a thousand hackerspaces and makerspaces around the planet, makers socialize as they create new objects. They emphasize generous interactions among people inhabiting the same physical space. This certainly isn't a rejection of the digital—makers eagerly work with cheap circuit boards and 3D printers to create computer-guided gadgets. What the movement rejects is the passive incomprehension in our everyday relation to high technology; makers take charge, learn by doing, and use their imagination.

Mark Hatch, who runs a chain of "fabrication workspaces" open to the public, articulates the spirit of the movement as follows:

> Making is fundamental to what it means to be human. . . . There is something unique about making physical things. These things are like little pieces of us and seem to embody portions of our souls. . . . You cannot make and not share. . . . There are few things more selfless and satisfying than giving away something you have made.

Dutch maker "Spider," who has organized a type-in at her hackerspace, adds that old machines are the past's gift to the tinkering present:

> Looking back to old technologies also makes you learn about the new ones. Repairing old machines, whether these are typewriters, mainframes, or telexes, really adds some spice! You can see every bit move, and follow the movement from the key you press until the type hits the paper. It's about the history of mechanics and society at the same time.

Jack Zylkin, of Philadelphia's Hive76 makerspace, notes that makers "practically refuse to throw anything away on the grounds that it could be useful for some fanciful project." He explains:

> The maker movement is about actively owning technology, instead of passively consuming it. Owning technology means having creative control over it, not only the electronics, hardware, and software, but the role it plays in your life. So, a common theme in the maker culture is to take some mass-produced technology and to find totally unexpected and individualized uses for it. Makers want the ability to pull

things apart and put them back together in new ways the original manufacturer never anticipated. If these new uses stop a product from ending up in a landfill, all the better.

Arthur C. Clarke once said that "Any sufficiently advanced technology is indistinguishable from magic." I think we have already reached the point where most gadgets are so high-tech that the average person feels helpless to understand them, let alone influence how they work or even repair them if they break. I love typewriters because, even though they are remarkably complex pieces of technology, it is still possible to look underneath them and appreciate the muggle magic of all the springs, levers, gears, and linkages that make them work. They are a tinkerer's dream. By contrast, looking inside an iPhone (if you are even able to open it) will only reveal a green piece of plastic, hosting a flea circus of generic-looking electronic components that reveal nothing about how the device actually works.

Like the slow-foods movement and the self-publishing movement, the maker movement tries to break down the perceived barrier between who makes a product and who uses it. It sets out to debunk the perception that high technology can only be created and disseminated by big specialized companies, like fire from Mt. Olympus, and bring the creation of technology back to the people who use it.

It's in that spirit that Zylkin invented the USB Typewriter—a way to hook up a real manual typewriter to a computing device, without harming either one. We'll look closely at his invention in Chapter Six.

Maker Dwayne Fuhlhage also thinks "the connection between typewriter culture and maker culture is logical":

> Unless one is in the rare situation of buying a restored and fully functional typewriter, a fair amount of learning is involved. Even changing out a ribbon is an entirely new experience for most.

The USB Typewriter is a great example of creativity and synergy. The project is empowered by cheap, open-source controllers like Arduino or one of the clones. These would not exist if not for collectives. While the USB Typewriter is the creation of one person, how much did being around other makers contribute to putting all the bits together?

Makers generally share a lust for knowledge; many enjoy deconstructing and reconstructing physical objects for the sake of the experience. The results may be worthless bits of junk, but practice and web-enabled sharing lead to useful things like typewriter parts and open-source robotic hands. Where others see discarded junk, makers see raw material.

**Carol Wax,
Writer's Blocks**

While makers enjoy blending digital and mechanical technology, others prefer to eschew computers for the sake of developing greater craft and self-reliance. They don't see this as nostalgia, but as a sustainable path forward that respects the earth and finds appropriate ways to produce things.

For instance, there's young San Francisco typewriter user Anthony Rocco, a self-described "analog guy in a digital world":

> One day I wish I could have a farm, a plot of land. I would love to have the time and ability to produce things. There's an importance to how things are created. Twenty-first-century fashion—clothing, food, whatever is in vogue—has to do with how it's made. Using an analog machine from the twentieth century or the nineteenth, or even further back, plays into that underlying commentary on how it's made. This is the most important artistic statement you can make in the twenty-first century.

Or there's author-farmer Wendell Berry, who published a contrarian essay back in 1987 titled "Why I Am Not Going to Buy a Computer":

> My wife types my work on a Royal standard typewriter bought new in 1956 and as good now as it was then. . . . I would hate to think that my work as a writer could not be done without a direct dependence on strip-mined coal. . . . To make myself as plain as I can, I should give my standards for technological innovation in my own work. They are as follows:
>
> 1. The new tool should be cheaper than the one it replaces.
> 2. It should be at least as small in scale as the one it replaces.
> 3. It should do work that is clearly and demonstrably better than the one it replaces.
> 4. It should use less energy than the one it replaces.
> 5. If possible, it should use some form of solar energy, such as that of the body.
> 6. It should be repairable by a person of ordinary intelligence, provided that he or she has the necessary tools.
> 7. It should be purchasable and repairable as near to home as possible.
> 8. It should come from a small, privately owned shop or store that will take it back for maintenance and repair.
> 9. It should not replace or disrupt anything good that already exists, and this includes family and community relationships.

Berry claims that using a computer to replace a typewriter would be wrong on all of these counts. Actually, by most of the Berry Rules, a typewriter makes a great replacement for a computer.

Let's face it: Don't typewriters kill trees? Doesn't going digital mean going green? Think of the classic image of the frustrated typist surrounded by balls of wadded-up paper. Planet-unfriendly, right?

First of all, I don't recommend ripping every imperfect text out of your typewriter and starting with a fresh sheet. Accepting imperfection and building on it is more in the spirit of the insurgency.

But where do you get your paper? It's a renewable resource and can be produced responsibly. But if you don't want to buy new paper, look no further than the recycle bin at work. The typical twenty-first-century "paperless office" actually generates reams of unnecessary printed material every day. Use the back of these documents. You can also find old paper in thrift stores; I've picked up five hundred sheets for ninety-nine cents.

If you mail a letter, it's true that its delivery will contribute carbon to the atmosphere, but a single letter makes only a microscopic difference.

A manual typewriter runs on your own muscle power, but your computer is shockingly thirsty for energy, as are the gigantic server farms

that satisfy our never-ending demands for information. Ask yourself: How is that electricity generated?

The pollution caused by the manufacture of your typewriter happened long ago, and your machine can last for decades. Not your digital devices; they'll be obsolete soon. The often unhealthy factories where they're made have to keep going, and the junk--well, consider this report:

> In far-flung, mostly impoverished places . . . children pile e-waste into giant mountains and burn it so they can extract the metals--copper wires, gold and silver threads--inside, which they sell to recycling merchants for only a few dollars. In India, young boys smash computer batteries with mallets to recover cadmium, toxic flecks of which cover their hands and feet as they work. Women spend their days bent over baths of hot lead, "cooking" circuit boards so they can remove slivers of gold inside.

Now who's the killer?

Buddhist and environmental activist Danny Fisher would agree:

> As non-electric devices, many of them built to last for far longer than a human lifespan or two, manual typewriters are "green machines," no doubt about it, and that's all the more reason to love them and consider being part of their renaissance. . . . Computers, tablets, smartphones . . . are

not innocuous technology; quite the contrary, in fact—their manufacture and use exact a heavy toll on the environment and on human beings . . . Typing away on the [Olympia] SM3 instead of staring at a busy, glowing, energy-guzzling computer screen sure feels like a practice whose time has come.

In an attempt to develop local, responsible alternatives to the global production system, Marcin Jakubowski's "Factor e Farm" in rural Missouri embodies a mix of self-reliance and collaboration, blending the maker movement's open-source ethos with a Berry-like earnestness: "We see small, independent, land-based economies as means to transform societies, address pressing world issues, and evolve to freedom." Part of the project is the "Global Village Construction Set." The idea is that the residents of every Jakubowskian village ought to be able to construct "the fifty different industrial machines that it takes to build a small, sustainable civilization with modern comforts."

No, the fifty don't include a typewriter—inexplicably. But the survivalist or "prepper" mood of the project is also shared by some typewriter insurgents who like the fact that their Remingtons have no need of the power grid, industry, or the tawdry aftermarket of e-waste. Typewriters are ideal for long-term, sustainable "permaculture"—or for the aftermath of culture. No wonder that the TV series *Revolution*, about the effects of the end of electric power on Earth, used a close-up of a typewriter in its marketing. As the title of Annalese Stradivarius's typewritten blog puts it, a typewriter is truly "A Machine for the End of the World."

While Factor e Farm buys into the ideal of the logical, useful, and efficient—one of the project's goals is to design a tractor that a small team can assemble in a day—there are people who are questioning this very ideal. They celebrate the gratuitous and the bizarre.

The prime example is Burning Man, the yearly art festival in the remote Nevada desert. Inheriting some of the spirit of the hippies and older American countercultural movements, Burning Man creates a bubble of weirdness within "the default world" of rational utility. It's not just a neo-Woodstockian free-for-all, but an experiment in creating a special place and time that operates under a different economy—an economy of the gift, where the ethos is to be generous and pay it forward. Burners devote themselves to the gloriously useless. Not unlike makers, they like to play and tinker for the sheer pleasure of seeing what will happen.

What better place for typewriters?

Stefano Corazza is a bioengineer, computer scientist, paraglider, and artist who likes typing personal letters. At the 2009 Burning Man, he set up a piece he called *Time Love Memory*. Inspired by the film *Naked Lunch*, he created a beetle-like carapace for a Royal portable, which he attached to a high table and accentuated with neon. The rest was up to the Burners, because "placing a typewriter in the middle of the desert unleashes a state of complete expressive freedom."

Visitors expressed themselves in a note to a dead grandfather from Sitka, the thought that "Time is sometimes sticky," affirmations ("I will not be silent and unseen / I am a person and I have a voice"), laments ("my boyfriend doesn! lovemezz"), and the uncategorizable ("I was born on the back of the man on the moon").

For Corazza, Burning Man is "the place where ideas outside reality can still take form." His typewriter served as a conduit for those possibilities, the portal through which they invaded the default world.

THE POWER OF THE LETTER

The rebellion against the logic of efficiency is also evident in the "slow movement," an idea that has been building (slowly, of course) since a protest against the opening of a McDonald's in Rome in 1986 started the "slow food movement," which celebrates locally sourced foods prepared with care. Although you can buy a fine ready-made dinner, some choose to make it from scratch—even to the point of hunting and gathering. The point is to develop a more mindful, appreciative participation in the food process, so that cooking and eating aren't just means to an end (energy or satisfaction), but activities to be cultivated and savored.

Today, people are exploring "slow" ways to create art and design, to run a business, to travel, and to raise children. Why not slow communication? John Freeman writes:

> We are here for a short time on this planet, and reacting to demands on our time by simply speeding up has canceled out many of the benefits of the Internet, which is one of the most fabulous technological inventions ever conceived. We are connected, yes, but we were before, only by gossamer threads that worked more slowly. Slow communication will preserve these threads and our ability to sensibly choose to use faster modes when necessary. It will also preserve our sanity, our families, our relationships, and our ability to find happiness in a world where, in spite of the Internet, saying what we mean is as hard as it ever was.

Stefano Corazza,
Time Love Memory

> Relying on screens, on typing at high speed, we have constructed an environment in which it is more difficult than ever to get a sense of context. . . . We comment glibly rather than engage; there just isn't time. . . . We check in with friends in short text messages about inane topics rather than sit down for a proper chat or withdraw to write a letter that can impart thoughts and emotions and give us a sense of our tangible selves in our handwriting, in our choice of stamp, that even the most elegantly composed e-mail will lack.

We need hardly add that choosing a typewriter, in this day and age, also sends a thoughtful and personal message.

The epitome of slow communication is the letter—old-fashioned snail mail that takes days to arrive in a physical mailbox. You might be surprised by the power of this humble medium.

That power is being explored by Universal Babel Service, an organization that defiantly declares: "Outdated, hard to transport and heavy, the typewriter is the perfect mascot of slow communication. That's why we love them so much."

The service is the brainchild of Arthur Grau, a self-described "mail geek" who grew up writing letters and simply didn't stop when others migrated to e-mail. Universal Babel Service began as "a gift project" that Grau and his friends contributed to Burning Man.

From Universal Babel Service's
Slow Communication Movement Manifesto

With this manifesto we intend to:

*Meet in person whenever possible and make eye contact during verbal interactions.

*Take a deep breath before responding to synchronous verbal messages.

*Allow ourselves the freedom to respond to asynchronous messages in any timeframe comfortable to our own preference.

*Allow ourselves the necessary time and comfort to draft, re-draft, think and rethink any communication before sending.

*Commit to take short-term or long-term breaks from any and all rapid communication as we see fit to maintain balance and integrity.

The gift economy is just great: We can share, we can be with each other! Part of the gift mentality is that you want to bring something to offer. What do I love to do that I can offer people? They already had a post office, so we thought: we'll type letters for people. It would be fun to hear people's stories, to put people into that state of having to dictate a letter to a typist, who then takes care of the magical act of putting words on paper and sending it out.

The idea was a success. By their third visit to Nevada, the Babelers came with eight typewriters in tow, which were put to work writing letters in the camp. Some burners chose the dictation method, others borrowed machines. Some wrote letters to themselves in the future. As is the routine at Burning Man, nothing was routine.

Grau and others have carried Universal Babel Service over into "the default world" at events such as art festivals, street fairs, and flea markets. The service is always free, including the assortment of old stamps that go on

the envelope. By now, Grau has typed some four hundred letters for strangers. At first, people may be shy. "Getting people to fess up, or say out loud,
is kind of cool. It breaks down a social barrier when they tell you what they
want to say to their loved one." The activity is more deliberate than the typical
casual text: "They sit and think about it." The mail medium encourages care
and decisiveness: "Once it's sent, then that's it, it's captured, it's recorded."

As for the recipients of the letters: "When I visit people I've sent letters
to, I see they cherish them. They put them up on their walls. A couple of
people have framed them."

The typewriter is an essential element of the Babeler process. When
Grau starts typing a letter in public, the sound brings out people's memories
and curiosity. They're attracted to the uncommon rhythm and to the intelli-
gible, visible mechanism of the machine. Grau says, "I'm so grateful that the
typewriters are so durable and they can continue to exist."

California journalist Keith Sharon is also grateful.

In early 2013, Sharon dreamed up Project 88. He lugged an italic
Smith-Corona Eighty-Eight that he'd bought on eBay to his desk at the
Orange County Register.

> A typewriter sounds either like a glorious calliope or a
> very old man slogging up stadium steps in metal shoes,
> depending on your perspective. More than one person in
> the newsroom complained about the rat-a-tat chatter of my
> typewriter. Take a minute to ponder the implications of what
> you just read. At one time, typing being frowned upon in the
> newsroom would have been a little like water being frowned
> upon in the ocean. . . . I bothered a few of my colleagues, who
> dared to try to talk on the phone while I was TYPING. Other
> colleagues stared at me and my typewriter like we were a
> black-and-white television show. Still others in the newsroom
> said they enjoyed the sound, like the clatter of rain.

Sharon was typing letters to friends, family, and the famous, attempting to
revive the art of correspondence on paper.

The result? One lone response to thirty-three letters.

Sharon mournfully reported in the *Register,* "If you want to be ignored by people you admire . . . If you have no desire to connect with your friends, no desire to share ideas, no desire to receive someone's deepest thoughts and feelings . . . If you enjoy sending unrequited love to all those around you . . . Type them a letter."

A failed act of insurgency?

No. After Sharon published the story of his experience, hundreds of letters arrived from around the United States—enough for him to start a whole new column, "Mail Bonding," where he shared stories from his correspondence. An author of erotica confessed to Sharon that "she" was actually a retired military man. A ninety-year-old woman wrote a letter in the voice of her brother, who went down with his submarine in World War II. A homeless woman described her "awesome" life.

So, although Project 88 didn't find immediate resonance, eventually it struck a nerve. There are people who will choose quality communication over quantity, who want to express themselves in a message to another individual in a way that slow writing can encourage, and e-mailing and texting often discourage.

Sharon types:

> I don't collect typewriters. Instead I collect pen pals. It feels subversive to be sitting in the middle of a modern newsroom whacking away on a typewriter. I get looks from the social media people, who think what I'm doing will certainly die soon (because of the effort it takes to keep up with this kind of communication). But I'm part of the insurgency now. I won't let it die. Going to the mailbox, opening letters, and responding is the best part of my writing day.
>
> I think the typewriter brings out the best in people because you can't use it quickly. You have to think. The machine forces you to consider. The machine forces effort. The slowness of the correspondence makes receiving a letter even more special. So, there is thoughtful effort on the front

end, and joyful acceptance on the back end. That's a pretty
good experience all the way around.

Writing a letter every day is like jogging. I'm in so much
better writing shape than I used to be.

He adds that his project is not ultimately about typing—"the typewriter is
the MacGuffin." It's about "a basic human need to connect with each other
on a deeper level than what feels possible via some modern technologies." In the age of the lonely network, "Receiving a real letter in the mail,
something other than a freaking bill or an advertisement, makes a person's
day." He also finds that "Twitter is mean while letters are nice. It seems that
personal attacks are more difficult when there are envelopes and stamps
and return addresses involved."

Then again, there's Attack of the Typewriters.

The attacks here aren't personal, but political. Hiya Swanhuyser of San
Francisco organizes the sessions at the city's Make-Out Room, a funky bar
and music venue. "Political letter-writing for everyone. We bring the typewriters—you bring the opinions, the rage, the questions, the frustration."
The combination of social letter-writing, drink, politics, and the merciless
hammering of steel type against inky ribbon makes for a cathartic form of
democracy. In addition to the typewriters, Swanhuyser provides stamps,
envelopes, paper, and "notebooks full of letters we've written in the past
and responses we've gotten; it's sometimes funny and sometimes sad." One
thing is safe to say: A typewritten letter is more likely than an e-mail to grab
the attention of its recipient—even a politician. And based on her conversations with congressional staffers, Swanhuyser reports that a letter has the
impact of at least a hundred votes. Type truth to power!

ACTIVISM, TYPEWRITTEN

Typewriters played a still more rebellious role in the Occupy Wall Street
movement in 2011. Mark Kronquist of Portland, Oregon, tells the story:

In mid-October, the Port-
land Police turned off the
electric vehicle charging
station that had been
powering Occupy Portland.
Many cheered that the
noisy radicals had been
silenced. Love the message
or not, because I believe
in free speech, I gave the
movement virtually my
entire collection of typewriters, ribbons (I have just
three left) and my only ditto
machine. These became
symbols of the ability to
communicate even without
laptops and Wi-Fi, and
hundreds if not thousands
of letters, flyers, missives

Occupy Portland

and poems were pounded out on these (and a thousand folk
in their twenties were huffing the smell of fresh-off-the-press
dittos!) . . . The typewriters and ditto machine and traditional
darkroom were destroyed during the raids. They died the
embodiment of a free press getting the word out. A noble death.

Local repair shop Ace Typewriter kept the machines running and sup-
plied with ribbons until the bitter end.

Meanwhile, in New York City, author and activist Robert Neuwirth was
having his own Occupy experience.

The typewriter is a great democratic object. The first time I
pulled out a typewriter in public was when I went to Occupy
Wall Street's encampment in Zuccotti Park in lower Man-

hattan. My partner, the choreographer Andrea Haenggi, was doing a performance there, and, since I'm not a performer, I needed something to do, too. So, at Andrea's suggestion, I brought my 1935 Remington 5. Once I started typing, it transformed me from one of a blank mass to an approachable person in the midst of the cacophony of the drum circle. People came up and wanted to know what I was typing. Others wanted to ask me about Occupy Wall Street and what it meant.

We started using typewriters regularly as part of a group we christened Direct Action Flâneurs. In our first action, we brought fourteen typewriters to Zuccotti Park in honor of the one-month anniversary of Occupy Wall Street being evicted.

Robert Neuwirth

The police first said we could go into the now-empty park, but we could only set up three typewriters. When we set up all fourteen, the cop came and threw us out. I put up a bit of a fuss and asked him what happened to free speech and the First Amendment and he said, essentially, "Don't start with that. If you want to go that route, I'll radio in and arrest you."

So we were thrown out of the park for having too many typewriters. In response, we set up on the sidewalk, just outside the boundary of the park. We spent the day running a typewriter lending library. If people were willing to give us their e-mail address and mobile numbers, we would loan them a typewriter for as long as they wanted. We set each machine up with stationery and carbon paper. When people were finished, they got the carbon copy and we kept the original. Perhaps forty people checked out a typewriter. Our suggestions to them were simple: Make lists of committed observations. Perhaps the types of slogans or buttons you see. Or the body types of the cops on duty. Or the colors of the banners people held. What people brought back were like observational poems—and some of them were inspirational.

We followed up with typewriter actions in Grand Central Station, in the New York City subway, and outside an art gallery. (Here, we encouraged people to type and then carry their finished writings around the neighborhood and do some textural rubbings on the paper, which we then taped to the center of the street, so cars would run over them—a kind of paean to the ephemeral nature of public expression and free speech.)

At two other events, we created giant scrolls of paper. At one, two typewriters each typed on the same scroll, one from each end, with the idea that the words would ultimately meet in the middle. In the other, we used a 1934 Underwood 6 with a twenty-six-inch platen to offer people the opportunity to write their own "Declarations of Interdependence" on a giant scroll of onion skin paper.

A *flâneur* is the Parisian ideal of an urban stroller, who walks the boule-
vards just for the sake of walking them, in order to experience city life.
To *flâner* is to embrace the slow transportation movement, just as typewriting is part of the slow communication movement. Together, when
linked to a social purpose, these practices are a potent duo whose pace
can be deceptive.

Andrea Haenggi theorizes the approach as follows:

> Direct Action Flâneurs is a politico/artistic effort in which
> we invite ourselves into public social fabrics to create tem-
> porary autonomous zones through committed observing,
> committed movement, and committed typing by allowing
> others to join us.
>
> To this day we have done more than ten Direct Action
> Flâneurs mobile constructed situation scores, each targeted
> to a certain event and surrounding. Quickly we noticed the
> typewriter's power to get people's interest and trust. The
> typewriter has the potential of "play," of being connected in
> the moment—being OK with the first instinct of writing—an
> act of improvisation—an act of taking risk. Participants
> expressed their voice on paper, and having carbon paper
> in the typewriter functioned as a souvenir—a gift to them-
> selves—a trace of proof for their ephemeral participation.
> Direct Action Flâneurs Interrupted Situations last until the
> legal owner of the public space tells us to stop the Action.

A slogan that Woody Guthrie wrote on his guitar has also been spotted
on one of the instruments of the Boston Typewriter Orchestra (more on
them in Chapter Eight): THIS MACHINE KILLS FASCISTS. Free expression
undermines any system of control, and typewriters are a great symbol and
embodiment of that fact. They're free not only from those who would dictate
the content of your speech, but from corporations that supply power, software, and communications platforms. Typewriters, particularly someone
else's, offer greater anonymity than any digital transmission, and invite the
author to be frank. It's no wonder that the very sight of a typewriter makes

people want to write freely—to type fragments of counternarratives that may someday disrupt the master story.

TYPING IT LIKE IT IS

It's this subversive honesty of the typewriter that The Bumbys have put to work in the service of another noble cause: learning how others really see you.

The girl wears a wig, the guy wears a ski cap. Sunglasses, bandannas, and headphones complete the garb. "Gill and Jill Bumby" sit down at a pair of typewriters. Their model of choice is new and electronic—they call the Brother GX-6750 "our axe." Their paper of choice: index cards, with a side of Sharpies and a rubber stamp. Their mission: to deliver "A Fair and Honest Appraisal of Your Appearance."

Andrea Haenggi

Instead of snarky takedowns, appraisals by The Bumbys are warm and funny; The Bumbys believe it's most interesting to look for the good in people, and then to help them see it, too. . . . The Bumbys are all about living in the present, letting go and taking creative risks; they are champions of the idea that you can find an authentic and sustainable meeting point between art and commerce.

Having come a long way from Gill's first performance in a Brooklyn subway station in 2008, The Bumbys are now in demand at high-fashion parties, shows, and art events from Vegas to Hong Kong, where people line up to be rated on a ten-point scale and told, with wit, what impression they create. "You could easily be a mid-level affiliate's colorful weatherman . . . 9.4." "Your wispy beard reminds one of a young rabbit in love . . . 8.9."

On The Bumbys' Tumblr blog and Facebook page, their trademark index cards also appraise everything from democracy to the first hangover of the year to art by celebrities ("Weirdly enough, you're not nearly as bad as you should be, Sylvester Stallone's paintings") to snow ("Sure you're lookin' good the day you fall, but after it warms up and the streets are lined with newspaper mush and soggy, half-frozen skunk carcasses, you KNOW Frosty the Snowman has some apologizing to do").

The Bumbys' "axes" help them function as all-around critics. Their associate producer, Mark Sussman, reflects:

> Besides the bandannas, sunglasses, and headphones, there's something a little intimidating about the typewriter.

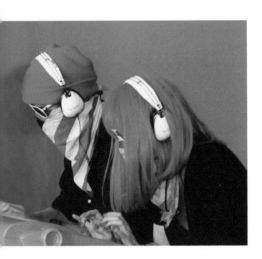

> It's a large piece of machinery and a loud one, so people who are being appraised are aware, if only unconsciously, that every time they hear a *clack,* that *clack* is a judgment about them. The experience is designed to be slightly unnerving, but we think of it as the sort of anxiety you feel before an amusement park ride—palpable but controlled. If all you heard was the soft tapping of fingers on a laptop keyboard, the effect wouldn't be the same.
>
> The fact that the technology is regarded as obsolete plays into it as well—it helps to further anonymize the Bumbys, maybe more than the outfits. Is there anything less stylish than a Brother electric typewriter? Whether you use a Mac or PC or whatever, people (for good or ill) use the kind of technology you carry to judge you. The typewriters both comment on that kind of judgment and interfere with it —the Bumbys aren't "Mac people" or "PC people," they're "Brother people," which is to say, no kind of people at all.

The notecards themselves, with their classic courier type-face and handwritten corrections, are a kind of commentary on the idea of judgment in the digital age as well. Gill Bumby came up with this idea during the heyday of websites like Hot or Not and party photography websites like Last Night's Party, and we think it's only become more relevant with the rise of social networking. People will not only tolerate being judged by large groups of anonymous people, they want to be judged. As a way to comment on this desire, Gill "dedigitized" the process. Instead of presenting a superficial image of yourself to a mass of anonymous strangers who would judge you based only on your posed image, the Bumbys type their appraisals using a medium that is totally personal. After the Bumbys hand over the card, it's yours to do with what you like—post it on Instagram, put it in a box and never show it to anyone, feed it to your dog, whatever. The analog, singular nature of the card and the typewriter encourage the people who attend our performances to rethink what these judg-ments mean here and now.

The typewriters also contribute an element of spontaneity. The Bumbys' performances happen on the spot, and with a typewriter, there's no way to cut and paste ready-made text. It's being written right there, in the moment—and for good. "The clicking sound makes it seem like things are being carved in stone," says Gill.

I'm sure that some of The Bumbys' customers feel their fingers itching to touch those Brothers. A typewriter is a constant invitation to write, and to write honestly. Several insurgent initiatives, such as Stefano Corazza's installation at Burning Man, have invoked this enticing power.

In 2013, Henry Goldkamp decided to use typewriters as sounding boards on a metropolitan scale. His project *What the Hell is St. Louis Think-ing?* set up dozens of manual machines around the city—in bars, barber shops, museums, and record stores—next to boxes where typists could deposit their reactions.

Henry Goldkamp

Goldkamp's typewriter story begins years earlier:

> It started simply. I just happened to have a typewriter, and for a writer there's something about how you can do nothing but move forward, you can't get stuck on one sentence. You have to keep going, that's that, there's no way around it. I lived in New Orleans for a couple of years and took street poetry [using a typewriter] back to St. Louis. It gained a lot of steam very quickly. I would see typewriters in shop displays, not working, not doing anything. "Damn it, these things still work, this isn't just a quintessential symbol of vintage—use one, document your life! Make your mark!"

The expressive potential of typewriters and the fascinating words and ideas people would contribute to his street poetry led Goldkamp to dream up *What the Hell is St. Louis Thinking?*

> From the street poetry endeavor I had ten or thirteen of my own typewriters, but I needed more. Demand got a lot higher; people heard about it, businesses were contacting me saying, "Hey, we want one of these, too." Great, but I had to build more of these stations and had to get more typewriters. It ended up being a wild success. I posted a Craigslist wanted ad for typewriters, explained the project, and the response was overwhelming. People gave them, lent them, sold them for five bucks. "I want to contribute, I want to give what I can." There were sixty to seventy typewriters total, with forty stations across St. Louis.

But there was a problem:

> The businesses where these typewriters were at would call me and say, "Hey, it's out of ink." I can't believe it—I set these all up with new ribbons. The guys weren't hitting the keys hard enough! You have to make that extra effort. It can be measured in the thickness of hair, it's so slight, but it made all the difference with honesty.

Once St. Louisans got used to the work that typewriters demand, that work proved to be one reason why typewriters, not e-mail, were the right medium for Goldkamp's project. There's a truth that comes with "physicality," as he puts it: "Physical effort leads to emotional effort." The writing was "tangible," the compelling strangeness of the machine "draws people," and the anonymity of the typing encouraged confessions: "One kid came out of the closet in one paragraph. Another guy said that after his late wife died, he'd been remarried—but every time he sleeps next to his new wife, he knows that it's cheating."

Then again, when others were around, the typewriters created community. One typist said, "It was interesting talking to the person next to me and trying to figure out how to work the typewriter. We're sharing this moment and it feels like we're kind of making a difference." As a bartender put it, "All of a sudden there's a typewriter, which sparks creativity and conversation. Then the next thing you know the whole table is laughing and typing, trying to figure out how to use a typewriter, and someone is yelling, 'No that's not how you do it. I took this class in high school and the shift button is over here.' So it creates a lot of fun."

But another problem arose: People wanted more, a broader representation of the city. Typewritten critiques started to turn up in Goldkamp's boxes, with complaints such as, "All these typewriters are located in areas with the same or similar demographics and don't really represent the community, as they will only get thoughts from white hipsters or tourists." Goldkamp felt this was constructive criticism. His new plan was to get a station for at least a couple of weeks into every one of the city's seventy-nine neighborhoods—and he did it, with the exception of some "dead industrial zones." With the help of his friend Robert Rohe, Goldkamp raced from one spot to the next, setting up typing stands, fixing machines, swapping good typewriters for bad ones—all while holding down a full-time job working with sheet metal.

He also encouraged individuals to bring a typewriter home and pass it on to someone else after a couple of days. "Responses got a lot more intimate with no friend peeking over their shoulder. People could take the typewriter into their room and unleash the hell that they have in their head."

The final product is a book that collects the best of *What the Hell is St. Louis Thinking?*—a unique record of the minds of a twenty-first century American city, gathered by typewriter. But maybe it won't be unique for long—Everett, Washington, has already hosted *Word on the Street,* a project that set up sidewalk typewriters on ten tables decorated by local artists and invited passersby to type responses to a daily question formulated by staff at the public library.

I expect some other cities will want to sponsor similar projects, maybe especially cities that need a shot in the arm. As Henry Goldkamp told the *St. Louis Beacon,* "If you think about it, the typewriter is symbolic of the city: Other people might write them off or consider them obsolete, but really it just takes some fixing up and it works just fine."

THE ROMANCE OF TYPEWRITING

No doubt about it: Typewriters elicit expression. They can even inspire confessions of love.

In 2008 in Lincoln, Nebraska, Christopher James dreamed up an event for Porridge Papers, his custom paper mill and letterpress print shop. "Love on the Run" would invite people to type love notes on typewriters and pop them into bottles, which James would deliver in person on Valentine's Day.

The event exceeded his expectations: Eighty-two people seized the opportunity. By 2015, Love on the Run had become a Lincoln tradition, with over five hundred people lining up at the typewriters to craft personal messages, typos and all, to be delivered by dozens of "valenteers." The idea has also been adopted by a kindred print shop, Flywheel Press in San Mateo, California—including typewriters as an essential ingredient, of

course. Christopher James points out, "The thought, care and consideration that goes into typing on them makes the result so much more meaningful than a store-bought card with a preprinted message or a text"—and "the charm of the old typewriters just makes it fun. If someone sees an old typewriter sitting there they just cannot help but start pecking at the keys."

The infectious fun of Love on the Run might just become a runaway trend.

Can typewritten love letters lead to matrimony? Iowan Alex Cooney bought his long-distance girlfriend a shiny, streamlined Remington 5 portable, and another for himself. The idea was that they would trade typewritten letters—something more tangible and personal than electrons. Today they treasure those letters, they still type to each other—and they're married.

Meanwhile, in Montana, Tyler Knott Gregson is a photographer who specializes in weddings. Small wonder that when he writes poetry, it's romantic. Nearly every day, he'll compose a haiku on love and a poem in his typewriter series. He scans the typewritten poems, posts them to his blog—and they typically get reblogged a thousand times within twenty-four hours.

Gregson adds to the tangible character of his poetry by typing it on miscellaneous found paper, including pages from old books, receipts, and envelopes. His online audience encounters all this in pixels, but feels the reality behind the digital images—except for the disbelieving readers who inevitably contact him after every poem to ask, "What app do you use to get that font?" Yes, there are faux-typewriter apps, as we'll see, but Gregson does it the honest way, on a Remington Rand Model 17 that he happened to find in an antique store one fateful day: "With technology making so many things so easy these days, the homemade, hand-made feel is so much more valuable to me."

If you press him for more about his use of a typewriter, you get a love story:

> I love the sound, the smell, the way the keys feel on my fingers, the bell at the end of a line. I love that mistakes are mistakes and even when covered up, stay that way. I love the urgency of it, the way your fingers pick up speed while you type and that you cannot go back and shuffle lines around, words around, or change the composition.

When Gregson started typewriting his poems, his online audience really took off, and eventually he secured a book contract. That in itself is a triumph for any poet—but a poetry book that sells by the tens of thousands is nearly unheard of. That's what Gregson achieved with *Chasers of the Light.*

The popularity of Gregson's poems is certainly due to their skill and their unabashed emotion, but the fact that they're typewritten adds materiality and genuineness—reminding the reader that the writer is finite, situated, and embodied.

The same dynamic is at work on a Facebook page called "Typewriter," which has garnered over seventy thousand "likes." The page features short thoughts and literary quotations, typed on pages that are usually pho-

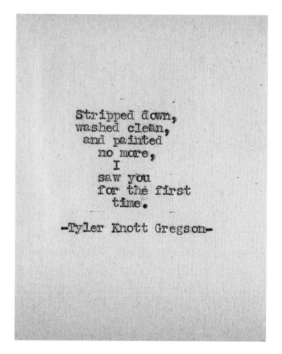

tographed while still in the machine. Sometimes the paper is beautifully colored; sometimes the typing is cut out and pasted onto images. The most common topic is romantic love and heartbreak.

"Typewriter" is the creation of Muhammad Abdullah Syed in Pakistan—and of his readers, who send him requests by the thousands. He gets into "real conversations about things like the meaning of life and why are we here"—all provoked by his carefully chosen, typewritten texts.

Syed's page inspired a similar Facebook project, "The Mad Typist," by teenager Yaser Khan from Peshawar. Khan's reflections on life and God break through the usual superficialities of social media and provoke passionate responses from his followers. One typewritten post reads, "In your light I learn how to love. In your beauty, how to make poems."

Paradoxically, the digital filter of the Internet and the mechanical filter of the typewriter can join forces to allow people to express their most intimate feelings, especially in societies that may discourage public displays of affection.

Typewriting touches the heart.

DIGITAL DETOX

We'll further investigate the peculiar magic of digitized typewriting in Chapter Six, but an introduction to the revolution wouldn't be complete without peering into some events where people are setting aside the digital altogether—at least for a while. The concept of observing a digital sabbath, or setting aside time for experiences that aren't mediated by ones and zeros, is making strides. An increasing number of creative and productive people advocate shutting down the phone and computer, focusing, and engaging with the physical.

The National Day of Unplugging urges us to put down our digital devices in order to "connect with the people in your street, neighborhood, and city, have an uninterrupted meal or read a book to your child." Participants from around the world testify that they unplug "to make memories," "to know myself," "to enjoy the present," "to arouse the senses," and "to be human! Duh!"

When it's shared with others, the redis-
covery of the nondigital becomes a social
event. Rob Roy, a Seattle bar, has been
holding musical Analog Tuesdays for several years: "Bring in records or a reel from
your own collection and play it for us!"

The idea was picked up and expanded
by a Toronto club, 3030 Dundas West:

> It's a celebration of all things
> analog. . . . You can come in, have
> a tasty snack or three, knock back
> a pint and play some board games,
> learn how to knit, and partake in a
> pinball tournament, all while lis-
> tening to DJ Nick Bandit spinning some great 45s. It's a good
> thing. It's a very good thing.

Board games? Knitting? It may sound like a sleepy Sunday at the retirement
home—but in fact, today's knitters have a sassy, "stitch 'n bitch" attitude,
and board games can be raucous fun.

"Sexy old typewriters" soon joined the advertised mix, thanks to Jamie
and Matt Chojnacki of Old Fort Typewriter, who made machines, paper, and
envelopes available to the crowd. On one Analog Tuesday, a society of poets
came in to type letters to Santa; on another, a girl typed a confession of love.

Sometimes it's the techiest people who most value the low-tech
approach. Some software companies make a point of using face-to-face and
paper communications as much as possible. And in San Francisco, at the
heart of the information economy, the need for "digital detox" is keenly felt
by citizens such as typewriter lover Anthony Rocco.

> At some point in time I know it existed: that iconic Main
> Street, with a tailor, a typewriter repairman . . . I knew my
> butcher's name, my postman's name. That type of community

can exist, but we first have to get over
our fascination with technology. Digital
technology is isolating; it just has the
facade that it's enabling communication or creating connection. Being
on Facebook all day is not physical
interaction. Where are you? Why aren't
you interacting with people around
you? On the bus the other day, a dude
from Louisiana starts talking to me. In
Louisiana, people just talk. That's what
they do, they start telling a story—that
happens. In San Francisco and New York, everyone has a
[expletive deleted] smartphone and iPad and is afraid of eye
contact. They're not present in what's happening. Put it down
for a sec. Stop and say hello to your neighbor! This is a very
scary concept. . . . San Francisco is in a unique position.
Because we're at the forefront of technology, we also get
bored of it quickest.

The irony, of course, is that online social media promise to provide human
connections. And they do—but the connections are filtered, skewed, and
spread thin. Beyond a certain level, sharing isn't caring, and more means
less. At that point, the overnetworked masses want something more personal and more direct.

San Franciscan Mike Zuckerman has addressed the problem through
a number of creative ideas that make space for the nondigital beside the
digital. He promotes rail travel as a way to reconnect with people and landscape. He was instrumental in creating a "pop-up community center" called
Freespace, a site for "civic hacking"—like a makerspace for community, by
way of everything from art to gardening. The San Francisco Freespace has
inspired similar initiatives in several countries.

Other projects and places are tackling our digital addictions head-on.
Aunt Charlie's Lounge, a disco in San Francisco, asks you to leave if

you're texting. For a more immersive nondigital experience, there's Camp Grounded, a three-day summer camp for adults in California that promotes "personal freedom, creative thinking, liberation from technology, and a space [away] from the working world where we can all once again be . . . human." Participants go by pseudonyms, never talk about work, and surrender their digital devices for the duration. People find that when they set Facebook aside, they enjoy actually looking into each other's faces. Phones and watches are taboo; typewriters are welcome. In fact, the old rifle range at the former Boy Scout camp has been converted to a typewriter range.

Camp Grounded is produced by The Digital Detox, an Oakland-based organization founded by Levi Felix and Brooke Dean that advises us to "disconnect to reconnect." Digital Detox is not a startup but a "slow-down"—"the ultimate decelerator." The group promotes events and places that encourage us to re-inhabit the present and rediscover our own bodies—such as tech-free

zones at high-tech conferences that serve as oases for physical interaction.

These are hardly the marginal ideas of a few cranks. A Digital Detox party at the San Francisco Freespace in July of 2013 attracted fourteen hundred people who indulged in dancing, singing, face painting, an art gallery, fresh conversation—and, of course, an "analog zone with typewriters." At a 2014 Unplug SF party, "idle thumbs met a parade of ways to stay busy. Twentysomethings wove friendship bracelets, painted faces, glued things onto rocks, played board games, listened to a live band, and drank beer. The typewriters were so popular that a chance to clack away at one required patience."

THE HIPSTER BROUHAHA

Hip • ster, n.

1. A long-unfashionable term for the fashionable, which became neofashionable but is now neo-unfashionable.

2. A term used ironically to refer to the overly ironic.

3. A label conformists apply to nonconformists to label them as conformist.

You know that a trend has some momentum when it attracts mockery—so we can take some pride in the nascent stereotype "hipster with a typewriter." Nothing provokes more irritation than a hipster, but who will admit to being one? You might describe hipsters as urban singles who adopt obsolete things and styles in order to create new trends, but that would be only a rough sketch of this elusive species. And still more baffling than hipsters is the anti-hipster campaign, which is often waged through online memes, and often involves a surprising amount of anger.

To some extent, the war is about familiar social paradoxes: Countercultural groups can be highly rigid, and rebelling against the norm can be a way of being enslaved to it, so nonconformists can often be accused, justly or unjustly, of being conformists.

What the hipster phenomenon adds to this dynamic is a hyper-aware process of rummaging through the past, reviving fashions for the third or fourth time, and exploring styles that can date anywhere from 1890 to 2000. The process is made easier and faster by the information age; you can find and buy endless images and objects from any year from the convenience of your smartphone. Some see this as the desperate flailings of a culture that has come unmoored, that no longer believes in itself but gets lost in its cast-offs. Others see the practice as a curious, appreciative attitude toward the good things of other times.

Whatever one's motive for rummaging through the detritus of the past, typewriters can be found there, and along with vinyl records, they've become one of the supposed markers of a hipster. Yes, if you use a typewriter it's possible that you'll be labeled a hipster, a poseur, an "attention whore"—not to your face, but in that haven for anonymous gossip, the Internet.

Damn the cultural torpedoes, I say, and full speed ahead! The view that typewriters are just a pose assumes that there can't be a legitimate reason to use them today—an assumption that couldn't be more wrong. Yes, probably some current typists have adopted their machines merely as a fad—but let them decide for themselves whether they like typing. Those who stick with it will be connecting to a technology and culture that go deeper than any fad and offer a durable alternative to the digital norm.

Many attacks on hipsters paint them as ironists. Yet for all the fun one can have with a typewriter, the typical typist is not ironic; we sincerely

YOU'RE NOT A REAL HIPSTER

UNTIL YOU TAKE YOUR TYPEWRITER TO THE PARK

appreciate the machine. Ryan Adney, an Arizona teacher who uses typewriters in the classroom, observes that they're part of a new culture of the authentic: "Pastiche and parody are far from the reason most people use these machines." Adney finds "honesty" in the spreading desire to compose on a typewriter.

Love should dictate your choice of writing instrument. So write as you wish, and let the chips fall where they may.

Case in point: writer Christopher Hermelin. Needing some cash, he tried going to Manhattan's High Line—an old elevated train line which has become a park—and setting up with his ten-dollar Royal Safari as "The Roving Typist," writing short stories on demand. His sign read: "One-of-a-kind, Unique Stories While You Wait. Sliding Scale—Donate What You Can!" The results were good: "Writing is usually a lonely, solitary act. On the High Line with my typewriter, all the joy of creating narrative was infused with a performer's high—people held their one-page flash fictions and read them and laughed and repeated lines and translated into their own languages, right in front of me."

But one day, Hermelin found that a snapshot of him was making the rounds of the Internet, labeled "You're not a real hipster until you take your typewriter to the park." Strangers heaped ignorant abuse on the image. When his former girlfriend published a story about what it was like to encounter her ex as a meme, the phenomenon was amplified.

To Hermelin's credit, he hasn't packed away his Royal and cowered indoors. "I prefer to let these little cesspools of cyberspace fester and then stagnate, forgotten as they should be, secure in the knowledge that I am doing something that matters to me."

Is Hermelin's public typing a cry for attention? In a sense, yes; he's seeking opportunities to interact. But is that so bad? As he told me:

There's this weird dislike of the pursuit of conversation. "That guy just wants someone to talk to him." "Just asking for attention." What's wrong with that? I want to talk to people, and this is the way to do it. Aren't we all trying to connect to each other in some way? I get a crowd collecting around me, talking about typewriters and stories. The fear of having nothing to say keeps people from talking to strangers, but with the typewriter, people immediately have something to talk about. People let their guard down. The sound of the typewriter is the point of entry for conversation.

My experience matches Hermelin's. When you type in public, most people are curious and friendly—and some may be eager to discover the pleasures of typewriting for themselves.

As for hipsters, Hermelin says:

I don't know what a hipster is, and that's kind of the point. It's a sort of a floating label that is used to describe someone who is interested in trends and fashion and what's coming up. It deals more in personal expression rather than what the fashion world is saying. Hipsters are interested in what's coming next, which is positive. Being at the cultural vanguard, at the spot where hipsters want to be, seeing what's going to take the world by storm, is cool.

And why are hipsters fascinated with the past?

We're living in a time period where everyone's sort of an emotional orphan. Things are moving so quickly, technology is changing so fast, that there's something nice about holding on to what's perennial, to what won't change. Having a typewriter is nice because it's a piece of machinery that works every time—and if it's not working, I can open it up and fix it myself. It's just moving parts. You just need a

basic understanding of tools. This is comforting for a group
that is constantly looking for some semblance of a baseline. Being aware of this dichotomy [between change and
continuity] is at the root of the hipster wink to the past.

In March 2013, an article on the website Gizmodo tactfully titled "Look at
This Idiot Using His Typewriter in a Starbucks" revived the "hipster with
a typewriter" controversy. Someone snapped a picture of a curly-haired
guy in a plaid shirt leaning back at a corner table in a coffee shop and
working on his Smith-Corona Skyriter. The author and many of the com-
menters lambasted the typist, sometimes claiming that he was disturb-
ing other patrons, but mostly denouncing him as an attention-seeking
hipster.

   The typist, Zachary Schepis, promptly stepped forward to identify
himself and answer questions—with cool, calm, and class. These are some
highlights from his interview.

> Just recently, one of my good friends moved in with me and
> brought his grandmother's antique typewriter. So I started
> messing around, and there were a few things I liked. When
> I'm using Microsoft Word, staring at that bright screen
> kind of zaps some of the creative process from me, and
> there are a lot of distractions with laptops. Plus, I'm one of
> the biggest self-editors. I'll write something and instead of
> forging ahead like you should, I'll go back and start tweak-
> ing things. With a typewriter, you need conviction. . . . So
> it helps me sustain momentum and get to the piece. Also,
> just listening to the rhythm of the keys—it's a completely
> different experience. . . .
>   I was in there for a couple hours working on this memoir
> for my best friend that passed away, and I was getting into it.
> I was kind of ignoring the fact that there were other people
> around me. But every once in a while someone would just

come over and out of curiosity ask me about the typewriter. You know, "why did you use the typewriter?", "how does it work?", basic questions like that.

I would just tell anyone out there to not worry what other people think about you. Go your own way, and do everything you do and do it with conviction.

Let's all take Mr. Schepis's words to heart.

Long after the term "hipster" has returned to the linguistic graveyard, there will be typewriters and typists. The revolution will continue—because our roots are deep, our goals are noble, and our passion outstrips any fashion.

In this chapter we've glanced at some highlights of the insurgency—some of the most visible ways in which typists have been challenging the system. From steampunks to burners, from makers to preppers, a wide range of creative people are looking for new frontiers of experience, imagination, and independence. That old invention, the typewriter, serves them all. Typewriters, these castaways from an obsolete industrial order, have found new lives to lead in strange contexts, giving us hazy glimpses of alternative worlds.

The insurgents we've met don't know each other, in most cases. Most wouldn't describe themselves as members of some worldwide movement. But they have each found their way to typewriters; they've discovered that these old devices offer something different, something full of unexplored potential. Something in the zeitgeist is turning us toward typewriters, and the typewriters are setting us free.

What will happen next? You and I, and thousands of other typists, will answer that question in our own ways.

But first we need some historical perspective. In our next chapter, we'll learn where these magic machines came from. In Chapters Three and Four, we'll get you set up with your own typewriter. Then, in Chapter Five, we'll return to some of these insurgent acts and look more systematically at the typing possibilities that await you.

Interlude #1

We assert our right to resist the Paradigm,
to rebel against the Information Regime,
to escape the Data Stream.

The enemy of the typewriter revolution is not computers—it's the all-embracing computing mentality, the Paradigm that threatens to dominate the way we live and think. This world view sees everything as a cluster of information, and information as a resource that can be processed for profit: From the Bible to the human genome, from Rembrandt to Rihanna, it's all just data—and success means crunching it effectively. Small wonder that information-processing devices are the essential tools for this way of life. In fact, they're more than tools: They control many processes with minimal human intervention, selling billions of dollars of stock or naming a million faces in a split second.

From this point of view, everything we do is a data stream, a flow of information to be tapped and sold. Your personal stream blends with countless others to create the Information Amazon where robotic predators fish.

When we're trapped in the horizons of the Information Regime, we're driven to manage our personal infostream as effectively as we can, to generate positive buzz about ourselves and take advantage of all the data we can accumulate. The first thing we do when we wake up, and the last thing we do before going to sleep, is check our messages. Developing influence and reputation means sending out a constant stream of data packets and hoping that they'll be retweeted, reblogged, or "liked." Success means going viral.

Of course, since we're just droplets in the global data torrent, and since the machines can process information unimaginably faster than our brains, our efforts are pathetic. The most "successful" human information processor is a lucky fluke, desperately treading water in the information ocean.

The typewriter insurgency doesn't ask you to chuck all your digital devices, but it does invite you to take time out from the Paradigm. Try digital detox for a day. Dance, cycle, garden, read a novel (on paper), take a walk in the woods—and sit at your typewriter, which doesn't process words at all, but just puts them on the page, mediating between you and the paper without remembering the information, without meddling with your choices. Write a letter, a poem, a journal entry. You may find that language and thought aren't just information processing, but a matter of waking up to your own situation and the world around you—a world that gets reduced and impoverished by the Paradigm.

Then, if you don't feel the need to keep what you've typed, you can have that special satisfaction of crumpling up the sheet in your fist and tossing it into the round file. You've just escaped the Data Stream.

2. The Typewritten Past

Let's stand back from the twenty-first century now to get some historical background. As a typewriter owner, you're a participant in over two hundred years of mechanical innovation, sophisticated manufacturing, and cultural transformation. Knowing something about that history adds depth to your typing experience. You may even find yourself coveting some early models for their style, ingenuity, or sheer weirdness. This chapter will give you a quick overview of the technical and social history of typewriters and introduce you to the hobby of typewriter collecting.

TYPEWRITERS AND TYPEWRITING: A MICROHISTORY

Maybe the typewriter was an inevitable invention. It's not hard to imagine that the idea could have occurred to Gutenberg on some afternoon when he was printing his Bible. We know that in 1714 a certain Henry Mill received an English patent for what sounds like a typewriter: "an artificial machine or method for the impressing or transcribing of letters singly or progressively one after another." We don't know what Mill's invention looked like, but surely the technology of the time was adequate to the task: Clockmakers were producing delicate and precise mechanisms, and they could have applied their wits to the creation of a writing machine if they'd wanted to.

But before the Industrial Revolution, a typewriter must have seemed like a luxury with little practical application. Only in the nineteenth century did inventors begin to build working models and dream of mass production. The earliest typewriter that we know existed was constructed by Pellegrino Turri in 1808 for his blind friend Countess Carolina Fantoni da Fivizzano. The device does not survive today, but numerous letters written by the Countess testify to the fact that it worked. (This first documented typist is the heroine of Carey Wallace's 2010 novel *The Blind Contessa's New Machine*.)

Later in the century, various pioneers invented writing machines from the simple to the extremely complex, from tiny to huge, and from practical to absurd. Some significant early developers of typewriters include William Austin Burt (whose invention dates from 1829), Charles Grover Thurber (1843), Alfred Ely Beach (1847-1856) and Samuel Francis (1857). Other notable inventors include the Italian Giuseppe Ravizza, the Frenchman Xavier Progin, and the Tyrolean Peter Mitterhofer—who carved his typewriter frames out of wood and trundled a prototype to Vienna by wheelbarrow to appeal for funds from Emperor Franz Joseph. These three inventors all came up with the concept of placing types on the ends of long, thin bars that would do the printing; today we call these "typebars." An American, John Jones, established a factory in 1852 to produce his "Mechanical Typographer"—a straightforward device that put the types

THE WRITING BALL IS IRON LIKE ME --
BUT ON TRIPS WE GET TWISTED EASILY.
PATIENCE AND TACT YOU NEED, SO MUCH,
TO USE US -- AND THE FINEST TOUCH.

                    FRIEDRICH NIETZSCHE

Sholes & Glidden

on a large, horizontal wheel—but the building burned down and most of the 130 machines were destroyed.

Finally, two inventors created machines that were successfully manufactured in a series. The first was Pastor Rasmus Malling-Hansen of Denmark, whose *skrivekugle* (writing ball) resembled a pin-cushion. The machine was a finely constructed piece of engineering that was patented in 1870. Its best-known user is Friedrich Nietzsche. Unfortunately, Nietzsche's machine was damaged before he ever got it, and he gave it up after using it for just six weeks in 1882. Malling-Hansen designed several models of the writing ball, including an electric version.

The next factory-produced invention was much more influential: It launched an enduring industry, and even introduced the term for the device that we use in English today. (Nearly every other language just calls it a "writing machine.") The Sholes & Glidden Type Writer was born in Klein-steuber's Machine Shop, a post-Civil War makerspace in Milwaukee. Its primary inventor was Christopher L. Sholes, who was also a newspaperman, printer, and politician. Sholes created the QWERTY keyboard, which is still very much with us today despite numerous attempts to overthrow it. We're still not sure why he came up with this arrangement, but one plausible the-ory among collectors is that he was trying to separate frequently-used pairs of typebars so they wouldn't get jammed at the printing point. (The claim that he was trying to slow typists down is slander; less jamming would mean more speed.) Remnants of an original alphabetic order can be seen in the DFGHJKL sequence in the center row of Sholes's keyboard.

The Sholes & Glidden was commercially manufactured starting in September 1873, by the Remington Arms Company of Ilion, New York, and reached the market in 1874. (Ever since, typewriters have been associated with firearms. In the Al Capone days, the machine gun got the nickname "Chicago typewriter." Even in the twenty-first century, US troops in Afghani-stan have dubbed the weapon a "Kandahar electric typewriter.")

The Type Writer was a fancy contraption, often sporting colorful decals and hand-painted decorations that were unique to a particular machine. Like the original writing ball, it wrote in capitals only. Its most famous early adopter was Mark Twain, who proudly sent his publishers a typescript of *Life on the Mississippi*. The machine was an expensive curiosity that attracted few buyers, but the novel idea of a keyboard for writing did make people sit up and pay attention. As far away as Australia, newsman J. H. Clark wrote in 1875:

> Who is the ingenious inventor of the type-writing machine
> that opens such a wide field of hope for the cautious caligra-
> phist while it takes from the feeble spellist his only safeguard,
> illegibility? My *Register* describes it as an instrument some-
> what resembling a family sewing-machine, with small keys
> by which you manipulate your correspondence. It also says
> that with practice a person can play upon it with as much
> ease and rapidity as a skilful pianist. . . . You can lounge over
> this silent but powerful agent of love and business, and as the
> seething thoughts crowd through your burning brain they will
> glide out at your finger tips and impress themselves on the
> rose-tinted paper ere you can say Jack Robinson! . . . If they
> could afford it, would not the poor compositors present each
> and every one of the *Register* staff . . . with such an instru-
> ment, and no more have to wade wearily through crabbed
> characters like dissipated Assyrian hieroglyphics!

Clark's fantasy came true; by the 1880s, the typewriter began to be accepted as a helpful and even essential tool for a modern newspaper, business, or government office, a tool that could produce multiple copies of easily legible documents in a short time. A typewriter industry gradually developed: not just factories but distributors, shops, salesmen, and man- ufacturers of accessories such as typing paper and ribbons. (Typewriter ribbon tins were produced in a wide variety of eye-catching designs, and they make great collectibles.)

    With the mechanical typewriters came human "typewriters" or "oper- ators" who had been trained to work the devices. These were usually unmarried young women, who had generally been banned from the business world before then, but who were considered to have the manual dexterity appropriate for the job. In a time when few women could work outside the home, the typewriter created new economic opportunities for them. Of course, these opportunities were limited: Women were unapologetically paid less than traditional male clerks, who resented being undercut by the new cheap labor. A

firm and low glass ceiling was in place, and the division of labor by gender—male boss, female secretary—persisted into the *Mad Men* days.

A natural product of these new office conditions was romance—and what today we call sexual harassment. The situation led to a whole genre of comic postcards picturing businessmen's fantasies and fears; on card after card, the boss's vengeful wife catches him with his "typewriter" on his lap. (That ambiguous word was eventually replaced by terms such as "typewritist" and "typist.")

The machines that these "typewriters" used in the 1880s included the Remington 2 (the successor to the Sholes & Glidden, which was retroactively called the Remington 1 once the typewriter company spun off from the arms manufacturer); the Model 2 introduced a shift key, to switch between uppercase and lowercase letters. Some of its competitors, including the Caligraph, Yost, and Smith Premier, spurned the shift and developed a "full" keyboard that assigned a separate key to each lowercase and uppercase character. The Hammond and the Crandall featured interchangeable type elements (called a shuttle and type cylinder) and two-row curved keyboards with double shifts—one shift for capitals, another for numerals and

New Model
Crandall

punctuation. With its inlaid mother-of-pearl, the New Model Crandall has often been called the most beautiful typewriter ever made. (It took me a decade before I could add a battered example to my collection.)

The decade of the 1890s sported the greatest biodiversity in the typewriter ecosystem. Hundreds of patents were filed and dozens of companies, mostly American, competed for a share of the growing market.

Inventors might put the type on typebars, swinging sectors, or typewheels. The greatest of the typewheel devices was an ingenious little machine with a long name, Blickensderfer. Dozens of different typewheels were available for "Blicks," which were made into the late teens.

Typewriters might have full keyboards, four-bank (four-row) keyboards, three-bank keyboards, or even no keyboard at all—as in "index" typewriters. These gadgets, such as the Hall, People's, American, or Odell, required the user to select a character on an index and then perform a separate action to print it. This concept survived into the twentieth century in cheap German machines such as the Mignon and Gundka, as well as in label makers and toy typewriters such as the Simplex.

Machines might use Sholes's QWERTY keyboard or another, supposedly more efficient arrangement, such as Blickensderfer's DHIATENSOR. They might use ribbons, ink pads, or ink rollers. There were expensive hundred-dollar machines (that's comparable to the cost of a high-end laptop today) and

Caligraph No. 1
(uppercase
letters only)

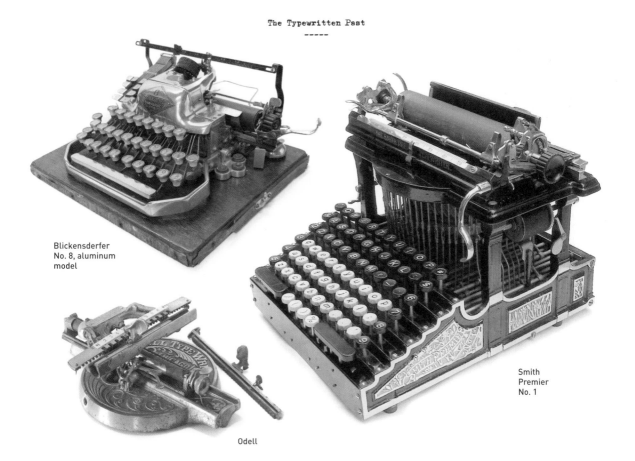

Blickensderfer
No. 8, aluminum
model

Odell

Smith
Premier
No. 1

trinkets that sold for a dollar. Most of these models were failures at the
time, and they are rare treasures for collectors today.

The typewriter factories of the 1890s experimented with modern production processes, sometimes employing hundreds of people on assembly lines.
They also used innovative materials such as aluminum and vulcanite—an
early plastic consisting of hardened rubber.

The greatest technical challenges for the inventors of the time were
durable alignment and immediate visibility for the typed text. The Sholes &
Glidden, the Caligraph, and many other early typewriters were "blind writers" that typed on the bottom of the platen (the rubber-covered cylinder),
so that you had to raise the carriage to see your work. Some inventors tried
typebars that stood upright in front of the platen (Bar-Lock, Franklin) or
behind it (Waverley, Fitch, Brooks, North's) and swung down onto the paper.

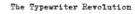

On the Williams, the typebars rested horizontally on ink pads and jumped like grasshoppers onto the paper from both front and back; unfortunately, only one or two lines of text were visible at a time. The Oliver found great success with its typebars shaped like inverted U's that swung down from the sides; this design survived into the late 1920s in the US, and into World War II in the UK. The Wellington used a "thrust" design that shoved typebars horizontally against the platen; this approach was eventually adopted by Adler in Germany, where the thrust mechanism was popular for decades.

But the best solution to visibility was the "frontstroke" design pioneered by the Daugherty (1891) and perfected by the Underwood (designed by Franz X. Wagner and introduced in 1896). In this arrangement, typebars are arranged in an arc above the keyboard, and swing up against the front of the platen. The speedy, well-engineered Underwood was eventually so successful that within a couple of decades, the vast majority of typewriters followed its model: They were single-shift, frontstroke, typebar typewriters with four-bank QWERTY keyboards, inked by a ribbon.

Underwood no.1

The creative chaos of the 1890s inevitably waned in the face of competition and consolidation. The Union Typewriter Company, also known as the typewriter trust, was controlled by Remington and included several other major producers of blind writers. The companies banded together to keep the price of their typewriters at a hundred dollars, and they succeeded in dominating the market for some time, despite various attempts by smaller enterprises to undercut them. By the

early twentieth century, however, independent makers of visible writers—including Underwood, Royal, and L. C. Smith (led by the same brothers who formerly made the blind Smith Premier)—were giving the trust a run for its money.

After the First World War, American typewriter manufacturing was led by a few large companies that had survived the challenging market of earlier years and the stresses of the war: Remington, Underwood, Royal, and Smith-Corona (the result of a 1926 merger between the L. C. Smith office typewriter and the Corona portable). Underwood and Royal built gigantic factories in Hartford, Connecticut, that employed thousands and produced millions of machines. There were a few smaller fish, such as the elegant Fox and the unique Hammond, which survived under the name Varityper and found a niche market as a "cold typesetting" machine all the way into the 1970s.

Oliver No. 5 (nickeled version)

Meanwhile, typewriter manufacturing had spread to Europe, especially Germany, where dozens of factories were built in the first few decades of the century. Major German companies included Adler, Triumph, Continental, Torpedo, Seidel & Naumann and AEG/Olympia. The largest British company, Imperial, exported many machines to other countries in the Commonwealth. Other European nations also got into the act, including France, Switzerland, and Italy (with the great Olivetti). Labor conditions at typewriter factories varied wildly; Remington was a notoriously ruthless strikebreaker, while Olivetti provided a spectrum of services to its workers.

How were these machines used? The romantic picture we have of the novelist or newsman smoking at the typewriter isn't wrong, but the majority of big typewriters were still used by secretaries and clerical workers, who weren't expected to do any creative writing. Often the boss would dictate a letter while his secretary took shorthand notes, or he'd speak into a recording device such as a Dictaphone; then the secretary would expertly turn those words into neatly typed sheets, making a carbon copy or two, and

bring the letter to the boss for his signature. In the accounting department, workers would type up spreadsheets with long tables of figures, sometimes using wide-carriage typewriters to handle big forms; some would manipulate monstrous devices that grafted typewriters onto complex adding machines.

Of course, not all uses of typewriters were prosaic. During the Cold War, behind the Iron Curtain, the machines were treated as controlled substances. When combined with mimeographs or photocopiers, typewriters could be used to produce samizdat, or illicit publications. In her memoir of growing up in Romania, Carmen Bugan recalls how her father kept a typewriter buried in the backyard; he would dig it out at night to write pamphlets against dictator Nicolae Ceausescu. The Stasi's obsession with controlling typewriters in East Germany is dramatized in the 2006 film *The Lives of Others.*

In the West, typewriters could create publications that were legal but offbeat: everything from rough, photocopied, fly-by-night zines to *The Match!,* a journal of ethical anarchism that Fred Woodworth has printed using Varitypers since 1969 (see Chapter Five).

Not all typewriters were standards, or big office machines. The early twentieth century saw the rise of portables, which could serve as ready tools for students, housewives, journalists, or traveling businessmen. Building on the success of the Standard Folding design, with a carriage that folds over onto the keyboard (1907), the Corona 3 was introduced shortly before World War I and went on to sell by the hundreds of thousands. It was succeeded by many other machines designed for personal or travel use. While the Corona and other early portables had a three-bank keyboard with double shift, the Remington portable of 1920 introduced a four-bank keyboard and was a big success. By the early thirties, the three-bank design was confined to a few offbeat machines and toys—that is, until its revival on smartphones and tablets of the twenty-first century.

In the mid-twentieth century, portables were further differentiated into machines that were as compact as possible (such as the Hermes Baby) and midsize typewriters that incorporated some of the sophisticated features of office machines. Styling evolved with the times. Olivetti was a style leader, employing first-rate designers such as Marcello Nizzoli and Ettore Sottsass and introducing iconic machines such as the Valentine—a bright red, informal portable marketed to countercultural youth.

In addition to developing portables, manufacturers sought advantages over their competitors by introducing inventions such as the "noiseless" typewriter, which reduced the shock of the type's impact, or Royal's "magic margin" device, which set the margin at the touch of a lever. Some companies developed specialized applications such as machines for stenography, musical notation, writing on flat surfaces, or typing Chinese or Japanese (using a gigantic tray of characters).

Another important development was the rise of electric typewriters. Malling-Hansen had already designed an electric *skrivekugle*, as well as another electric machine, the Takygraf, which was capable of a mind-boggling twelve hundred strokes a minute. The Cahill Electric (1900) and Blickensderfer Electric (1902) were produced in series, but flopped in the marketplace. Electric typewriters began to gain wide acceptance only in the 1930s, led by IBM's massive Electromatic. The famous IBM Selectric of 1961 followed the Blick Electric in providing interchangeable elements that could type in different styles or alphabets. Electronic typewriters, which use integrated circuits to control the behavior of the machine, were

No. 23   MAKING A RECORD OF THE CUSTOMER'S ORDER.
SEARS, ROEBUCK & CO., Chicago, Ill.

Sears headquarters in 1907: "The work of transcribing customers' orders to merchandise order tickets is performed on special typewriters [Elliott-Fisher book typewriters]; four hundred of these typewriters being in use at the present time."

Remington
Rand Model 1

introduced in the 1970s. Most electronics use interchangeable daisy wheels. (The daisy wheel concept actually dates back to the 1891 Victor index typewriter.)

By the seventies, typewriter production was no longer centered in American and European factories. The machines were cranked out around the world, including in Japan, India, Brazil, Mexico, and South Africa. They were mass-produced, affordable, and usually less durable than the iron wordmills of old.

Meanwhile, a few electronics hobbyists with names like Jobs, Wozniak, and Gates were tinkering in their garages. Their work would spell the beginning of the end of the typewriter's popularity. Since the early eighties typewriter sales have steadily declined, despite some attempts at hybrid word processor–typewriters. In 2009, manufacture of big manual office typewriters finally ended when the Indian company Godrej & Boyce announced it would no longer produce them. In 2012 the last typewriter made in the United Kingdom (an electronic Brother) rolled off the assembly line in Wrexham. As of this writing, a few manual portables are still being manufactured in China, but most typewriters produced today are electronic; the major brands include Swintec, Nakajima, TA Adler-Royal, and Brother.

Why do typewriters still get made at all?

Because there are some niches in business and government where they still get used. Typewriters fill out forms and envelopes in a variety of situations. Police may type up paperwork such as reports, property receipts, and warrants. The NYPD and seventeen other New York City agencies use over a thousand typewriters today, to the amazement and scorn of many. ("They still have a function and your belief that typewriters have gone away is just erroneous," said pugnacious Mayor Michael Bloomberg in 2012. "It's like books. Some people, believe it or not, still read books in

paper.") Prison inmates, forbidden to use computers, use typewriters with transparent shells that can't hide contraband. Libraries type labels. Funeral homes type official death certificates. You may find typewriters lurking at hospitals, banks, law offices, or dentist's offices. Even spies and diplomats use typewriters for sensitive documents, to avoid electronic theft and snooping.

THE BEGINNER'S TYPEWRITER COLLECTION

You know you're a typewriter collector when you find yourself inventing reasons why you "need" a blue Royal Quiet De Luxe to place next to your pink one, or wishing for a machine with a Greek keyboard even though you don't know the language. If that's you, welcome to a hobby that offers endless variety and a community of supportive fellow obsessives. (Tips to keep your significant other from losing patience: Store your typewriters neatly arranged on shelves, not underfoot, and point out that every one of them is an investment. As the insurgency grows, so does the value of the machines.)

Dedicated, deep-pocketed collectors may spend five figures on a rare Victorian machine. But happily, it's easy to build a modest and affordable typewriter collection that illustrates some historically significant mechanisms. The following typewriters can be found for fifty to two hundred dollars in decent condition. (A fine place to research the varieties and values of these machines is eBay. Before buying online, check the advice in our next chapter.)

- **Hammond**: These machines feature a swiveling, interchangeable type shuttle and a hammer that hits the paper against the ribbon from behind.

- **Blickensderfer**: the most successful of the typewheel machines, inked by a roller, usually sporting the "Scientific" DHIATENSOR layout. Most common model: No. 5.

- **Smith Premier**: a superbly constructed full-keyboard under-stroke. Most common model: No. 2.

- **Oliver**: the "iron butterfly," with an unmistakable look. Most common model: No. 9.

- **Corona No. 3**: a popular portable with a folding carriage.

These typewriters are great conversation starters, and you can even write on them if you're a little patient and hold out for a nice one. Of course, you'll have to adapt to their systems. None of the above uses a four-bank keyboard; the Smith Premier has a double keyboard, and the others usually have three-bank keyboards with double shift (Hammonds also came in a curved two-row layout). None of this will deter a true steampunk or a dedicated iconoclast.

Your collection might branch out to include index typewriters. (The Simplex is a cute toy, made in a wide variety of slightly different designs that you can pick up for as little as ten dollars.) Or you might decide to specialize in typewriters from a certain manufacturer, country, or inventor, or machines of a particular size, color, or decade.

There's no end to the discoveries you can make as a typewriter collector, even if you limit yourself to just a few machines. Every typewriter is a rich field of research: You can investigate its history, its styling, its mechanism—and of course, you can use it to write something the world has never seen before.

There's always room for one more: a small selection from Robert Messenger's collection in Canberra, Australia

COLLECTORS' RESOURCES

ETCetera and *The Typewriter Exchange* are quarterly color magazines in English. (I edited *ETCetera* from 2006 to 2012, took a break to write this book, and began again in 2015.)

European collectors' organizations include IFHB (*Internationales Forum Historische Bürowelt*), ANCMECA (*Association Nationale des Collectionneurs de*

Machines à Écrire et à Calculer Mécaniques), SHBS (Sammlerclub Historischer Büromaschinen Schweiz), and Associazione Italiana collezionisti macchine per ufficio in genere d'epoca.

Helpful online resources include my site The Classic Typewriter Page, the Yahoo! groups TYPEWRITERS and The Portable Typewriter Forum, the Facebook group Antique Typewriter Collectors, and The Typewriter Database, which offers serial number information and the opportunity for collectors to upload and discuss photos of their machines.

FURTHER READING

The most complete books on technical typewriter history are Michael H. Adler's *The Writing Machine* (1973) and, for those who read German, Ernst Martin's *Die Schreibmaschine und ihre Entwicklungsgeschichte* (1949).

The Typewriter and the Men Who Made It by Richard N. Current (1954) is a fine account of the invention of the Sholes & Glidden.

On typewriters and the new forms of work and social organization that arose in the late nineteenth century, see Margery Davies, *A Woman's Place is at the Typewriter* (1982) and Nikil Saval, *Cubed: A Secret History of the Workplace* (2014).

For postmodern takes on the meaning of the typewriter see Friedrich Kittler's *Gramophone, Film, Typewriter* (1999) and Darren Wershler-Henry's *The Iron Whim: A Fragmented History of Typewriting* (2007). Janine Vangool's *The Typewriter: A Graphic History of the Beloved Machine* (2015) highlights the cultural and design aspects of typewriters through the years.

On the transition from typewriters to computers as writing tools see Michael Heim, *Electric Language: A Philosophical Study of Word Processing* (1987) and Matthew Kirschenbaum, *Track Changes: A Literary History of Word Processing* (2016).

For the collector, Darryl Rehr's *Antique Typewriters and Office Collectibles* (1997) is a great beginner's guide; just multiply the values by a factor of four or five. Michael H. Adler's *Antique Typewriters: From Creed to QWERTY* (1997) is a long catalogue of older makes as well as designs that were never commercially produced, with some reasonable guesses at value.

<u>Interlude #2</u>

We strike a blow for self-reliance against dependency.

You work a typewriter, a computer works you. Typewriters you can own. I think a computer owns you.

—*Manson H. Whitlock (1917-2013),*
typewriter repairman

Plato's *Phaedrus* recounts the story that the Egyptian god Theuth, who invented writing, boasted that it would bring memory and wisdom. The god Thamus retorted that it would create forgetfulness and foolishness: Mortals would rely on texts to store their supposed truths, instead of finding them within.

In "Self-Reliance" Emerson complains: "The civilized man has built a coach, but has lost the use of his feet. He is supported on crutches, but lacks so much support for muscle. He has a fine Geneva watch, but he fails of the skill to tell the hour by the sun . . . it may be a question whether machinery does not encumber; whether we have not lost by refinement some energy."

Plato and Emerson are right. When traditional oral bards in India are taught to write, they start to forget their epics. When drivers rely on GPS, they fail to learn the basic topography of their own cities.

Of course, Plato *wrote* his dialogues, and Emerson consulted watches. The point is to remember that every invention can erode our resourcefulness at the same time as it brings convenience. The trick is to benefit from inventions while denying them the power to chain and

William Kentridge, *Large Typewriter*, 2002

define us. To retain our strength, we have to remember the danger of crutches.

Our computing devices are amazingly convenient and powerful. By the same token, they can sap our inner power. If you want to learn how to spell, don't use spell check and autocorrect as crutches; use them sparingly, to train your own memory. If you want to develop accurate typing, use a typewriter, precisely because it's hard to correct your errors.

The dependency fostered by digital devices goes far beyond writing techniques. We jump when the hardware and software manufacturers tell us to, buying the latest model, upgrading our operating system, downloading the latest virus protection. Or we can refuse—and watch our devices grind to a halt as they get out of sync with the times. Many of these updates come with long, turgid legal agreements that nobody reads; we click away our rights and accept obligations without even knowing what we've done.

A typewriter is made to require a ribbon, paper, a little oil, and occasional maintenance. A good one was made to last for decades. The fact that Remington is out of business doesn't stop me from using my 1937 Remington portable today. And when the power goes out, the insurgents happily work off the grid: They draw on their own mind and muscles, working with the trusty tools at their disposal, tools that don't presume to think for us or act for us.

3. Choose Your Weapon

The typewriter kingdom is diverse, with hundreds of designs to choose from. The quest for The Perfect Typewriter is part of the excitement of joining the insurgency.

What defines perfect? Your taste, needs, and passions. Your own ideal typewriter will probably include the right kind of touch, typing that pleases your eye, and some extra features that will sweeten the deal. You may have to date lots of models before you settle on a long-term partner. I also have to warn you that you may find yourself wanting more than one. How about a hefty one for your office desk, a medium one for your den, and a little one to strap on the back of your Harley? (Watch out, though—they breed and multiply. I have no other explanation for the fact that, at last count, I owned 287 typewriters.)

Choosing a writing machine may seem daunting, but if you're equipped with some basic technical knowledge and you're aware of the most popular choices, you'll be off to a good start.

ESSENTIAL VOCABULARY

We'll get into more mechanical details in the next chapter, but here are the basic parts and features to keep in mind when you're hunting for your very own typer—as some insurgents affectionately call them. The location of controls often varies by make and model; pictures of one of my favorite portables and one of my favorite standards will illustrate some typical control locations.

Keys are the buttons you hit on the keyboard. Keep in mind that a manual typewriter and a computer keyboard call for different typing techniques. You'll need to move your fingers with a bit more force, using a staccato touch (pretend the keys are red hot), and more vertical movement is required. Typewriter keyboards are also banked on a slope. Prewar keys typically have round metal rings and glass tops; "keychoppers," much despised by the insurgency, may buy an old typewriter just to cut off these keys for use in jewelry. Postwar keys are typically plastic and cupped to fit your fingertips.

The **carriage** moves from right to left as you type on most typewriters. On a manual typewriter, you use the **carriage return lever** to push the carriage back to the right when you reach the end of each line, which is signaled by a bell. This lever simultaneously advances the paper vertically, so it's also known as the **line space lever**. A **line space selector** on the left end of the carriage determines how many lines up the paper will rise when you return the carriage. As you return the carriage, you are also winding up the **mainspring** that pulls the carriage along when you type. Most older typewriters make a zipping sound as you return the carriage; silent carriage return became more common in the fifties. The mechanism that controls the space-by-space movement of the carriage is called the **escapement**.

A **carriage release** lever or button disengages the carriage from the escapement (the mainspring will then tend to pull the carriage quickly to the left); it's convenient to have such levers on both sides. Most portables have a **carriage lock** that consists of a lever on the left or right end of the carriage, a lever in the upper left corner of the keyboard, or sometimes a position of the line-spacing control that may be marked by a dot; the point of

Carriage return lever
Typeslug
Typebars
Paper guide
Platen
Paper table
Margin stops (behind paper table)
Paper bail
Paper release lever
Carriage release lever
Margin release
Keyboard
Platen knob
Backspacer

the carriage lock is to center and immobilize the carriage during transport.

The **platen**, also known as the roller or cylinder, is the rubber-covered shaft that your paper wraps around. You roll the paper in from the back, upside down and back side toward you. Smaller **feed rollers** behind and in front of the platen press the paper against it. Left and right **platen knobs** can be turned to move the paper up and down.

The **paper release lever**, usually on the right of the carriage, should be in the closed position when you type; you put it in the open (released) position to move the feed rollers away so that you can straighten your paper or pull it out of the typewriter.

The paper rests on a **paper table** or **paper rest** behind the platen, where you'll often find the name of the typewriter.

Older typewriters may use **paper fingers**, vertical devices that press the paper against the platen. Many typewriters use a **paper bail**, a horizontal bar with a couple of rollers that holds the paper against the platen more effectively but does interfere a bit with your view of your typing. When you insert a new sheet of paper, you usually have to lift the paper bail and tuck the top of the sheet under it. Typewriters of the fifties and later often have transparent **plastic paper guides** on either side of the printing point.

Typebars (sometimes inaccurately called keys, hammers, arms, or strikers) are the bars with **typeslugs** on their ends that swing up to the platen.

A **carriage shift** mechanism changes from lowercase to uppercase by moving the carriage (or part of it) up. There's always a spring to assist your pinkies, but you will notice the mass of the carriage on these machines, and some typists find a carriage shift visually distracting.

Segment shift changes from lowercase to uppercase by moving the semicircular slotted segment that holds the typebars. This system is also known as **basket shift**, since it moves the typebasket, or collection of typebars. Since the typebasket is lighter than the carriage, segment shift is easier than carriage shift, and it's preferred by many who are used to the delicate touch of a computer keyboard. Most larger typewriters adopted segment shift by the 1950s. Smith-Corona poetically called it Floating Shift, and Royal called it Shift Freedom; sometimes you find these trademarks on their shift keys.

A **tabulator** moves your carriage to positions or **stops** that are set in advance. A **keyset tabulator** gives you some way to set and clear tab stops from your keyboard, at any point on the typing line; simpler tabulators have a limited number of stops that are found in the rear of the machine, and that you place at your desired points on a rack.

A **touch regulator** or **tension adjuster** controls a spring, or springs, that pull your typebars back into place after each keystroke. If your typewriter has a touch regulator, you can set it for a light and easy feel or a more springy, resistant touch. A springier touch may allow for faster typing.

Margin stops determine the left and right edges of your typing. They are often in back of the carriage. The margin stop controls may peek up over the top, or may be accessible when you tilt the paper table forward or back. A few models, such as Underwood standards, put the margin stops in the front of the typewriter. A warning bell should ring around five spaces before you reach the right margin.

Automatic or **spring-set margin setting** was introduced by Royal with its "Magic Margin" system. You position the carriage at the desired place while pulling a lever or pushing a button.

You can bypass the left and right margins by holding down the **margin release** key, which may be marked with the letters MR, a double-headed arrow, or four dots.

A **typebar release** is a key or lever that gives you a quick way to disentangle typebars when, sooner or later, they get jammed at the printing point. You can also just reach up and flick them back into place with your fingertip. On some models, the margin release key doubles as a typebar release.

Snap is a term typists often use to describe the feel of a manual typewriter. When a typewriter offers a "snappy" experience, keys are easy to depress, but you feel some pleasant, springy resistance; a staccato touch will bring the typebar in a smoothly accelerating motion to the platen and immediately back. The degree of snap depends on your typing technique, as

Tabulator bar

Line space selector

Paper guide

Type guide and printing point

Typebar release

Automatic margin key

Shift lock

Ribbon color selector

Touch regulator

Margin release

OVER THE RIBBON Max Rudiari

Office Digest's
centerfold in 1966.
Best Choice Award
1967 and 1968!

Two novels
and four
short stories.
Two by the hands
of Hemingway!

Tennessee Williams
kissed me once
and Bukowski
spit on me twice!

Now I'm yours for 5 bucks
or buy the stoned little
Gandalf over there
and take me home
for free.

well as on the system of leverage used by a typewriter and the condition of your particular machine.

Now let's take a look at some popular choices in several categories. With all the typewriter models that have been produced between 1870 and now, you'll never run out of new ones to test in the hunt for the ideal machine. But most of the models below are commonly available machines from the mid-twentieth century. They were made when typewriters had reached a high degree of technical excellence, many useful features had been introduced, and the industry was using top-notch materials and manufacturing. (Things went gradually downhill afterwards. Some of the worst typewriters you can buy are new manual portables made today.) I'll start each list with some of my personal favorites.

STANDARDS

Standards, a.k.a. office or desk typewriters, are big, heavy machines designed to stay put and get extensive, professional use. They were built to produce millions of words and last for decades. Good standards have the most features and the best touch—a snappy, speedy, springy feel that most typists like.

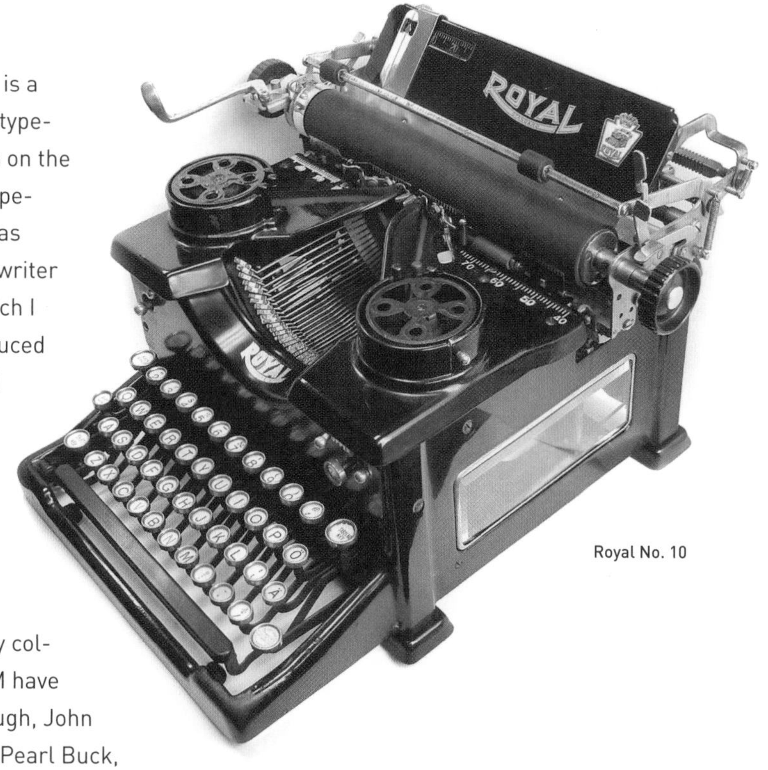

ROYAL: The No. 10 is a beautiful carriage-shift typewriter with glass panels on the sides; some longtime typewriter repairmen see it as the finest standard typewriter ever. Segment shift, which I recommend, was introduced in the thirties. The KMM model introduced the Magic Margin system and includes a keyset tabulator and touch regulator. My own KMM is one of the snappiest, fastest typewriters in my collection. Fans of the KMM have included David McCullough, John Ashbery, Ray Bradbury, Pearl Buck, and Rod Serling. Later Royal standards, which are all good typewriters, include the KMG (Saul Bellow, Joan Didion), HH (George Burns, Truman Capote, Eudora Welty), FP, and Empress. The serial number of a Royal standard can usually be found by moving the carriage all the way to the left and looking at the area revealed on the right; it will begin with a letter or letters that indicate the model, such as KMM-, X- (for the No. 10), or SX- (for the segment-shifted No. 10).

Royal No. 10

Royal KMM

More than forty years later I'm still at it and on the same
old Royal. It has been my sturdy tool of the trade through
every book I've written. . . . More than forty years in
service <u>and there's nothing wrong with it!</u> . . . Lots of
good-hearted, well-meaning friends and relatives have tried
to point out, in an effort to be helpful, how much better
off I would be, the time and effort I could save, using a
word processor. I can't dispute that. I <u>would</u> save time and
effort, no question. But I don't want to go faster. If
anything, I probably ought to go more slowly. Besides, I
like the effort involved. . . . I've always loved making
things with my hands. It's often when I'm happiest, and
that's the feeling I have working at my typewriter. . . .
Who knows, maybe after all it's writing the books!

--David McCullough

OLYMPIA SG1 AND SG3:

The model name is not marked on these West German machines; the SG1 has a bulbous, fifties look, while the SG3 has an angular sixties design. These typewriters are massive and luxurious, with some unusual features such as a paper injector (a lever that quickly advances your paper into typing position) and e x t e n d e d   s p a c i n g (used on several German machines for emphasis). The carriage is huge but runs very smoothly. It comes off in a few seconds for easy cleaning and repairs. (On the SG1, twist the knobs on the sides; on the SG3, lift the front housing and move the locking levers on the sides toward the back.) Features include segment shift, keyset tabulator, touch regulator, and a margin release that doubles as a typebar release. Olympia users include Philip K. Dick, William S. Burroughs, Elmore Leonard, Danielle Steel, and Wallace Stegner.

Olympia SG1
(repainted)

REMINGTON:

Remingtons are known for their solid construction. I recommend the segment-shifted Model 17 from the thirties (a favorite of sportswriter Jim Murray) or, even better, the similar KMC (Keyboard Margin Control), with automatic margin setting; it's recognizable by the KMC keys at the upper corners of the keyboard. After it was sued by Royal, Remington dropped the

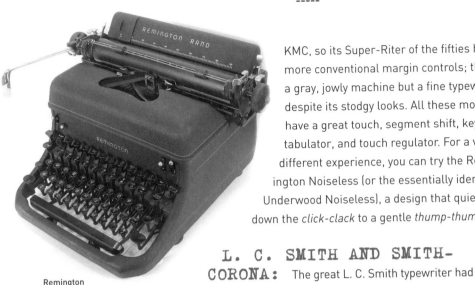

Remington
KMC

KMC, so its Super-Riter of the fifties has more conventional margin controls; this is a gray, jowly machine but a fine typewriter despite its stodgy looks. All these models have a great touch, segment shift, keyset tabulator, and touch regulator. For a very different experience, you can try the Remington Noiseless (or the essentially identical Underwood Noiseless), a design that quiets down the *click-clack* to a gentle *thump-thump*.

L. C. SMITH AND SMITH-CORONA:
The great L. C. Smith typewriter had segment shift from its start in 1904. The company merged with Corona in 1926, becoming Smith-Corona. Available in various models with minor variations, but all are snappy and well-made. L. C. Smith users include H. L. Mencken, Mickey Spillane, and eccentric mystery writer Harry Stephen Keeler. Early L. C. Smiths have the carriage return lever on the right.

UNDERWOOD:
The No. 5 (1900-1933) is the prototypical early twentieth-century office typewriter and the most influential design ever. It's a fine, snappy typewriter when well adjusted. This is a carriage shift machine; segment shift was introduced in the forties. Avoid early No. 5s, on which the right shift key functions only as a shift lock. Visibility on Underwoods isn't perfect due to hardware between you and the paper. The margin stops are easily accessible above the keyboard. Since they're located on the body of the typewriter

L. C. Smith
Super-Speed

instead of on the carriage, the left stop counterintuitively controls the right margin, and the right stop controls the left margin. The many Underwood users include Erle Stanley Gardner, Carson McCullers, Carl Sandburg, and James Thurber.

OTHER OPTIONS:

Woodstock was a smaller American manufacturer that made sturdy, high-quality machines (later called **R. C. Allen**). Most common German standard typewriters are very good; these include **Adler, Triumph,** and **Torpedo**. **Olivetti** standards are also fine, including the Lexikon 80, which is common in Europe and Latin America but hard to find in the US. **Imperials** are good British machines with the interesting feature of an exchangeable keyboard/typebasket unit.

Underwood No. 5

SEMI-PORTABLES

Semi-portables or midsize typewriters come in a case and can be carried around, but may be pretty bulky and heavy. The best midsize machines have almost all the features of a standard, and a nice touch. They're a good solution if you want a companion you can take with you on a drive or bring to a type-in. This is the most popular class of typewriter today.

OLYMPIA SM SERIES: As usual with Olympias, the model isn't indicated on these typewriters, only on the accompanying owner's manual (if you're lucky enough to have one). SM1-5s have a rounded fifties

Olympia SM3
(repainted)

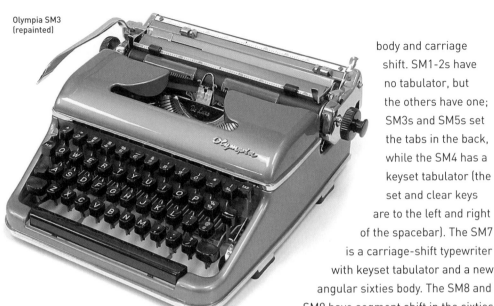

body and carriage shift. SM1-2s have no tabulator, but the others have one; SM3s and SM5s set the tabs in the back, while the SM4 has a keyset tabulator (the set and clear keys are to the left and right of the spacebar). The SM7 is a carriage-shift typewriter with keyset tabulator and a new, angular sixties body. The SM8 and SM9 have segment shift in the sixties body; the SM9 has a keyset tabulator. I recommend the "De Luxe" versions of all these models, with features such as a touch regulator and a paper support that pops up when you push a button. You might also want to look for versions that have carriage release controls on both ends of the carriage; many have the release only on the right (it's a chromed tab that you push down). All are high-quality, durable typewriters. The SM3 has been favored by writers including Woody Allen, Don DeLillo, Robert Penn Warren, John Updike, and Patricia Highsmith. The many users of the SM9 include Paul Auster and J. G. Ballard. If you had to pick just one typewriter to use for the rest of your life, you wouldn't go wrong with an Olympia SM9.

Olympia SM8

SMITH-CORONA: This American company made popular segment-shifted semi-portables for about half a century, starting in the early thirties. The keyboard has an easy, comfortable touch and a system that keeps the keytops horizontal. The earliest models are "flat tops" with a horizontal ribbon cover; then, curvy "speedline" styling was introduced. The beefy machines of the fifties have the sturdiest construction; among these, the Silent-Super model has the most features, including a keyset tabulator. Models of the sixties and seventies such as the Galaxie have a ribbon cover that slides forward; the

Smith-Corona
Silent-Super

The reason I use a manual typewriter concerns the sculptural quality I find in words on paper, the architecture of the letters individually and in combination, a sensation advanced (for me) by the mechanical nature of the process—finger striking key, hammer striking page. Electronic intervention would dull the sensuous gratification I get from this process--a gratification I try to soak my prose in.

--Don DeLillo to David
Foster Wallace

quality of materials and the fit and finish declined a bit in these models, but these are still good typewriters that are easy to find in the US. Late Smith-Coronas may include extra features such as a half-spacer (useful for inserting a missing letter), power spacer (keeps spacing quickly as long as you hold it down), two typebars with changeable type, and a typebar release. All Smith-Corona carriages make some noise when returning, and they are sometimes downright rattly. Smith-Coronas were also sold by Sears under the Tower name, often with nifty styling. Users of Smith-Corona portables include David Mamet, Arthur Miller, T. S. Eliot, and e. e. cummings.

TORPEDO: an excellent German make with a springy, snappy feel. The best and most popular models have segment shift. The company was controlled by Remington beginning in the early thirties. Some sixties Torpedoes are labeled Remington Ten Forty or Remington Mark II and have plastic bodies; the best of these are marked "Made in Western Germany." Later, production moved to Holland. No touch regulator. The Torpedo most commonly found in the US is the Model 18, pictured at the start of this chapter (the model number doesn't appear on it; it's only marked "Torpedo"). Gabriel García Márquez used one of these.

ROYAL: The Royal portables of the twenties and thirties are carriage shifted and sometimes develop escapement problems (they may skip spaces); they are sturdy but not very sophisticated machines. They got some dazzling paint treatments, including two-tone colors and wood grain. Keep an eye out for the "Vogue" sans-serif Deco typeface on these early Royal portables. A more reliable option is the segment-shifted Quiet De Luxe and sim-

Royal Quiet

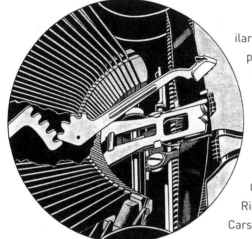

ilar models, with Magic Margin, which were very popular in the forties and fifties. Yes, the Quiet De Luxe actually is pretty quiet, and some were finished in great colors—or even gold plated! Later models with similar mechanisms but new, space-age bodies include the Futura (push the Royal logo to lift the ribbon cover), Safari, Sabre, Sahara, and Caravan. Writers such as Ernest Hemingway, Richard Wright, Edward R. Murrow, and Rachel Carson used Royal portables.

REMINGTON: The Remington semi-portables fall into three very different groups.

From 1920 to 1949 the company produced a variety of carriage-shifted portables with **geared typebars**; when you push a key all the way down, you'll see that the base of the typebar has gear teeth on it. The twenties machines have a knob on the right side that has to be pulled out and pushed back to raise the typebars into typing position. (Another nonintuitive detail: If a geared-typebar Remington portable has a locked carriage, try pulling the right platen knob out. The knob will pop back into the carriage-locking position if you push it in while pulling forward on a small lever near the left end of the carriage.) The curvaceous Remington 5 is especially popular today. All these type-writers are tough and reliable, but less sophisticated than some later models. Their users include Agatha Christie, Allen Ginsberg, Langston Hughes, Margaret Mitchell, and George Orwell.

Remington Streamliner

Remington **noiseless** portables were popular in the thirties and forties. (By arrangement with Underwood, some noiseless portables are labeled with that name, but they are the same Remington design.) They create a quieter, though not silent, typing experience by slowing down the typebars just as they approach the platen. These elegant-looking typewriters have dedicated fans, and my own first typewriter was a Remington Noiseless Model Seven. They require a light staccato touch to avoid skipping and double-printing. Disadvantages: Some typists dislike the feel of the keyboard, finding it unsatisfying or jarring; and the typing may look blurrier or fainter than that of a conventional typewriter. (Make sure you have a well-inked ribbon.) Users of these portables include Arthur C. Clarke, Stanislaw Lem, George Bernard Shaw, and Flannery O'Connor.

Segment-shifted Remington portables were introduced in 1949. The most popular model is the Quiet-Riter of the fifties, which is not especially quiet but is very solidly built; it features a touch regulator and a tabulator that is set and cleared with a lever next to the keyboard. Hermann Hesse used one of these. Some

Remington Noiseless Portable (special two-tone version)

Remington Quiet-Riter
(repainted)

segment-shifted Remingtons made in Germany or Holland, including the
Travel-Riter, are actually Torpedo designs (see above).

Visit The Classic Typewriter Page online for a rundown of all prewar
Remington portables.

UNDERWOOD: The 1920s-1940s Underwood carriage-shifted portables are sturdy, snappy, and well made. Most 1920s machines have only
three rows of keys and are very cute, but
less practical than the later four-bank
models. Fans of these speedy typewriters have included William Faulkner,
Jack Kerouac, and Orson Welles. The
best model is the Champion. Postwar
segment-shifted models introduced
some dramatic styling, but fit
and finish declined a bit
while some other brands
of the day were improving.
The company was acquired

Underwood
Champion

Underwood
Deluxe
Quiet Tab

Underwood-
Olivetti
Studio 44

by Olivetti in 1963, and some late "Underwoods" such as the 315 and 319 are actually Olivetti designs.

OLIVETTI: The postwar
Olivetti portables feature innovative modern styling and segment shift. The Lettera 32 is on the smaller end of the semi-portable class; the unique-looking Studio 44 is on the large end and could be called "luggable." Both are full-featured, good machines. (But choose a Lettera made in Italy or Spain rather than the later, lower-quality ones made in Mexico or Yugoslavia.) Later models, including the famous red Valentine, employed lots of plastic and may be less reliable, but they are

When I started working on the
Grinderman record, I decided that I
would forgo the computer altogether
and write my stuff either in
notebooks or on the typewriter.
The great thing about a manual
typewriter is that it is so
time-consuming to change a line
or a verse, as you have to type
the whole thing over again and
can't simply "delete," that one develops a
renewed respect for the written word. The other thing is
that you never really lose anything. One problem with the
computer is that you can sit down in front of something you
have written in a particularly self-loathing mood and start
hitting delete left, right, and centre and stuff is
consigned undeservedly to oblivion just because you're
having a bad hair day.

--Nick Cave

worth exploring. Olivettis, in my experience, are less snappy than some
German and American machines, but they have many admirers. After the
company acquired Underwood, some of its machines were labeled Olivetti-
Underwood or Underwood-Olivetti; the Underwood 21 is just a Studio 44 in
a new skin. Ralph Ellison and Tennessee Williams used a Studio 44, among
other typewriters. Nick Cave uses a Lettera 25. Francis Ford Coppola and
Cormac McCarthy have favored the Lettera 32. (McCarthy's sold at auction in
2009 for $254,500. He got an identical replacement for under twenty bucks.)

Hermes 3000
(second version)

HERMES: The 3000 model is a Swiss segment-shifted typewriter with excellent alignment, smooth carriage return, and quality manufacturing, introduced in the fifties. You'll find it in a wonderfully bulbous body, painted in a color that some call "sea-foam green," a more angular body (introduced in 1966) that is grayer in color, and a still more angular seventies design. Not the very fastest or snappiest typewriter, but "buttery" in its smoothness, as fans like to say. The controls are in unusual locations; they include an automatic margin mechanism. The margin locations are shown by a red ribbon inside the paper bail. Users include Larry McMurtry, Sam Shepard, Eugene Ionesco, and Stephen Fry. The older 2000 is a good carriage-shift machine.

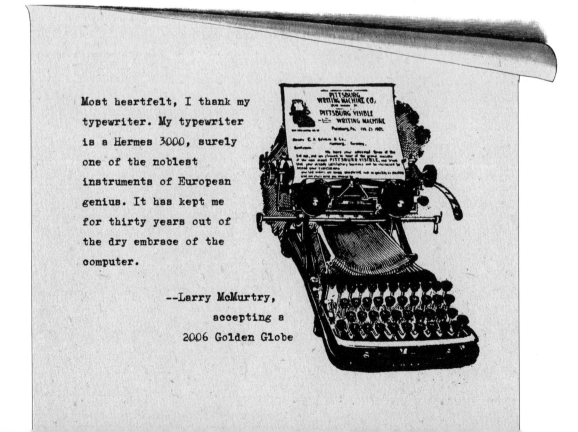

Most heartfelt, I thank my typewriter. My typewriter is a Hermes 3000, surely one of the noblest instruments of European genius. It has kept me for thirty years out of the dry embrace of the computer.

--Larry McMurtry,
accepting a
2006 Golden Globe

FACIT: a Swedish make with distinctive styling, precise engineering, and the smoothest carriage you've ever experienced (the carriage rod rides inside a tube, cradled in ball bearings). The Facit's construction is a bit delicate, in my experience, and may be hard to repair, so make sure it's working when you buy one. Its prede- cessor, the Halda, is also a fine typewriter; make sure it has its original ribbon spools, each with a hinged tab on the bottom.

Facit TP1

VOSS: a midcentury West German make, common in Germany but pretty scarce elsewhere. Vosses of the fifties feature dramatic, biomor- phic styling and a very smooth and comfortable carriage return. The earlier fifties Vosses have "gull wing" ribbon covers; to open them, engage shift lock, push them toward the back of the typewriter, then flip them outwards. Vosses are carriage shifted, and their alignment is not always ideal. Writer James Jones was a Voss user.

Voss De Luxe

Imperial Good
Companion 5

The British **IMPERIAL GOOD COMPANION** series, based on two Torpedo designs and used by writers such as Dylan Thomas and J. B. Priestley, are very nice. I particularly recommend the segment-shifted Models 3, 5, and 7. Some are found in streamlined fiberglass cases.

SIGNATURE was Montgomery Ward's label for typewriters made by several manufacturers. Look for midsize machines with a pushbutton ribbon color selector and a paper injector (a lever on the right end of the carriage that advances the paper several lines), made in Nagoya, Japan, according to a label on the back. The manufacturer of these typewriters is Brother. They are high-quality machines with lots of features, but their touch and carriage return can be a bit heavy and stiff.

OTHER OPTIONS: Most West and East German semi-portables are worthy machines, including **Adler, Alpina, Continental, Erika, Groma, Optima, Rheinmetall,** and **Triumph.** Some of the East German typewriters made it to North America under the name **Aztec.**

OVER THE RIBBON Max Rudiari

ULTRAPORTABLES

Ultraportables are devoted to minimization; they're the laptops of the typewriter world. (Some of us call them "laptaps.") Because of their tiny levers, these mobile devices probably won't have the satisfying feel of a larger typewriter, and they won't have as many features, but some of them are still very good writing machines that can take a beating.

Olympia SF

The **OLYMPIA SF,** like other Olympias, keeps its model name a secret except on the user's manual. You can recognize it by its small size and its carriage shift. For a tiny typewriter, the SF is snappy and sturdy. Some have a very sensitive touch regulator under the ribbon cover, which I'd recommend putting on the easiest setting. These machines are sometimes labeled Splendid and Socialite; a later, boxier, and somewhat less pleasant version is the Traveller. Ian Fleming used an SF when he wanted a small typewriter.

OLIVETTI LETTERA 22: This segment-shifted small portable with tabulator has been acclaimed for its modern design and its overall excellence. For best performance, look for one made in Italy and make sure it's clean. Lettera 22 users have included Leonard Cohen and Sylvia Plath (but you're allowed to type happy thoughts on yours).

GROMA KOLIBRI: a solid East German flat typewriter with attractive styling and good mechanics,

Olivetti
Lettera 22

including the refinement of keys that remain horizontal as you type. Kolibris are common in Germany; some were exported to North America, where today they often sell for a couple hundred dollars. Despite the name, which means hummingbird, Kolibris are fairly heavy for their size. Will Self writes on one. A Kolibri hides under the floorboards in the film *The Lives of Others*.

Groma
Kolibri

TIPPA: German ultraportables by this name were first made by Gossen, then by Triumph-Adler. The earlier Tippas are all-metal and use carriage shift; a plastic body was introduced later, and the Tippa S has a segment shift (it is also labeled Royal Sahara). All are well made. Stanley Kubrick used a yellow Tippa S.

Gossen
Tippa Pilot

BROTHER: The small Brother machines with metal bodies are fine typewriters—precisely made, but a bit on the loud side. They also carry names such as Webster, Signature, Remington 333, and—for when you're feeling particularly devilish—Remington 666. You can recognize Brothers by the label in back saying they were made in Nagoya, Japan.

Remington
333 (made by
Brother)

My Old Flame

An olive green Olivetti 22 portable typewriter, with black
keys and white letters. I bought it in London for forty
pounds in 1959. It's the same typewriter I used for my first
book and my best works. . . . I once had drawn a bath and I
put pine oil in it and I noticed the pine oil stained the
water the same color as my Olivetti. I was in a mood of some
extravagance and I put the typewriter in the bathtub and
tried to type under water. . . .
Then I took the typewriter out
of the bathtub and in a rage
over some imagined injustices
a woman had done to me,
flung it across the
room. . . . The Olivetti
cracked. I thought it was
finished and I just stowed it
in a corner of the house.
About a year later I went to the
Olivetti factory . . . and brought
the thing to the front desk. The man there just looked at it
and said "not a chance." Then--I don't know why--when the
fellow's back was turned I walked in the factory proper,
toward a workbench where an elderly man was working on some
typewriters. I approached him and I said I really needed
this typewriter. He told me to come back in a few weeks, and
when I did he had repaired it meticulously.

--Leonard Cohen

PRINCESS: Slightly larger than most typewriters in this category, and on the heavy side, this is a solid, smooth, top-quality West German machine with carriage shift; the 300 model has all the trimmings. Later produced in Bulgaria (with a bit less precision) as the **Maritsa** and **Omega**. Scarce in the US.

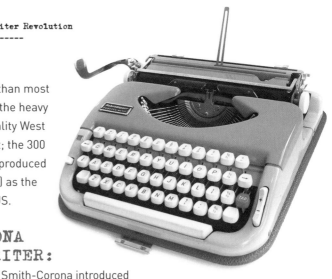

Scheidegger (name variant of the Princess 300)

SMITH-CORONA SKYRITER:

Smith-Corona introduced the ultraportable Zephyr in 1938. Redesigned as the Skyriter in 1949, the rugged little typewriter was advertised as the perfect machine to bring on an airliner. The Zephyr is a good little typer, but much harder to disassemble than the Skyriter, which can be pulled right out of its shell once you remove two screws. The Skyriter's successors were manufactured as late as the seventies in the UK under names such as Corsair, but these later, plastic-bodied machines are flimsy. Ingrid Bergman used a Skyriter.

Smith-Corona Skyriter

ROYAL: In the 1950s, Royal bought the small Halberg typewriter factory in Holland and turned its curvaceous little portable into a bestseller under a plethora of names including Royalite, Dart, Fiesta, Crescent, 590, Parade, Lark, Skylark, Forward, and Eldorado (this last model sports black

Royal Eldorado

and gold paint). All these Dutch-made typewriters have carriage shift and a carriage return lever that pivots on a horizontal axis. In my experience, they have unusually smooth carriages but may have imperfect alignment. Later Royal ultraportables made in Japan are tiny, angular machines that will get the job done but aren't particularly pleasant.

Hermes
Baby

HERMES BABY: Popular for decades, the Baby started an ultraportable trend when it was introduced in the 1930s. Its feel is not especially snappy, but it is compact and very light. Similar models: Featherweight, Rocket. Licensed clones: Montana, Empire Aristocrat. Baby users include John Steinbeck, Joseph Brodsky, and Ho Chi Minh.

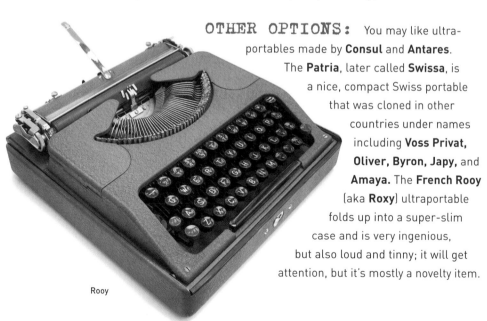

Rooy

OTHER OPTIONS: You may like ultraportables made by **Consul** and **Antares**. The **Patria**, later called **Swissa**, is a nice, compact Swiss portable that was cloned in other countries under names including **Voss Privat, Oliver, Byron, Japy,** and **Amaya.** The **French Rooy** (aka **Roxy**) ultraportable folds up into a super-slim case and is very ingenious, but also loud and tinny; it will get attention, but it's mostly a novelty item.

ELECTRICS

Classic electric typewriters are typically powered by a constantly
spinning internal roller or shaft that makes typing
a breeze. Purists may insist on human-
powered technology, but many typists enjoy
the power that comes from plugging in.

IBM Selectric I

IBM SELECTRIC: This design
revolutionized office typing when it was
introduced in 1961. It uses an interchangeable typing element, nicknamed the "golf
ball," which spins to the right character
and moves across the page as you type.
Other manufacturers imitated this system,
but their machines aren't as reliable. Selectrics are fast, and can use carbon
ribbons that create crisp writing in a variety of typefaces. The Selectric I (a.k.a.
Model 71) has a stylish, rounded shape designed by Eliot Noyes; the II and III
are boxier. The Correcting Selectric II introduced easy error correction. All
are big and heavy. If you want a Selectric, consider investing in a professionally reconditioned one, because when they've been sitting around for years
they almost inevitably need service—and these are mechanically complex
devices, not easy for the amateur to work on. Many writers have used Selectrics, including Isaac Asimov, Erma Bombeck, Ray Bradbury, John Irving, P. J.
O'Rourke, Harold Robbins, David Sedaris, and Hunter S. Thompson. Look up
Charles Bukowski's tribute to the machine, his poem "IBM Selectric."

SMITH-CORONA ELECTRIC PORTABLES:

Smith-Corona introduced the first electric portables in the fifties, based on
their semi-portable manual design, and made them through the seventies.
These are fine machines, heavy but totable. The earlier ones still require
manual return of the carriage. SF writer John Brunner favored 1970s
Smith-Corona electrics, labeling each typewriter with a note to self: "NEVER
UNDERESTIMATE THE STUPIDITY OF EDITORS."

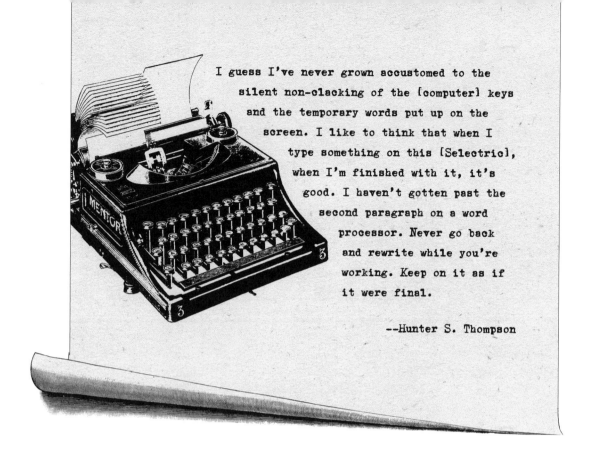

I guess I've never grown accustomed to the silent non-clacking of the [computer] keys and the temporary words put up on the screen. I like to think that when I type something on this [Selectric], when I'm finished with it, it's good. I haven't gotten past the second paragraph on a word processor. Never go back and rewrite while you're working. Keep on it as if it were final.

--Hunter S. Thompson

OTHER OPTIONS: Most major manufacturers offered electric standards. IBM's typebar (non-Selectric) electric typewriters are high quality; keep an eye out for the IBM Executive, with elegant proportional spacing (a *W* is wider than an *I*), recognizable right away by its two spacebars.

Electronic typewriters (electrics with electronic circuits, which typically use interchangeable daisy wheels) are the most common typewriters made today. They get little love among insurgents, who often dismiss them as "plastic wedges," but The Bumbys use them, as do novelists Frederick Forsyth and Javier Marías and singer-songwriter John Mayer. I view electronics as inanimate, while other electrics are on life support and manuals are fully alive. On the more literal level, daisy wheels can be slow, and the visibility usually isn't good.

Electronic typewriters sometimes have a small screen and memory, so they are essentially word processors, computers with a single app. If you're interested in a portable word processor (neither a typewriter nor a full-fledged laptop) consider a gently used AlphaSmart, a discontinued device meant just for writing that will run for hundreds of hours on a couple of ordinary batteries; it can be connected to a normal computer or a printer. A similar, stylish word processor called the Hemingwrite (pictured in Chapter Six) is billed as "a distraction-free writing tool" that is "dedicated like a typewriter."

Alive!

HOW TO IGNORE EVERYTHING I JUST SAID

I've been recommending typewriters that tend to get users' highest ratings for durability, performance, and overall quality. But you know what? Maybe you're not the average typist. Maybe a 1970s K-Mart 300 swathed in funky turquoise plastic will speak to you. And when it calls, you must follow.

On life support

Choosing a typewriter is an act of love. Write on a machine you love, and don't let anyone, including me, tell you that you're wrong.

Speaking of love, for a lovingly detailed description of one man's favorite writing machines, along with other advice for the budding typist, I recommend Scott Schad's Kindle book *Typewriters for Writers.*

Inanimate

K-Mart 300

KEYBOARDS

The typical typewriter has between forty and forty-four typing keys. As for the arrangement of characters, a typewriter keyboard is similar to a computer keyboard, but older English-language typewriters have the apostrophe over the 8 and quotation mark over the 2. A frequent question is, "Where's number one?" If your typewriter doesn't have a special numeral 1, just use a lowercase L. If it doesn't have an exclamation mark, you can type apostrophe-backspace-period—or hold down the shift key and spacebar (immobilizing the carriage), then type apostrophe-period.

Typewriters can also include characters you won't find on a computer keyboard, such as ½ and ¼. British typewriters simply love fractions, and are packed with useful ones such as ⅝. Standard Olympias often include a superscript th and a 1/ key so you can create a new fraction. All sorts of specialized symbols are also possible.

There are national differences between keyboards, many of which survive in the digital era. The English-language standard is QWERTY, introduced on the very first "Type Writer," the Sholes & Glidden of 1873. The German variant is QWERTZ, the French is AZERTY, and the old Italian typewriter keyboard is QZERTY. Of course, typewriters were also made

OVER THE RIBBON Max Rudiari

with non-Roman alphabets; the easiest to find are Cyrillic, Greek, Hebrew, and Arabic.

Since the nineteenth century, various alternatives to QWERTY have been proposed, such as Blickensderfer's DHIATENSOR or the Dvorak keyboard, but the force of habit means that the layout of the Sholes & Glidden still dominates even the most advanced smartphones.

A refinement found on Smith-Corona semi-portables, many Erika portables, and the Groma Kolibri, among other makes, is a system that keeps each keytop horizontal as you type, for a sensation that some find comfortable and appealing.

Once in a while you'll find a teaching keyboard that color-codes the keys to help you remember which fingers to use, or has blank keys to force you to develop your memory.

TYPEFACE AND PITCH

While we refer to computer *fonts*, we talk about typewriter *typefaces* or *type styles*; and instead of *font size* we refer to *pitch.*

Most typewriters use ten-pitch type (ten characters to the inch), also known as "pica," or the smaller twelve-pitch type, called "elite." You can

often recognize the pitch of the type from the scale on the machine's paper table: On a normal-width carriage, a pica scale will go up to about eighty, and an elite to about one hundred. Some typewriters, especially European ones, use pitches between these two. You'll also occasionally find extraordinarily small or large type.

Typewriter manufacturers often bought their typeslugs from independent type foundries, such as Germany's RaRo (Ransmayer-Rodrian). You may find a tiny foundry logo and a number indicating the typeface stamped between the upper and lowercase characters on the typeslug.

abcdefghijklmnopqrstuvwxyz
ABCDEFGHIJKLMNOPQRSTUVWXYZ
0123456789"#$%_&'()-*½¼¢@?

abcdefghijklmnopqrstuvwxyz
ABCDEFGHIJKLMNOPQRSTUVWXYZ
0123456789*"/@£_&'()-?$\frac{31}{44}$%+

abcdefghijklmnopqrstuvwxyz
ABCDEFGHIJKLMNOPQRSTUVWXYZ
0123456789;"+%&()_§/ß£$?!öüä

abcdefghijklmnopqrstuvwxyz
ABCDEFGHIJKLMNOPQRSTUVWXYZ
0123456789+"#$%_&'()*!?¢@½

abcdefghijklmnopqrstuvwxyz
ABCDEFGHIJKLMNOPQRSTUVWXYZ
0123456789"#$%_&'()*½¢@?¼;

abcdefghijklmnopqrstuvwxyz
ABCDEFGHIJKLMNOPQRSTUVWXYZ
0123456789!"#$%_&'()-=+¢?*

abcdefghijklmnopqrstuvwxyz
ABCDEFGHIJKLMNOPQRSTUVWXYZ
0123456789"#$%_&'()-*½¼∧@?

abcdefghijklmnopqrstuvwxyz
ABCDEFGHIJKLMNOPQRSTUVWXYZ
0123456789!"#$%_&'()*-½¢@?

abcdefghijklmnopqrstuvwxyz
ABCDEFGHIJKLMNOPQRSTUVWXYZ
0123456789¿&"'()_è^çà+½¼!?

abcdefghijklmnopqrstuvwxyz
ABCDEFGHIJKLMNOPQRSTUVWXYZ
0123456789!"#$%_&'()-*=+¢?

abcdefghijklmnopqrstuvwxyz
ABCDEFGHIJKLMNOPQRSTUVWXYZ
0123456789@#$%¢&*()-=+!;"/?

abcdefghijklmnopqrstuvwxyz
ABCDEFGHIJKLMNOPQRSTUVWXYZ
0123456789*"/@£_&'()$\frac{3}{8}\frac{1}{8}\frac{7}{8}\frac{5}{8}\frac{2}{3}\frac{2}{3}\frac{1}{3}\frac{3}{4}\frac{1}{4}\frac{1}{2}$

abcdefghijklmnopqrstuvwxyz
ABCDEFGHIJKLMNOPQRSTUVWXYZ
0123456789"/()_¿?!ꞟ₤ªℓ%=;

abcdefghijklmnopqrstuvwxyz
ABCDEFGHIJKLMNOPQRSTUVWXYZ
0123456789+"#$%_&'()*⅌°∧√?

abcdefghijklmnopqrstuvwxyz
ABCDEFGHIJKLMNOPQRSTUVWXYZ
0123456789"#$%_&'()*-½¢@½¼?

abcdefghijklmnopqrstuvwxyz
ABCDEFGHIJKLMNOPQRSTUVWXYZ
0123456789¾!"#$%_&'()-*=+

abcdefghijklmnopqrstuvwxyz
ABCDEFGHIJKLMNOPQRSTUVWXYZ
0123456789+"#$%_&'()*¾½¼¢?

1ςερτυθ**ιοπ**˜ασδφγηξκλ'`ζχφωβνμ
QWEPTΥΘΙΟΠ˛ΑΣΔΦΓΗΕΚΛ¨˙ΖΧΨΩBNM
)23456789-ʿ(CSDRGUJFL˅V'"″

§№-/":,.‿?%!+1234567890=
йцукенгшщзхъфывапролджэячсмитьбюё
ЙЦУКЕНГШЩЗХЪФЫВАПРОЛДЖЭЯЧСМИТЬБЮЁ

جحخهعغفقثصضكمنتالرزوسش

ةؤرﻻءيلاىةوزظذدجحبا؟
:طظدذ×حعفقرؤ؟١٢٣٤٥٦٧٨٩٠ ١٢٣

ששאבגדהוזחטיךכלמנסעפצקרת,
9876543210
ששאבגדהוזחטיךכלמנסעפצקרת
~.:;[]ʾ()-

The typical "typewriter typeface" has no single name, and in fact it varies, as you'll see if you compare characters, especially numerals, on typefaces produced by different foundries.

The main alternatives to the standard typefaces include:

Print-style typefaces with slightly broader vertical strokes. These typefaces are very elegant, although the effect may be hard to see if you're typing through a coarse ribbon. They include Oliver's Printype and Olympia's Congress.

Cursive or *script* typefaces became popular in the fifties, especially on portables meant for women's personal correspondence. There are several styles of script. I myself find it charming in small doses, but wouldn't want to read a long text in cursive. Some script typefaces require a single-color ribbon because of the vertical extension of some of their capitals.

Sans serif typefaces include Royal's Vogue type, in the Art Deco style, and so-called techno typefaces, with squared-off letters, which gained popularity in the sixties.

Italic typefaces are unusual, as are other exotic styles such as German *Fraktur* (blackletter).

You may find a typewriter that types in caps only. It may be a low-budget Depression-era machine without a shift, or a machine used by telegraphers (a so-called "mill").

Typewriters with interchangeable type elements will let you switch from one style to another nearly as quickly as we change fonts in our word processing programs. The most famous such modern typewriter is the IBM Selectric.

Most typewriters are *monospaced,* assigning the same width to each character, but several manufacturers have tried marketing *proportional* (or *differential spacing*) typewriters that vary the width of characters. The only proportional typewriter that had a significant market presence was the IBM Executive, a top-of-the-line electric typebar machine. The Varityper DSJ was a specialized machine with interchangeable, proportional type shuttles that was typically used to prepare copy for offset printing. The main challenge for users of proportional typewriters is memorizing the width of every character, which is necessary when you need to go back and correct an error.

CASES

Until around 1920, standard typewriters were usually sold with a wooden base and a metal cover. If you're buying an antique, a cover and base are definitely desirable, especially because they will have protected the machine from the environment.

Portables are often in better condition than standards because they were made to be kept in a case. A portable without a case may show more signs of age.

Older portable cases are usually made of wood covered in black cloth; the cloth is often peeling and the wood may be coming apart, but wood glue can do wonders for both problems. Newer cases may be leatherette, plastic, or fiberglass. Whatever the material, you'll almost always find that they have only a little handle, as if shoulder straps hadn't been invented. For comfort, consider toting an ultraportable in a laptop case with a shoulder strap. You can also often fit a typewriter into a wheeled carry-on bag.

Take a look inside every typewriter case when you're on the hunt. You might find not only a great machine, but supplies (carbon paper, erasers, correction tape, brushes), literature (owner's manual, warranty, official factory typing test sheet), and writings by a former owner.

WHERE TO FIND THEM: ONLINE AND OFF

The Internet makes a bounty of pre-Internet objects available to the world. Auction sites, predominantly eBay, offer thousands of typewriters for sale every day. The risk of buying a typewriter at a distance, though, is that you can't check it out in person and it may get damaged in shipping.

Even if you never buy online, I recommend spending plenty of time exploring eBay to educate yourself and develop a sense of various models' scarcity and value (check completed auctions for prices). To dig deeper, search for misspellings ("typewritter," "typerwriter," "type writer," "typewrighter" . . .). Sometimes sellers neglect to put "type-

The Urban
Legend Institute,
Cincinnati, Ohio

writer" in their auction title, so go to the categories (*Collectibles: Pens and Writing Instruments: Typewriters* and *Antiques: Mercantile, Trades & Factories: Typewriters*) and search for "-typewriter" to catch a few more listings. Don't miss the opportunity to search for *Schreibmaschine* (and the common misspelling "*Schreibmaschiene*") on German eBay (ebay.de) to learn about a wide variety of German and other European typewriters. Other European sources include *macchina da scrivere* on ebay.it, *máquina de escribir* on ebay.es, and *machine à écrire* on ebay.fr. (You may leave out the accent marks.)

Once you're educated, try finding a typewriter locally. See whether anyone offers typewriter repair in your area, either as an individual or as part of a larger office machine business. (I maintain a list of repair shops on The Classic Typewriter Page.) Some people only offer repair services, but others will also have machines for sale. They won't be the cheapest typewriters around, but you'll get a professionally cleaned and tuned machine, and you can start a relationship with someone who has a wealth of knowledge about these objects. There's more on typewriter shops in our next chapter.

Local sources of unrestored typewriters include thrift stores, estate sales, and antique malls. Check the local classified ads, including sites such as Craigslist.

Sometimes buying online is the only way to get the typewriter you want. If you find a good-looking machine on eBay at a fair price from a seller with a good reputation, you can "buy it now" if that's an option, or "snipe" by bidding the maximum price you're willing to pay within the last ten seconds of the auction. Sniping is always the smartest bidding strategy, as it prevents others from reacting to your bid and trying to outbid you; of course, it does not guarantee that you'll win. If you can't stand the high drama of sniping or the ending time is inconvenient, use an automatic bidding service that will snipe on your behalf.

There are many smaller online sources beyond eBay. One popular site for typewriters is Etsy, where prices tend to be higher but the average quality is better. A good number of typewriters on Etsy have been carefully restored or repainted.

When you've bought a typewriter online, you'll have to get it shipped. This is a perilous moment: Typewriters are delicate, and the heavier an object is, the greater the risk of damage in shipping. I usually ask the seller to follow some simple rules:

1. Lock the carriage, if possible. (Most portables have a lever on the left or right, under the carriage, that locks it in place in the middle of the machine. On Olympias, the lever may be in the upper left corner of the keyboard.)

2. If the typewriter is a portable in a case, make sure it is attached firmly to the bottom of the case, and surround it with enough packing material *inside* the case to make motion impossible. If it doesn't have a case, put it in a snugly fitting box, again with enough packing material to immobilize it.

3. Put the case or the box inside another strong box, allowing at least three inches on all six sides for packing material. The safest packing material is bubble wrap. Foam peanuts may or may not be sufficient; they can shift around, and some kinds are easily crushed. Again, the heavier a typewriter is, the more protection it needs.

You may want to promise the seller a small bonus and positive feedback *if* the machine arrives correctly packed and unharmed. Be polite, and wish on your lucky star.

KICKING THE TIRES

A typewriter lies before you. Is it The One? What should you do?

Feed in a piece of paper. If it won't feed smoothly or skews to the side, there may be an obstruction, or the feed rollers may be flat and need replacing.

Hit a few keys, of course. Does the carriage advance after every keystroke and every touch of the spacebar?

If the carriage doesn't move at all, and it's centered, maybe it's locked. If that isn't it, look for a broken or disconnected strap or cord under the carriage; it can be replaced if need be. You can still push the carriage gently to the left and see whether everything else works.

If the carriage moves only occasionally, the typewriter may need cleaning and adjustment, or its escapement may be damaged (a bad problem).

Go ahead and test every key on the keyboard. Do the typebars get stuck at the printing point? That's not unusual—they may just need a little cleaning or alignment—but nonsticking typebars are a sign of a machine that's been well cared for.

Smith-Corona typebars sometimes get detached from a link that connects to their bottom end; fortunately, the link can easily be reattached. Royal portables have a weak point in their key levers, so you may find that a key is broken and dangling down; replacing the lever is very challenging, and such a typewriter is best considered a parts machine.

Find the carriage release and run the carriage back and forth a few times. It should run smooth and easy. A slightly resistant or squeaky carriage probably just needs cleaning and lubrication; grinding or scraping is a bad sign (but it may easily be fixed on Olympia midsize portables by replacing the squashed rubber bushings near the feet).

Rub and tap the rubber on the platen. Ideally it will feel a little bouncy, not rock hard. We'll discuss what to do about a hard platen in our next chapter, but other things being equal, let's hope the platen isn't petrified.

Can you set the margins and move past them using the margin release key? When you approach the right margin, does the bell ring? When you reach the margin, you should be prevented from typing any more.

Don't be concerned if the ribbon is old and faded, but see whether it's advancing when you type, rising up properly to the black and red positions and coming down quickly after each keystroke. Everything is fixable in theory, but ideally you shouldn't have problems in the ribbon department.

Type out several lines and see if you like the look and feel. A classic test sentence is "Now is the time for all good men to come to the aid of the party" (a common variant is "of their country"). Amazingly, this typing tradition dates back to the development of the Sholes & Glidden in the 1860s, according to Charles E. Weller, who was there. It's also fun to type a pangram, a sentence that uses all the letters in the alphabet. The most famous one is "The quick brown fox jumps over the lazy dog." My favorite is "Blowzy night-frumps vex'd Jack Q.," which uses each letter only once.

Pay attention to the sound of the machine, too. Does it grate on you? Hurt your ears? Or is it glorious percussion? As typewriter lover Tom Hanks puts it, when you get a good typewriter rhythm going, "the muscles in your hands control the volume and cadence of the aural assault so that the room echoes with the staccato beat of your synapses." (Ironically, his favorite machine is a forties Corona Silent.)

Every used typewriter is unique. It's been touched a million times by its owner; it has shivered, rattled, and sung as the muscles in the writer's fingers have shot typebar after typebar to the ribbon, machine and human becoming one. As the habits of its user create nicks and quirks, the typewriter's behavior becomes more individual. A computer gets packed with data, but it's just a disposable vehicle; a typewriter remembers nothing that you type on it, but your personality rubs off on it.

Take a little time to discover the particular character of the typewriter you're examining. Maybe it will match your own personality and desires, inviting you to add a new layer of character as *you* use it, creating your own physical bond with the machine.

At last you've chosen a typewriter. Congratulations! With a little care, this machine will be a life companion, a partner in your storytelling, a witness to your most intimate thoughts.

Your relationship is just getting started.

Interlude #3

We strike a blow for privacy against surveillance.

Digital creations can be found in a split second. But what if you don't want to be found? Think of every e-mail you've sent, product you've rated, video you've uploaded. Our phone calls, purchases, and driving are digital. In cities, digital cameras record us at every step. The Internet is constantly crawled by bots that crunch data far more efficiently than any old-fashioned Ministry of Truth could. Social networks and spy agencies identify faces in your snapshots; video sites pinpoint the song that's playing in your home movie. Some digital picture frames have been found to transmit data from owners' PCs back to China. In 2012, the director of the CIA himself was exposed as an adulterer because he communicated with his mistress electronically.

To quote Edward Snowden, "Any unencrypted message sent over the Internet is being delivered to every intelligence service in the world." And thanks to spyware, the fact that you didn't put a document online doesn't mean that it's safe on your personal computer.

But your humble typewriter has the power to circumvent this entire system. File your typescript in a safe place, and there will be no copy unless you want one. No one will see it unless you choose. Mail it to a trusted correspondent, and only the two of you will be the wiser. (But be aware that the exterior of every piece of US mail is now scanned.) This is why, in 2013, the Kremlin's Federal Protective Service invested in a phalanx of machines capable of outwit-

ting the latest, greatest algorithms. Yes: typewriters (twenty Triumph-Adler Twen 180s). Other government units relying on typewriters for security include MI6's top secret facility at Hanslope Park, England, and the High Commission of India in London. Privacy-sensitive Germany has seen a spike in typewriter sales.

Of course, offices can be burglarized, mail can be opened, and it's well known among forensic document examiners that every manual typewriter creates distinctive work. Carbon ribbons retain a record of your writing, and in the eighties the Soviets even devised a way to bug the Selectrics used in the US Embassy. But these physical methods are so inefficient that a typist's privacy is highly reliable unless you have already been identified as an important target.

The privacy problem also extends to the voluntary oversharing that the Internet encourages. The default setting for our existence is worldwide publicity. Snowden warns: "A child born today will grow up with no conception of privacy at all. They'll never know what it means to have a private moment to themselves, an unrecorded, unanalyzed thought." The consequences of the principle that "all that happens must be known" have been explored in all-too-realistic dystopias such as Gary Shteyngart's *Super Sad True Love Story* and Dave Eggers's *The Circle*. Let's just say that it isn't good.

The typewriter insurgency insists that we have the right to keep our words our own. In a time of publicness run amok, typewriters build a space for privacy.

The Typist's Creed

This is my typewriter. There are
many like it, but this one is mine.
My typewriter is my best friend. It
is my life. I must master it as I
must master my life. My typewriter,
without me, is useless. Without my
typewriter, I am useless. I must type
true. I must write better than my
rival who is trying to outwrite me.
I must outwrite him before he outwrites
me. My typewriter and I know that
what counts in writing is not the
number of pages we type, the noise we
make, nor the ribbons we wear out.
We know that it is the words that count.
My typewriter is human, even as I,
because it is my life. Thus, I will
learn it as a brother. I will learn
its weaknesses, its strength, its
parts, its accessories, its carriage,
and its keys. I will keep my
typewriter clean and ready, even as
I am clean and ready. We will become
part of each other. Before God, I
swear this creed.

4. Learn It as a Brother

Your typewriter is a tool for innovation. You'll write things on it that no one has ever written before. You may even create art and music with it. But in order to get the most from it, you need to learn what it was meant to do. You'll appreciate the craft that went into it as you explore its every feature.

You'll also eventually want to learn how to keep your machine running well. You'll be able to make little adjustments to bring it back to top condition when it gets out of whack. You may even find yourself becoming a typewriter-repair expert.

As you and your typewriter learn to coexist, you'll enjoy developing skill and power in conjunction with this mechanical companion that, for all your knowledge, is never completely under your control; it remains an independent, sometimes stubborn thing that develops quirks and scars over the years.

The experience of developing a close relationship with a mechanical thing is one of the most satisfying aspects of the typewriter insurgency. As Anthony Rocco puts it, "When you sit down at a typewriter, it's never the same experience. It's always going to be a little different. You have to be a dancer that's ready to make a split-second difference." Yancy Smith reflects:

> Typewriters have no mechanical signature fresh out of the factory; that signature is lent to them by those who use the specific machine. That mechanical fingerprint can be nearly as unique as an actual fingerprint. . . . Each product one makes on a typewriter not only depends on how the user physically interacts with the machine, it depends on how all users have interacted with the machine. . . . It is a machine that mass produces words, but this very property imbues it with a particular aura.

A typewriter's specific aura incorporates the history of the people who've used it before you, as well as the history of those who made it and the company that employed them. Spend some time researching that company and the models that it put on the market.

You may recognize the general era of a typewriter from its style, but it's always gratifying to learn the particular year it was made. Although we don't have data on every make, the online Typewriter Database dates many models by serial number.

But where is the serial number? You may have to do some searching. Try running the carriage all the way to the left and right and looking at the areas that were covered by the carriage; look on the bottom of the typewriter; open or remove the ribbon cover and look in the areas near the ribbon spools; check the slotted comb behind the keyboard.

Search for an owner's manual, if you don't have one yet; it will point you to the machine's major parts and functions. I provide quite a few on The Classic Typewriter Page.

SUPPLIES

Is there a mom-and-pop office store in your town that's been there for decades? Stop by and check it out. My own local store, Spitzfaden's on Cincinnati's Main Street, has a whole corner devoted to typewriter ribbons (which I've raided repeatedly), stacks and stacks of paper for many purposes, and a trove of other old-fashioned office supplies.

If you're not lucky enough to have such a place, you can still find lots of good supplies at a big box store or online.

RIBBONS

"Do they still make those, uh, ink strips?" may be the number one question you get from people puzzling over your writing tool of choice. Happily, the answer is yes. The Internet, of course, makes it easy to locate typewriter ribbons for sale.

Fully understanding your ribbon options and needs is not quite as easy, but it's worth learning, since the ribbon plays an essential part in the appearance of your typed words.

MATERIAL: Most cloth ribbons these days are nylon, which works very well. A more traditional material is cotton, which holds a lot of ink but is a bit less durable and sometimes has a coarse weave that will show up on the paper. A traditional luxury material is silk. Then there are film ribbons

OVER THE RIBBON Max Rudiari

(also known as carbon ribbons), which are very long strips of thin plastic with a one-time-use layer of pigment on one side. Film ribbons make for crisp, clean typing, but they won't work with every typewriter. IBM Selectrics are made to accept them, as are some other electrics and a few manual standards. If your manual typewriter advances the ribbon quickly enough to avoid overlapping characters, then you can probably install a film ribbon for a Selectric and get beautiful results. Use a noncorrectable ribbon for the IBM Selectric I (also known as the Model 71).

INK: Ribbons come in various colors. If your typewriter has a color change switch, you can use a bicolor ribbon. The switch will typically be marked with a blue position (for the upper half of the ribbon), a red position (for the lower half), and a white position (for using no ribbon at all, a setting meant for typing stencils to use with a mimeograph). A few typewriters even give you the option of typing right in the middle of the ribbon. The point of this setting is to get the most out of a single-color ribbon: Type on the top until it's worn out, type on the bottom (or flip and switch the spools), then type in the middle. The most common bicolor ribbons are black and red, but you may also find them in black and blue, or other combinations. As for single-color ribbons, I've found purple, green, brown, and red ones when digging through old stock at Spitzfaden's; FJA Products makes them in exotic colors such as orange and pink. Sometimes ribbons are over-inked (especially if they're intended for printing calculators); this can be remedied by wiping the ribbon firmly with a paper towel. As for re-inking a worn-out ribbon, I don't particularly recommend it—not as long as new ribbons are still cheaply available. However, if you want to give it a try, use ink made for metal stamps (not rubber ones) and apply modest quantities. You may also find that your ribbon is dry but still contains plenty of ink; you can freshen it up. Unspool the ribbon into a box, keeping both ends out of the box; spray moderately with WD-40; respool the ribbon and let it sit overnight. (This is the only use that the insurgency has for WD-40. Don't spray it on your machine.)

SPOOLS: The spools, or reels, on which the ribbon is wound must be appropriate to your typewriter. Older spools are metal; today they're made of plastic, of course. If you have some metal spools that fit your typewriter, it's smart to keep them; you can wind a new ribbon onto them. You usually attach a ribbon to a spool by forcing it onto a little arrowhead at the center of the spool or holding it on with a clip. The most common American spool design originated on Underwoods and fits many other makes. Some German typewriters require a spool known as DIN 2013, which has a wider central hole. Royal and Smith-Corona standards have special spools just for them. Noiseless portables and post-1950 Remingtons wind the ribbon onto a small metal core, which fits over the ribbon mechanism and is then covered with a removable circular lid (if you don't have a metal core, it may be enough just to tuck the end of the ribbon into the mechanism). Olivetti spools are also unique, and are held on with a round nut that mustn't be lost. As you can see, this can all get a bit confusing; fortunately, some modern plastic spools are "universal" spools that will fit almost any portable typewriter (note that they may have a central element that can be removed so they'll fit those Remingtons and some late Underwood standards). And when you're really stuck, a typewriter repair shop or your fellow insurgents will give ready advice.

WIDTH: Ribbon widths varied a great deal in the nineteenth century, but in the twentieth most manufacturers adopted a standard half-inch width (13 mm). Some film ribbons are narrower or wider, and some typewriters, particularly late Royals, call for a 9/16" ribbon (14.3 mm). If you find that the tops of your letters keep getting cut off, it's possible that the device that holds the ribbon and moves it up and down as you type—excitingly called the ribbon vibrator, or more prosaically the ribbon carrier—is not rising high enough; but it's also possible that it's intended for a 9/16" ribbon.

EYELETS: These are little metal grommets that are inserted near the two ends of a ribbon. Many typewriters use eyelets to trigger the automatic ribbon reverse mechanism. If your ribbon passes through a narrow fork near the spool, and that fork can be moved back and forth to trigger the ribbon reverse (either immediately or when followed by striking a key), then you usually need a ribbon with eyelets; if not, you don't. An unwanted eyelet can be removed by cutting off the end of the ribbon and reattaching the remainder to the spool. A missing eyelet can be replaced by tying a knot in a ribbon, by inserting a brass fastener and cutting its legs short, or by using a proper eyelet-installing tool, available at craft shops.

INSTALLING A RIBBON: If there's an old ribbon on your typewriter, observe and take notes. You want to note how the spools turn, and exactly how the ribbon is threaded through the mechanism. Most typewriters have retaining arms that push the ribbon against the spools and hold the spools in place; these arms can simply be pulled out of the way. The ribbon may need to go around a post and/or pass through a fork

Some typical ribbon paths

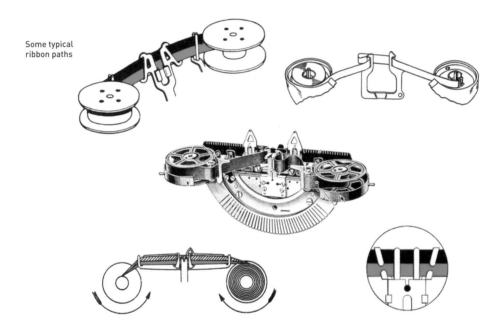

before it reaches the ribbon vibrator. The ribbon must weave in and out of the vibrator, in such a way that the portion of the ribbon in the center of the vibrator is as close as possible to the paper. When installing a bicolor ribbon, the more frequently used color (usually black) should go on top to avoid unnecessary and distracting motion of the vibrator. And you may need to wind your new ribbon onto a different spool; I'm sure you can figure out how to do this—you're an insurgent!

Changing a ribbon is a messy but loving operation. Some typewriters make it a bit easier by letting you pinch open the vibrator, which will then close when you type. To get the best access to the vibrator, depress shift lock, set the color selector on red, and push two typebars together at the printing point in order to keep the vibrator in its highest position. But no matter how you do this job, you'll end up with inky fingers that could use a squirt of hand cleaner.

PAPER

Ordinary printer or copy paper will work fine on a typewriter. Of course, many other kinds of paper are available and are worth checking out. These include vintage papers such as onionskin—a thin, crinkly paper that was used for making multiple copies or for saving weight in airmail letters. Other sorts of old paper can be found on eBay, including erasable typing paper (such as Eaton's Corrasable Bond), which allows you to do just what it says, but can be smudgy.

Customized paper—everything from fancy personalized stationery to reproductions of vintage letterhead that you can find online—can provide extra entertainment for the lucky recipient of your letter. Have fun browsing through stationery shops and art stores.

One or two backing sheets are a smart way to provide some cushioning. This is especially helpful if you have a hard platen or you're not quite satisfied with the evenness of your typewritten impressions.

CORRECTION

If you can train yourself to play a melody on an instrument without making a mistake, you can also type without mistakes. Our computers have made it so easy to hit "delete," though, that many of us have developed speedy but sloppy typing. A typewriter is less forgiving. "Mistakes are like tracks in new fallen snow," as typewriting blogger Mark Hinton has put it. Still, even snow can be smoothed over.

Ways to correct a mistake include:

1. Plastic film rectangles, coated on one side with white cover-up material. Slip one behind the ribbon, retype the offending character, and the error is hidden. These are known as typewriter correction tabs or typing correction film, and they are my favorite way to fix mistakes. Paper correction tabs were also made, but the plastic film works better. I'm not aware of anyone who makes it anymore, but old stock by manufacturers such as Ko-Rec-Type, Tipp-Ex, Wite-Out, and Liquid Paper turns up on eBay.

2. Erasing: Special typewriter erasers were made in a circular shape with an attached brush, or in the form of a pencil. You often find eraser crumbs in the innards of typewriters—the leavings of users who ignored manufacturer instructions. The proper way to erase is to move the carriage to the left or right so the crumbs won't fall into the sensitive heart of the machine. Careful typists also used eraser shields, little cards that would let the eraser affect only the part of the typing that appeared through a hole in the card. The problem with erasing is that it rarely makes the mistake disappear completely, and it often damages the paper. If you want to use this method, you might want to look for erasable paper.

3. Correction fluid: messy and tedious. You often find streaks of this white liquid on typewriters' transparent plastic paper guides. The stuff is one of the most despised memories of those who grew up using typewriters.

4. IBM Correcting Selectrics and some other electric typewriters can use correctable film ribbons and a special correction tape that actually lifts the unwanted carbon off the paper. A very nice method if you like using these machines.

5. Cloth typewriter ribbons with a white correction strip on their bottom half. It must have seemed like a good idea at the time, but I don't recommend these; the white stuff eventually flakes off, turning your typewriter into a dandruffy disaster zone.

6. Modern correction tape comes in little plastic dispensers that will stick a neat white ribbon over the problem. These are the best readily available solution. In order to use them while typing, you may need to roll the paper up to the flat paper table of your typewriter.

A missing letter can often be squeezed in, especially on typewriters with a half-spacing feature (the carriage advances half a space when you hold the spacebar down or if you push a special half-space button).

Some typists like to aim for perfection and will actually enjoy correcting all their typos. Myself, I'd rather xxxx over a mistake. Let the typescript reflect your humanity and imperfection, I say—everything that poet Les Murray, a typewriter devotee, calls "the spoor of botch." Then go over it with a pen and add corrections, insertions, deletions, arrows. There is a certain beauty to a typescript that shows a creative mind at work. Seamlessness can wait for the edited version that you retype on a computer.

COPIES

The traditional tool for making typewritten copies is carbon paper. A vestige of this tradition can be found in the "cc:" field on an e-mail; it originally stood for "carbon copy." If you want to try this, you can still readily find vintage or even new carbon paper. Just slip the carbon between two sheets of typing paper. You can also make more copies, with more carbon paper and more sheets—but the typing requires progressively more force. Electric typewriters usually have a force setting that can be amped up. Thinner paper will work better. Carbon paper can be used multiple times.

Of course, you can also copy a typescript by photographing, scanning, or photocopying it. All these methods are digital these days, so if you don't want any yucky ones and zeros sticking to your typing, carbon copies are the way to go.

For completely nondigital home publishing, you could invest in a mimeograph machine, a simple printing system invented by Thomas Edison. You'll need mimeograph ink and stencils, which are sheets with a waxy coating. To type stencils, disengage your typewriter ribbon by setting the color selector on the white position. The area where the coating is displaced by your typing will hold ink and make a copy. Mimeograph paper should be uncoated, so that the ink will sink in quickly and dry. Stencil correction fluid can be used to alter a stencil. Finding these supplies is a challenge; old office supply stores and eBay are possibilities.

TYPING PADS

Pads have three advantages: They quiet down your typing, they prevent the typewriter from sliding around when you return the carriage, and they protect the surface of your desk or typing table. A traditional typewriter pad is felt, about 12" x 13" x 0.5", and has a layer of rubber on the bottom.

If you can't find such a pad, grip liner (made for shelves and drawers) will work. Another solution is a high-quality felt carpet pad with a rubber base. They are typically thinner than the traditional typewriter pads, but they work well. The felt is treated to be a bit rough on top, so it may stabilize your typewriter even better than the traditional pads; if not, put squares of self-adhesive felt on the typewriter's feet and they will grip the pad perfectly. A little carpet pad can be cut up into several typewriter pads for you and fellow insurgents.

You can also equip your typewriter itself with the equivalent of a pad. I like to take a strip of self-adhesive soft foam rubber (made for insulating windows) and cut squares of it to stick on a typewriter's feet. The nonsticky side is slick and needs to be cut off to expose the foam rubber inside. These "typewriter slippers" are a little delicate, but they make a big difference.

TYPEWRITER COVERS

To keep your typewriter as clean as possible, stash it in a case when it's not in use—or cover it up. Typewriter companies and stores used to sell cloth and plastic covers for the machines, which you may be able to find on eBay. You can also easily make your own if you know your way around a sewing machine.

I admit that I don't cover up most of my typewriters. I like looking at them too much!

USING YOUR MACHINE

INSERTING AND REMOVING PAPER

It bears repeating that you insert your paper behind the platen, upside down, with the back side toward you. There is probably a sliding paper guide on the paper table (which you might as well set at zero) to show you where to put the left edge of your paper.

You can usually keep the paper release lever closed so that it grips the paper from the start; if this gives you trouble, you can open the paper release, push the paper down under the platen, then close the release. As you roll the paper in, you probably need to lift up the paper bail to get the paper under it. If you have a fancy machine with a paper injector, you can have the fun of zipping the paper to the right position in one move.

If you need to straighten your paper, open the paper release. By lining up the left and right edges of the upper part of the page with those of the lower part of the page (which is behind the platen), you can get the page perfectly straight.

How will you know when your typing is nearing the bottom of the sheet? You may be able to eyeball it, but some typewriters give you a way to be sure. There may be a scale on the left end of the platen that tells you how much space is left—along with a scale that marks the correct position of the platen when inserting paper, depending on the length of your sheet. Other models provide an extendable paper support that pops up behind the carriage; with just a little experimentation, you can set the holder to the right height so that the paper reaches the top of the holder just when it's time to put in a new sheet. The simplest solution is found on some typewriters that have openings in the curved metal tray or "paper pan" that holds the paper, through which you can glimpse the approaching end of the page. If your machine has none of these features, you can fold a sticky note around the edge of your page at the spot where you want the bottom margin.

If you want to type as close to the bottom of the page as possible, your machine may have a device that helps to hold the paper after it's left the secure embrace of the feed rollers. Standard typewriters often have little metal fingers on either side of the printing point that can be flipped up to hold your paper. This is particularly useful when writing on a postcard. (Thinner, more flexible postcards will work best.)

Don't rip your paper out of the typewriter. Satisfying though it may feel, this can damage your document or the machine. Turn a platen knob, or open the paper release lever to allow a smooth and easy exit.

TYPING TECHNIQUE

The question of how to type has been around ever since the Sholes & Glidden hit the market. Initially no one dreamed that we could use all ten fingers, or "touch type" without even looking at the keyboard. But, of course, these methods were soon developed, and many of us use them today.

There are also plenty of people who've never learned to touch type, but can produce text fast enough. Reporters are well known for typing with four fingers, two, or even one. (Charlie LeDuff says, "I'm not a journalist, I'm a reporter. The difference between a reporter and a journalist is that a journalist can type without looking.")

Cell phones and touch screens have led to new typing techniques, which often depend on autocorrect to fix the inevitable errors due to tiny keys, a three-row keyboard, or a glass surface that provides no tactile feedback.

Some kids approaching their first typewriters have been seen to try typing with their thumbs only. I wouldn't recommend that.

A computer keyboard can be used in a gliding, mostly horizontal motion. In contrast, a manual typewriter's keyboard is banked, and the typing requires a bit more force and vertical movement. The most important thing is to use a quick, staccato touch on each key; otherwise, typebars can jam or double-print. You'll get used to it as you practice. Take inspiration from typing champs of the past such as Albert Tangora, who typed an average of 147 words per minute on his Underwood for an hour in 1923. (That's after subtracting for his very few errors.)

To avoid arm strain, keep the typewriter at a medium distance from you and at a height that keeps your forearms comfortably level.

Here's some more good advice from *50 Common Typing Faults and How to Avoid Them*, a booklet written by Tangora and published by Royal in 1939:

- "The typist who works fastest and most accurately appreciates the value of rhythm and continuity in typing—even to the
  point of *slowing down* to a natural *continuous rate* of speed
  that can be maintained without muscular strain. . . . Type as
  fast as you can accurately, and never faster."

- "The fingers should be naturally curved—the keys should be
  struck with the ball of the finger-tip and the tip of the nail."

- "Study your typewriter's 'feel' and try as best you can to
  adapt *your* touch to the touch of the machine. 'Know your
  typewriter'—learn to feel that it is a part of you."

Typewriters with touch regulators let you experiment with that feel. You might enjoy a light and easy touch (especially when you're starting out), or a tight and springy one.

The convention is to type two spaces after a period. This isn't necessary when using a proportionally-spaced computer font, but on a monospaced typewriter, it helps to differentiate sentences.

SETTING MARGINS

Your margins are determined by left and right *margin stops.* If the left edge of your paper is at zero on your scale, you might set your left margin at ten, and the right margin five to ten spaces from the right edge of the paper. But you may prefer wider or narrower margins. You're in charge.

The margin stops may be located in front (as on Underwood standards) or in back of the machine. If they're in back, the sliding buttons that control the stops may poke up from behind the paper table for easy access. If not, you can usually get access to the margin stops by tilting the paper table forward or back without turning the typewriter around.

If the margin stops aren't located on the carriage but on the body of the machine (as on all but the last Underwood standards, as well as a few other models such as the Remington 17 and the Brosette portable), then, counterintuitively, you control the right margin by moving the margin stop on the left, and vice versa.

A warning bell should ring a few spaces before the right margin, and when you reach the right margin a lock should engage, preventing you from typing anymore. The lock should automatically disengage when you return the carriage.

To bypass the margins, hold down the margin release key.

Automatic margin setting was pioneered by Royal. Remington developed a similar system, KMC (Keyboard Margin Control), until a lawsuit by Royal put an end to it. You'll find automatic margins on some other makes, too. The idea is that you activate the automatic margin key or lever, then move the carriage to the position where you want the margin to be. So to move the left margin farther to the left on an automatic margin typewriter, you need to hold the margin key or lever while pushing the carriage to the right. To move the right margin farther to the right on an automatic margin typewriter, hold the margin key or lever *and* the carriage release while moving the carriage to the left.

Confused yet? Some see automatic margins as a gimmick rather than a convenience. Many of these machines also have the disadvantage that you can't see where the margins are set except by moving the carriage itself and finding out where it stops. The Hermes 3000 shows the margin locations with a unique system: a length of red ribbon visible inside the transparent paper bail.

LINE SPACING

Just about every typewriter gives you the option of single or double spacing between lines, normally set with a little lever or knob on the left end of the carriage. More sophisticated line space selectors will give you the option of triple or quadruple spacing, or even advancing the paper by 1.5-line or 2.5-line increments. No choice is wrong; do what feels best. But if you plan to edit your typescript, you may want to leave room for handwritten corrections between lines.

There's also normally a *variable spacing* mechanism that lets you turn your platen up or down to exactly the position you want. The mechanism is often controlled by a button that pushes into the left platen knob or pulls out of it; sometimes the whole knob moves in or out.

Better typewriters actually offer two kinds of variable spacing. The first, described above, will permanently change the position of your writing line. The other, sometimes called a line retainer or ratchet release, is typically controlled by a small lever on the left end of the platen or by setting the line space selector to the zero position; it will let you freely move up and down, but then return to your original position when the device reengages. You might want to do this in order to type a superscript, for instance, and then return to the original writing line.

Optima M10 with decimal tabulator

TABULATING

From the Latin *tabula* (table), a tabulator is a device for typing tables—that is, text or numbers arranged in columns. It makes your carriage jump to predetermined places on your typing line, which are determined by *tabulator stops*.

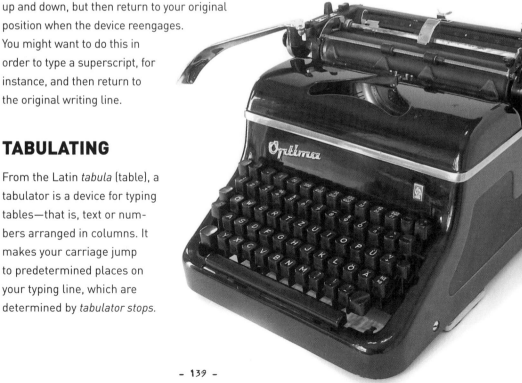

Sit facing your machine,
with both feet on the
floor . . . no crossed
knees, no curved spine. Sit
erect.

Keep your fingers well-
curved. Strike keys with ball of
finger. "Anchor" each hand on home keys with the little
fingers serving as pivots. Keep your wrists down and "hug"
the keyboard. Let your fingers do it . . . keep your hands
down and watch speed go up!

Typewriter keylevers are so beautifully balanced--only a
light tap is needed. It's never necessary to "hit bottom"
on a typing stroke. The mechanism carries the stroke through
and you save a lot of energy.

Develop a good sense of rhythm when you type and you'll
save nervous tension and getting all tired out. Start in
by determining your average speed and then try to type
smoothly, with as few pauses or spurts as possible.

Start carriage with a quick firm "throw" of line space
lever, then let the momentum finish the job. When carriage
is about half way across, your left hand
is back on guide keys without loss
of rhythm.

Here's a quick run-through on
paper. The letterhead should be
clean-cut, simple, dignified.
The usual standard is a bond

stock, 8¼ x 11. For sales letters
a 7¼ x 10¼ two-fold sheet is
frequently used. Intra-office
memos often use a half-sheet
8¼ x 5¼. "Club Size" strictly
male and personal is 7¼ x 10¼.
And of course legal size is
8¼ x 14.

A short letter looks skimpy if single-spaced.
Double-spacing with wide side margins does it. Single-space
a long letter with double-spacing between paragraphs.

Set your spaces for margins two spaces farther apart
than the number of spaces in your average line. That's
because the warning bell rings four or more spaces before
the stop--depending upon the number of letters to the inch.

Set your tabulator stops for date line, paragraph
indentations, signature, etc. See how much time it saves
you when you have a flock of
letters to turn out.

To test out writing position,
put ribbon indicator on
"stencil" and tap key lightly.
Enough impression will show to
indicate proper position.

--from "Tips to Typists from Smith-Corona,"
circa 1954

These stops are a form of mechanical memory; the typewriter will "remember" where you want the carriage to stop when you hit your tab key or tab bar (which is found above the keyboard on many standards).

Your computer keyboard also includes a tab key, and word processing programs let you set tab stops wherever you like, but most of us use this feature only to indent paragraphs. The average typewriter user may have little use for a tabulator, too. Many simpler typewriters, especially older portables, don't have one. Some prewar Remingtons have a "self-starter" key that advances the carriage five spaces from wherever it currently is.

If your typewriter does have a tabulator, how are the tab stops set? A few machines have fixed tab stops that you won't be able to change. Many older machines have systems that require you to slide tab stops to the desired position, or pull them off a rack and put them back on where you want them; you may need to turn the typewriter around or push the paper table back to get access to these tab stops. It's not very convenient, but then again, you may not need to change the locations of the stops often.

A more modern refinement is a *keyset tabulator.* A typewriter with this system has a separate stop for every position in the typing line, and each stop can be activated or deactivated independently. The tab setting and clearing devices may be keys or buttons above the regular keyboard, keys located on either side of a tabulator bar, a lever next to the keyboard, keys located on either side of the spacebar (as on some Olympia portables), or a rocking switch next to the keyboard (as on some midsize Smith-Coronas). There is also often a lever at one or both ends of the carriage, or a key, that will clear all the tab stops at once. You may also be able to clear them all by holding down tab and clear simultaneously. The Voss uses a unique system: A knob on the right end of the carriage is twisted toward you to set a tab stop, twisted away from you to clear it, and pushed in to clear all tab stops.

Then there are *decimal* tabulators. Their purpose is to type columns of figures that are aligned on the decimal point—a common bookkeeping need during the heyday of typewriters, but a feature that the average typist today is unlikely to use. The typical decimal tabulator uses four or more keys, located above the regular keyboard; the most elaborate and impressive decimal tabulators have a full row of keys. They are typically labeled

1, 10, 100, 1000, etc. To use a decimal tabulator, you set tab stops where you want the decimal points. Then, if you want to type the figure 5476.23, you hit the 1000 key, which will bring you to a spot four spaces before the decimal point. When typing 338.02, you hit the 100 key, which will bring you to a spot three spaces before the decimal point, and so on.

Most typewriters with tabulators also have a tabulator brake, which prevents possible damage caused by a carriage whipping to the left at full speed. There are many ways to slow a carriage down. If your carriage moves very slowly or not at all when you hit the tabulator, locate the braking mechanism and see whether it needs lubrication or adjustment.

Is a tabulator just a luxury? I find it useful myself, and not just for indenting paragraphs. I usually set a stop in the middle of the page, for centering titles, and another towards the right where I begin to type a date on letters. If I know I'm going to be filling out many copies of the same form, such as a piece of paperwork or a check, I set tabs at the appropriate places; it makes the job easier and more fun.

CENTERING AND JUSTIFYING TEXT

Centering text on a typewriter is a matter of dividing by two. Count the number of characters in the text you want to type, move the carriage to the middle of the page (you may want to set a tab stop at this point for convenience), back up for half the number of characters required, and type. A numbered scale on the paper bail or under the printing point can help you find the right spot.

Is a justified right margin possible on a typewriter? Yes, if you think ahead, count carefully, and hyphenate. By inserting extra spaces or half-spaces between words, you can make every line end at the same location.

```
This is an example of
right-justified type-
writing, created by
inserting some extra
spaces where needed.
```

You may find it easier to type your text without justification first; then decide where the extra spaces are needed, and retype it.

FORMATTING A LETTER

One of the jobs typewriters most commonly did in the last century was writing letters. I recommend searching online for images of typewritten letters, so you can see the many traditional options that were available. Here's one common format for business letters:

- The name and address of the sender are centered at the top, either typed or preprinted on letterhead (custom stationery).

- The date comes next, typed on the right side of the page.

- Then come the name and address of the recipient, over on the left.

- There's a salutation: "Dear X." (The greeting "Hi" marks you as an e-mailer.)

- Paragraphs are indented by five spaces or more. They're single-spaced, or double-spaced if the letter is short. There may be two lines between paragraphs.

- The complimentary close or valediction ("Sincerely," "Yours truly") is separated from the body of the letter by a couple of lines and begins in the center of the page. The name of the author is typed about five lines farther down, again beginning in the center. In between the valediction and the name comes the signature.

- A letter typed for a boss would include, at bottom left, an indication of the boss's initials in capitals and the secretary's initials in lowercase, separated by a colon with no space. (All too symbolic of the power difference between "dictator" and typist!) The existence of a carbon copy would be signaled by "cc" on a final line—possibly followed by a colon and the names of those getting a copy, if the copy wasn't simply filed.

- Fold the letter into thirds, folding up from the bottom and then down from the top.

- Type the name and address of the recipient in the center of the envelope, with each line starting at the same point.

REPAIRS AND CLEANING

TYPEWRITER REPAIR SHOPS

If you've chosen your typewriter well, you won't have to fix problems often; these machines were built to last. But they can get out of perfect adjustment with use, or parts can give way. That's the nature of the tool. Chances are good that a just-purchased old typewriter needs some cleaning and work—work that you may be able to do yourself, or that you may want to entrust to a professional.

I am currently aware of some two hundred shops and individuals that offer typewriter repair in the United States (see my worldwide list online on The Classic Typewriter Page). What a contrast to half a century ago, when every decent-sized town would have several typewriter repairmen (they were and are primarily men, though not exclusively). The typewriter shops that have held on into the new millennium have usually branched out into printer and photocopier service, or office machines more broadly; typewriter repair has become a small part of these businesses' income. A good number of repairmen are retired, but fix machines now and then from their homes. Despite the understandable decline in business, today's number of active typewriter technicians is surprisingly high, considering you might well expect it to be zero. Their customers include a steady trickle of computerphobes and offices that maintain Selectrics—as well as "an eclectic clientele of collectors, design enthusiasts, prison inmates, and tweenage girls," as a 2010 *Wired* story put it. In many areas, increasing numbers of young people are bringing their machines in for service. In San Diego, Mitchell Vassiliou says, "There are ten-year-olds that want typewriters, twelve-year-olds, twenty-five, thirty, writers, upcoming writers; it's all age groups now. People are just getting mesmerized with typewriters. I just can't keep up with them, which is a good problem to have." Here and there, some young people are apprenticing with the experts or training themselves to become the next generation of typewriter technicians. So I no longer believe that this art is in imminent danger of dying out. The typewriter revolution is keeping the trade alive.

You'll find that many techniques for typewriter repair and maintenance can be learned at home, and you may even discover that this becomes one of the most enjoyable aspects of owning a typewriter. But don't hesitate to go to a professional when you want to be sure the job is done right; you'll be supporting a traditional trade that demands experience and skill, and a typewriter shop can be a fascinating place to visit, too.

Ask for a clear statement of prices and labor rates before you leave your typewriter in the shop. This is skilled labor, and you may find that your machine costs more to repair than it did to buy initially—but it may well be a wise investment.

OVER THE RIBBON Max Rudiari

Many typewriter repair shops will also sell refurbished typewriters, usually for between one hundred and five hundred dollars, depending on the model. This isn't the cheapest source, but you can trust what you're getting, test it before you buy, and perhaps get a limited warranty.

THE HOME SERVICE STATION

A computer typically works perfectly, until suddenly the hardware or software fails. Then there's little that the layman can do, except the old trick of shutting it off and starting it up again. The particular workings of a digital

Ken Alexander
at California
Typewriter

device are mysterious to all but a few experts. In contrast, a typewriter may come down with this or that ailment, but its parts can be seen with the naked eye and understood even by those who aren't mechanically inclined. (I was never the kind of kid who took apart alarm clocks, but I was able to teach myself typewriter repair as an adult with patience and logic.) Gaining the ability to under-stand your machine is one of the empowering pleasures of owning a typewriter. As Anthony Rocco says:

You can't see the parts in your cell phone; it's a magical piece of wizardry. It's just a piece of plastic and glass and metal that is able to do countless numbers of actions. Being separate from what happens in the phone—"I don't need to know how it works, it just comes from magical elves in China, the Apple store will just give me a new one if it breaks"—just encourages igno-rance and lack of presence. But in my typewriter, I see every moving part. People are a little scared of taking the clothes off; they're shy, they're intimidated. When you can't see it you can be the "master" of it, but now that it has all these moving parts, it's a little different.

A typical typewriter has around two thousand parts, and none of them is pointless. It's not unusual for a typewriter to grind to a halt because one little spring is disconnected. If that's daunting, consider the good news about manual typewriter repair: Although it's a complex machine, your typewriter operates using mechanisms you intuitively grasp—mostly levers, springs, and gears. Attentive observation, reasoning, and experimentation will usually give you the answer to a problem.

Once you get into cleaning and repairing typewriters, the hours spent at the workbench can provide almost as much enjoyment as the hours spent typing. And the more you work on your typewriter, the better you'll understand the whole of it—the synergy of its synchronized movements.

How should you set up your own little typewriter makerspace?

Good lighting is essential so you can see into the innards of the typewriter.

A lazy Susan, or turntable, is very helpful—especially to avoid throwing out your back when you're working on a big machine.

I recommend a roll of white paper to cover your worktable. You'll easily see small parts on the paper, and you can also take notes on it.

Now, here's your shopping list:

HARDWARE/HOME IMPROVEMENT STORE

- Good-quality **screwdrivers** with magnetic tips, at least one medium and one small. Thin blades are desirable. A set of gunsmith's screwdrivers would be pricey but excellent. A set of tiny screwdrivers might also be convenient.

- **Pliers:** Narrow duckbill pliers are the most useful. You may want one pair of straight pliers and one that is bent so that you can reach into tricky corners.

- **Lubricant:** Good lubricants include gun oil, sewing machine oil, light machine oil, or liquid (not spray) lubricant with Teflon. Some brand names popular with insurgents include MPL Multi-Purpose Lubricant, Marvel Mystery Oil, LPS Greaseless Lubricant, and Liquid Wrench Super Penetrant. As for the first product that comes to many people's minds,

My typewriter
repair station

WD-40, run away and don't look back! Originally developed for water displacement (WD), the stuff is not appropriate as a lubricant for fine machinery. It will eventually gum up and leave your typewriter worse than it was.

- **Degreaser:** Various petroleum products dissolve thick, old grease, including mineral spirits (commonly used as paint thinner, and known as white spirit in the UK), naphtha (often used as lighter fluid), and kerosene. Of course, observe all safety precautions and ensure ventilation when using hazardous chemicals. See the auto store shopping list below for more degreaser suggestions.

- **Superfine steel wool:** very helpful for cleaning metal.

- **Emery (fine sandpaper):** likewise.

- **A rotary tool** (such as a Dremel) with attachments including wire brush, grinding stone, and cutting wheels. I got by without a rotary tool for years, but it will make your life easier if you're working on typewriters that need lots of restoration. Just be aware that the bristles from that wire brush will get into everything, so use it outdoors.

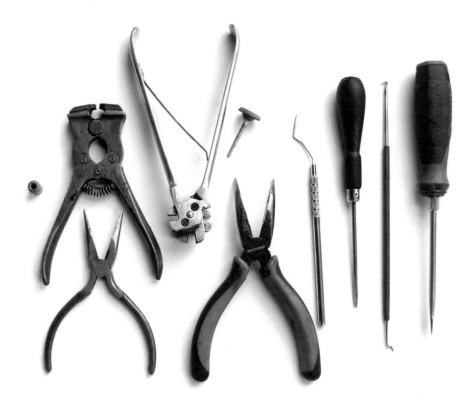

- **Small rubber grommets and rubber feet or stoppers** may also be useful; they can be trimmed with an X-Acto or other sharp knife.

- **A small air compressor** will be useful if you plan on blowing lots of dust out of many typewriters; otherwise, a few compressed air canisters from the office supply store or supermarket will do the job.

AUTO SUPPLY STORE

- You'll need plenty of **soft white cotton rags**.

- **PB B'laster:** This stuff loosens up even thick residue, and leaves a light lubricant behind. In fact, I usually use it instead of oil. I love the smell of PB B'laster in the morning!

- **Degreaser:** Sometimes you don't want any lubricant left behind. Some degreasers are listed above, but you can also find effective products at the auto store: carburetor cleaner, brake cleaner, or an electric motor parts cleaner such as Lectra-Motive. This last product is my favorite; the others may damage plastic and decals, and may be flammable. It's a good product for cleaning plastic paper guides smeared with correction fluid.

The Art of Screwing

A typewriter is mostly held together by screws. That very basic pair of tools, a screw and screwdriver, call for a few comments for those who may not be mechanically experienced. You'll want at least two good screwdrivers—one medium, one small--with magnetic tips that will help you hold little screws in awkward places. Look for screwdrivers with fairly narrow blades, as sometimes the slots on these typewriter screws can be tight, and you want the blade to fit the slot accurately. Sometimes you may need a tiny screwdriver.

A tool called a screw starter is very helpful for inserting screws; you use a screwdriver only for the final tightening.

If a screw resists being unscrewed, try not to strip it. Push in hard while trying to turn. If that won't work, apply a product such as Liquid Wrench or PB B'laster to loosen it up. You can also try tapping the end of the screwdriver, grabbing the screwdriver tip with pliers to apply torque, and using a screwdriver as if it were a chisel to loosen the side of the screw, tapping the screwdriver against the side at an angle.

When a screw is out, don't lose it! The best way to keep track of screws is to replace them in the hole they came from as soon as you've removed the part you wanted. If you can't do that, put the screws in a place where you know where to find them, or in a labeled baggie.

When replacing screws, if several of them are holding a piece on, don't tighten them until they are all in, as you may need to shift the piece around a little. Then tighten them, again being careful not to strip them.

And of course, make sure screws go back in straight, not at an angle.

- **Metal polish:** I use Mother's Mag and Aluminum Polish.

- **Touch-up paint**, matching the color of your typewriter, if needed

- You can find good **lubricants** at these stores, too. Again, don't use WD-40.

SUPERMARKET

- Toothbrushes

- Strong cotton swabs, such as Q-Tips

- Mild liquid abrasive, such as Soft Scrub

- Spray furniture polish, such as Pledge

- Foaming cleanser, such as Scrubbing Bubbles Bathroom Cleaner

- Compressed air canisters, meant for cleaning electronics (if they're not in the office supply aisle, you can find them at an office supply store)

HOBBY AND CRAFT STORE

- Soft medium paintbrushes and stiff small ones, for cleaning

- Needle-nose tweezers (look in the jewelry section)

- Sheets of self-adhesive felt to dampen sounds

ONLINE

You may find these products in a local store, but the Internet may be easier:

- **Renaissance Wax:** a museum-grade polishing wax from the UK

- **Evapo-Rust:** This is the only rust remover I recommend. It's nontoxic, dilutable, and reusable. Just a quart will handle many little parts, but if you want to dunk an entire typewriter, you'll need to invest in five gallons.

- **Spring hook** (a long, thin tool designed for pulling and pushing springs)

- **Captive spring hook** (a spring-loaded little hook at the end of a long tool, meant for handling small springs)

- **Dental pick** (for getting into tricky places)

- **Hemostat** (for holding small pieces in tight places)

CLEANING YOUR MACHINE

Even if your new typewriter looks good, take some time to clean and polish it. You'll get to know it along the way, and start to form an intimate bond.

1. The first step in cleaning a typewriter is to get as much **access** as you can. The ribbon cover is often removable; other body panels sometimes lift off. Engaging the shift lock will provide better access to the area under the carriage. If the interior is nasty, I recommend unscrewing as many body panels as you can. (Keep track of those screws by putting them back in their holes as soon as the panels are off.) Some typewriters even allow you to remove the entire carriage with ease. The Olympia SG1 makes it easiest: Twist the two knobs on the side of the machine and the carriage lifts straight up. (The Hermes 3000 carriage can be removed easily too, but I don't recommend it unless it's really necessary because jiggling the carriage back into place is a real pain in the neck.)

2. **Loose dirt:** This includes dust as well as other delights, like hair and spider webs. When there's a lot of this crud, I've

been known to blow it out with a leaf blower. Gentler tools include a compressed air canister, toothbrushes, paint-brushes, and cotton swabs (I go through dozens of these on every typewriter). Who knows what you'll find inside a type-writer? I've found a wasps' nest and former owners' address labels. Other collectors have found everything from a decapi-tated, mummified mouse to five hundred dollars in cash.

3. **Old grease:** Bits of it will usually come off if you rub them with a cotton swab dipped in degreaser. You may have more than bits, since it was a common practice for shops to dip an entire typewriter in a slightly oily solution. Of course, this made the typewriter run great in the short term—but by now the oil has turned into a brownish film (often mistaken for rust). If you have a typewriter with this syndrome, you may want to spray generous amounts of electric parts cleaner into the works, and clean individual surfaces with rags moistened with this product.

   What about a total cleaning? The pros have traditionally dipped typewriters into baths of often highly hazardous chem-icals. Some technical manuals sing the praises of a cyanide solution! The amateur who really needs to give a typewriter a thorough cleaning can remove all the body panels and platen, then dip the machine in a kitchen sink full of very hot water and plenty of dishwashing liquid. If you have old-fashioned keys with metal rings and paper key legends, angle the typewriter so the keys aren't underwater. Clean the machine gently with a tooth-brush, being careful not to detach little springs. Rinse in hot water, then dry the typewriter immediately to avoid rust, using a hair dryer and finishing it off in a warm oven. Lightly oil the linkages and carriage rails while the typewriter is still warm.

4. **Rust:** In order from milder to stronger methods, try: rubbing with a metal polish; rubbing with superfine steel wool or em-ery paper; scrubbing with a wire brush; removing the parts

and soaking them in Evapo-Rust (rust will be replaced by a
dark residue that is easily wiped or rubbed off); and grinding
heavy rust off with a Cratex wheel on a rotary tool.

5. **Dirty paint:** Again, try the more conservative methods first,
   and test all techniques on inconspicuous areas (be especially
   careful when working on and around decals). The gentlest
   approach is simply a clean, white cotton rag dampened with
   water or furniture polish. One step up would be very diluted
   dishwashing detergent. A typewriter that's caked in grime,
   as old standards often are, can benefit from a liquid abrasive, such as Soft Scrub; diluted or even pure liquid abrasive,
   with repeated scrubbing, will eventually remove nearly every
   deposit that has accumulated on your typewriter. Don't be
   surprised if it takes dozens of rounds before your rags come
   away white. Note that you shouldn't apply Soft Scrub to
   clean, glossy paint, as it will leave tiny scratches.

   Wrinkle paint (also known as crinkle paint) is harder
   to clean, as the little crevices want to hold onto their dirt.

Scrubbing Bubbles is best for this type of paint, but it will tend to dissolve the paint a little, and it can harm decals. Protect decals with wax if need be, and wipe off any Scrubbing Bubbles from the decal right away. Several rounds, wiped off with a cotton rag, will lift the dirt out of the paint. This product is also sometimes excellent for cleaning glossy paint, but test it first, as it sometimes damages such paint.

6. **That smell:** There's a certain aroma of ink, oil, and rubber that is perfume to a typewriter lover's nose. As UC Berkeley profes-

sor Leigh Raiford writes of her red Smith-Corona, "It smells like grease and archives," evoking the power of writing as an "engine of history." But sometimes there's also an offensive reek of mold. Mold can grow on cloth and felt, such as an old ribbon or the cloth that covers a typewriter case. Get rid of it by throwing out the old ribbon, along with the felt if need be (it can be replaced with the self-adhesive felt you got at the hobby store); clean a case with disinfectant wipes, Scrubbing Bubbles, or other home cleaning products. Some hours in fresh air and sunlight wouldn't hurt your typewriter (or you) either.

7. **Touching up paint:** Little chips in black paint can easily be touched up with a black permanent marker. A more truly permanent solution is some type of enamel paint (auto touch-up paint or nail polish, or bring the typewriter to a store where they can custom-mix a matching color).

8. **Polishing:** Metal polish will bring out the shine on nickeled or chromed parts. The safest, best polish on flat painted areas is Renaissance Wax. A spray furniture polish such as Pledge can also look very good, particularly on wrinkle paint. Try letting a fine layer of furniture polish dry on the typewriter before you rub it; this can create a deep gloss. Don't polish until you've gotten the paint as clean as possible.

9. **Cleaning the type:** The "grungy old typewriter" look beloved by advertisers comes from misaligned and dirty type. We'll discuss alignment below, but in order to clean your type, the simplest and most effective technique is to take a pushpin and gently clean out the crevices of each individual type. Don't be surprised if there's a chunk of ink and ribbon bits squatting in your *e* or *o*. After removing such stuff, brush the type with a dry toothbrush. If you want, you can use Silly Putty to pull out more junk from the types, or get them to shine by brushing them with a degreaser.

LUBRICATION

Most typewriter parts were made to work with *no* lubrication. Don't overdo it. The part that's most likely to benefit from lubing is the carriage rails. Use cotton swabs to clean the rails with a degreaser and apply a lubricant. As I've mentioned, I use a degreaser/penetrant (PB B'laster) to remove old grease and leave a light lubricant behind (get the front and back rails on the carriage as well as those on the body of the machine).

Other spots that might benefit from a little lubricant, if they seem sluggish, include the ball bearings on which the carriage rides, the mainspring, all the hinges and pivot points that are activated when you depress a key, the escapement, and the ribbon advance mechanism. A little drop applied with an oiler, oil syringe, or cotton swab is probably enough. And first, try cleaning these parts with a degreaser and see if that does it. Oiling the slotted segment that holds the typebars is not a good idea.

REPAIRING AND ADJUSTING YOUR MACHINE

Literature on typewriter service typically involves detailed technical diagrams and vocabulary; it requires close study, but can save you from guesswork and errors. ("Typewriter hunters" on The Typewriter Database have access to downloadable repair literature, and you can also find some on The Classic Typewriter Page.) One good resource is *War Department Technical Manual TM 37-305*, published in 1944, covering essential service for Remington, L.C. Smith, Royal, Underwood, and Woodstock standards of the time. This manual, written by Clarence LeRoy (Rocky) Jones, was eventually reprinted by Ames as *Typewriter Mechanical Training Manual*. A second volume by Jones describes the most common portables of the time, and a third by Byron L. Wolfe discusses noiseless standards. A later guide is *Ames Basic Training Manual for Standard Typewriters* by Murray Harris (1968). Another helpful book on common American standards and portables is

David E. Fox's *Typewriter Maintenance and Repair* (1950).

When working on a typewriter, don't act blindly: First observe, then think, then tinker. When something isn't working, inspect how all the relevant parts are connected and see if you can pinpoint where something is stuck, maladjusted, or out of place. Take your time and use your brain; in a typewriter (unlike in a computer) nothing ever happens for reasons that are impossible to understand.

If you're stumped, try sleeping on it; many a solution has come to me in my dreams. But don't count on remembering tomorrow exactly what you did today. Be sure to document complicated disassemblies with notes and photos.

Here's some sound advice the late Manson Whitlock gave me after eighty-three years of experience fixing typewriters: "Don't force anything, ever. If it doesn't come easy, don't use a hammer to take it apart." However, this doesn't preclude gentle, intelligent bending (repairmen prefer the word "forming"). Even what looks like a sturdy metal part can get out of whack and may need to be coaxed back to its original position.

Finally, listen to Sherlock Holmes: "When you have eliminated the impossible, whatever remains, *however improbable*, must be the truth."

Below are a few tips on dealing with common typewriter problems. I can't cover every variation of every typewriter model, and can't give instructions on advanced repair. Professional typewriter techs and fellow insurgents will often be very helpful.

CHARACTERS ARE TOO FAINT OR RIBBON IS BEING TORN TO SHREDS: Assuming you have a fresh ribbon, these problems may indicate that your carriage is respectively a little too far back or too far forward. On many typewriters there is no way

to change the position of the carriage, but check whether there are some screws on either side of the carriage that permit a small adjustment.

What is the right position of the carriage? Note that (usually) when a typebar comes up, a point in the middle of the typebar hits an arc of metal that stops its motion; this arc is called the anvil or ring, and the sound of typebars hitting the anvil is actually what makes most of the click-clacking. In a perfectly adjusted typewriter, if you press the middle of the typebar against the anvil, the type head should not be hitting the platen; if you push the type head, it should move far enough to make a clear impression by pushing the ribbon firmly against the paper, but ideally the type should still not go far enough to contact the platen itself. Test this at several points on the writing line, with several typebars. The pros call this the "ring and cylinder" adjustment, where ring=anvil and cylinder=platen.

VERTICAL POSITION PROBLEMS: The top or bottom

of every character you type may be faded, showing that the vertical position needs adjusting (take a close look at *f, p,* and */*). Finding the right vertical position is known by the pros as getting the machine "on feet." Another problem is that lowercase and uppercase may not line up (try typing hHhH and see if the bottom of one letter is higher than the other). Fixing this is called adjusting the

Manson
Whitlock

"motion." The correct order of adjustments is (1) ring and cylinder, (2) on feet, (3) motion.

The on-feet and motion adjustments can both be made by way of stops that control the vertical position of the carriage or the segment, depending on your shift mechanism. Many typewriters have upper and lower stops on both left and right, so there are four stops total. Sometimes, such as on Smith-Coronas, there are just two stops, underneath the typewriter near the center. Keep moving the shift up and down, slowly, and look closely until you find the stops on your machine. They can usually be adjusted with a small screwdriver (you'll probably have to loosen a little nut first, using your pliers). Try modest changes first—such as half a turn clockwise or counterclockwise (on both left and right, if you have stops on both sides)—and try typing again until everything is lined up right. This will make a great difference to the neatness of your writing.

Earlier L. C. Smith and Smith-Corona standards do not have slotted segments for the typebars; instead, pairs of typebars are held in place by large screws. If a character is printing noticeably above or below the typing line, loosen its screw and lightly wiggle the typebar up or tap it down to get it into place.

TYPEBARS STICK:
Typebars will often get stuck at the printing point or on the way back from it. If you tap the keys while holding down the space bar (thus reducing the tension that pulls the typebars back into position), you'll easily find out which typebars have a tendency to stick. Try this in both the lowercase and uppercase positions.

If a typebar sticks only at the printing point, it may be bent a little to the side. Move it up towards the printing point and see whether it hits the type guide on the left or right instead of shooting straight up the middle. Give it a light push to the right or left to correct this. It's also possible that there are small burrs that are making the typebar stick and should be filed down.

If the typebar gets stuck or moves slowly on the way to or back from the printing point, the slotted segment that holds the bases of the typebars may be dirty. Clean the slots with a pin or razorblade and see if that helps. Often some degreaser is needed—maybe just a few drops, maybe several good drenchings. Do not squirt lube into the segment; it may help temporarily, but in the long run it is liable to get sticky or dirty and make things worse.

If the segment is made of cheap, soft metal, you may have to pry a slot a bit farther open by wiggling the tip of a little screwdriver in it.

If a previous owner sprayed something sticky into your segment, degreaser may not be enough; you may have to do some serious disassembly and take out the typebars to clean them. A curved rod typically runs through the segment and through holes in the typebars. On some typewriters, though, such as Smith-Corona portables, the typebars merely hook onto this rod, so they can be worked out of the segment individually with a little finesse.

The problem is also sometimes in the keyboard rather than the typebar or segment. The key levers pass through a slotted comb, and the slot for a particular key may be too narrow so the lever is getting stuck. Inserting a screwdriver and wiggling it in the slot may free it up. You also want to make sure that the comb is free of dirt and grease.

Other parts of the linkage between key and typebar can also get dirty or jammed. Sometimes a little friction is causing the trouble, and the problem can be eliminated by some gentle forming.

CARRIAGE WON'T ADVANCE: First, make sure the

carriage lock is released. Now, does everything work OK as long as you push the carriage gently to the left? If so, you have lost carriage tension. Normally the mainspring pulls the carriage via a drawband—a cord or strap that winds around the mainspring housing, or drum, and attaches to the bottom right end of the carriage.

If your drawband is intact and attached but you don't have tension, your mainspring may need tightening. The method varies; you may need to turn the central shaft with a screwdriver, advance some gear teeth using the tip of a screwdriver (on noiseless portables for instance), or turn a crank. Sometimes you have to loosen a stop before the spring tension can be adjusted. On simpler typewriters, you often just tighten the mainspring by turning the drum; you have to detach the drawband and reattach it when the spring is tight enough, or else slip part of the drawband off the spring while turning, then slip it back on at the appropriate time. Tighten the spring until it's just strong enough to let you type all the way to the right end of the carriage, without letters overlapping. If the spring will not tighten or keeps coming loose, it may be broken or detached from its housing; you'll have to open the drum and take a look. This can be a challenging repair, sometimes requiring you to make a new hole in the end of the spring using a cutting attachment on your rotary tool.

It may well be that your drawband has snapped after decades of use. You can use fishing line or a flat shoelace as a replacement. If the shoelace frays when it's cut, some super glue can stop further fraying; the lace can be folded over and stapled if a loop is needed.

The drawband is attached to the spring and to the right end of the carriage with knots, hooks, or screws; there may be some hardware on either end of the band that you can remove and attach to your new band. The trickiest part of this repair is usually passing the drawband under the carriage; you may want to find or fashion a long, straight rod with a hook on the end to help you do this. (A bike spoke or part of a wire clothes hanger may work.) You can also use a wooden skewer with a slit cut in one end that can hold the cord. Once you have attached the new cord or strap, tighten the mainspring as explained above.

If the carriage won't budge even if you hold down the carriage release, there may be a blockage somewhere. Finding it can be challenging in the dark complexity of your machine. Keep gently moving what you can, use a flashlight, observe carefully, and don't force things. One possibility is that the tabulator has been activated, has hit a tab stop, but has failed to go back to its original position.

Everest K2

LETTERS OVERLAP ON THE PAGE:

Your carriage may not be moving fast enough to keep up with your typing—you speed demon, you! Make sure that the carriage rails are well lubricated, and the escapement is clean, and try increasing the tension on the mainspring a bit (see above). There may be a screw that adjusts the point at which the escapement is tripped, and this may also improve performance. When you raise a typebar slowly to the printing point, the escapement should trip roughly half an inch before impact.

SHADOWING (DOUBLE PRINTING): It's a bit embarrassing, but the most common cause of shadowing is the typist's technique. Make sure you are typing with a quick, staccato movement and you aren't holding the key down when the type hits the ribbon.

RIBBON WON'T LIFT: It may be in the stencil position (typically indicated by the color white on your ribbon color control). If not, a linkage may be disconnected.

RIBBON GETS STUCK IN THE RAISED POSITION: Make sure you've installed the ribbon correctly and the spools are turning easily. The ribbon vibrator is thin and can easily get bent, so see whether there's some friction between it and the type guide on which it rides up and down. You can form the vibrator back into shape to eliminate the friction. Your dental pick or small screwdriver can come in handy for this task.

RIBBON TOO HIGH OR TOO LOW: Type the slash and underline characters: / _. Every part of them should create an inky impression, and if you have a bicolor ribbon, the typing should all be one color. If you're having problems, make sure the ribbon is properly threaded through the vibrator; observe the mechanism that raises the ribbon when you depress a key, and look for adjustable parts. Missing tops of letters can also be a sign that you're supposed to be using a wider ribbon (9/16" instead of 1/2").

RIBBON WON'T ADVANCE: Remove the ribbon and spools, and observe how the mechanism is activated when you depress a key. Is something disconnected or jammed? Often the spool fits down onto a toothed wheel whose motion is controlled by two pawls, one to turn the gear in the correct direction and another to stop it from turning in the wrong direction. These pawls should be engaging the wheel on the uptake side of the typewriter (the side toward which the ribbon is going), and should be disengaged on the other side, where the wheel should spin freely in either direction. Sometimes the pawls fail to engage. Usually the solution is simple: A little spring needs to be put back into place, or the pawls have gotten gummed up and need some degreaser to get them moving freely again.

Olivetti ribbon spools are held down by nuts, both of which need to be tight. Some very early portables require you to screw down a nut that holds the uptake spool in place, while the nut on the other side is loose; to reverse the ribbon, you simply loosen one nut and tighten the other.

RIBBON WON'T REVERSE AUTOMATICALLY:

Almost all typewriters made after 1920 have an automatic ribbon reverse mechanism that is tripped when the ribbon is almost unspooled from one side. (Exceptions include early Underwood portables.) If the ribbon passes through a narrow movable fork, an eyelet in the ribbon is probably supposed to catch on that fork to reverse the ribbon. There may also be a less obvious mechanism that does the trick. Sometimes, as on Royal standards, the mechanism is tripped by a tab that hangs down from the ribbon spool when there is no ribbon left to hold it up. On noiseless portables, later Remingtons, and late Underwood standards, a small piece in the center of the round ribbon platform is supposed to drop down; dirt may be preventing it from moving freely. Observe the mechanism on your machine, noticing the possible role of special ribbon spools, and see if some part needs to be cleaned, unjammed, or lubricated. Even if your typewriter has an automatic ribbon reverse mechanism, it can always be reversed manually by flipping a switch, moving a ribbon fork, or moving a rod that protrudes from the side.

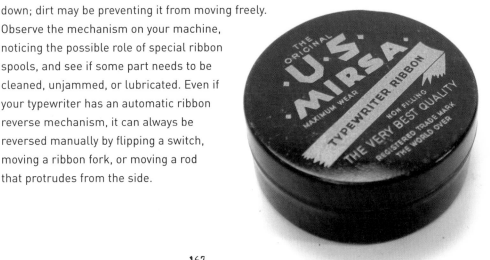

CARRIAGE SKIPS:

If your typewriter is throwing in an extra space here and there, first check your typing technique. You should type staccato and should not be holding the keys down; by the time the type reaches the ribbon, your finger should not be pushing the key.

If your technique is OK, your escapement may be broken, or it may just need adjusting (a delicate task, but if you're good with small mechanisms, take a close look and observe how it works). Escapement mechanisms vary quite a bit. On midsize Smith-Coronas, there's a little prong parallel to the back of the typewriter that is bumped every time you strike a key, activating the escapement; it may be that it's being bumped a bit too hard. Try gently bending the prong toward the back of the machine.

If the skip always occurs at the same point on the line, it's likely that the toothed rack that runs along the bottom of the carriage has a damaged or missing tooth. If so, the rack must be replaced.

SPACEBAR WON'T WORK:

The spacebar may not work at all, or not unless you hit it hard or push it deep. You can usually adjust the sensitivity of a spacebar so that it will respond quickly to a gentle touch. Look at how the motion is transferred from the spacebar to the escapement. You may be able to adjust a connection, or you may see a connecting wire with a V-shaped bend in it; by tweaking that bend with pliers, you can make the connection tighter or looser. You may also be able to form the spacebar upwards a little to give you greater depth of motion.

NOISY SPACEBAR:

The spacebar may have lost its rubber bumpers. An easy solution is to attach bits of self-adhesive felt in the right places.

BELL WON'T RING:

Take a close look at the right margin stop and how it's supposed to trip the bell. Is everything connecting? Some part may need to be formed back into place. In particular, the clapper may need to be closer to the bell—or maybe it's too close, so that it continues to touch the bell after striking it, and the bell doesn't get a chance to resonate properly. You may also be missing a little spring. (Whenever you see an unused pair of little holes or hooks in your typewriter, there's a good chance that a spring ought to connect them.)

MARGIN PROBLEMS: Your left margin may be ragged, your margin stops may not actually stop the carriage, or the margin release lever may not work. Some small adjustments may fix these problems. The rack on which the margin stops are located may need to be moved slightly to the left or right. The stops and the margin release mechanism may need gentle forming. You may need to return the carriage with more consistent force in order to have an even left margin.

KEYS WON'T GO ALL THE WAY DOWN: Your carriage lock may be on, or your line lock may be stuck. This device is supposed to engage at the end of a line so you don't pile letters on top of each other; it is activated by the right margin stop, and it should release immediately when you hit Margin Release, return the carriage, or even backspace once. The line lock often consists of a horizontal bail that flips into place under the key levers to block them. Sometimes it is a piece near the back of the machine, on the underside, that blocks the normal operation of the escapement. Find the line lock, observe what connects to it, and look for jams, friction points, or possibly a missing spring. The Olivetti Studio 44 has its own Achilles' heel: When typebars are activated, they make a tube slide over a shaft that you'll see on the underside of the machine; if the tube sticks, you will feel resistance when typing, so it must be clean and may need lubrication.

ALIGNMENT PROBLEMS: Individual typed characters may tilt, or part of the character may be clear while the other is dim. Fixing these problems requires gently twisting the type head (the top of the typebar, with the typeslug on it). Professional repairmen used special tools for this purpose, but I find that narrow pliers are effective. Fixing the problem may take finesse and patience.

HEAVY SHIFT: This is usually an easy problem to fix; it's an adjustment, not a repair. The shift action is normally assisted by one or two springs that can be tightened or loosened on many typewriters. Modern pinkies will probably prefer an easier shift. Just make sure that the typewriter returns to the lowercase position promptly, without bouncing, when you release the shift.

TYPEWRITER DOESN'T FIT IN ITS CASE:

Sometimes the carriage return lever needs to be tucked away, pushed down, or (on many Olivettis) folded back. It may also be that your shift lock is engaged and is raising the carriage too high. Some prewar Remington portables require you to push in the right platen knob, which will lock the carriage and let the machine fit in its case; the knob will go in if you pull forward on a small lever near the left end of the carriage.

PLATEN CARE:

The rubber on your platen should be, well, rubbery, so it grips the paper and provides good typing. But often platens have hardened over the years. A hard platen can slip against your paper, make a racket, punch holes in your ribbon and paper, and even damage the type. An old platen may also be pockmarked by the effects of millions of keystrokes over the years, causing irregular impressions when you type.

It never hurts to clean a platen using a little liquid abrasive on a rag, rubbing vigorously. This will remove dirt and even a little hard exterior rubber, revealing fresher rubber below. The pros traditionally use fine sandpaper (emery paper) and denatured alcohol (also known as methylated spirits).

In order to clean the platen and feed rollers it helps to take the platen out, although this isn't essential. On some typewriters this is very easy: You move a lever or two on the end(s) of the platen and it will lift right out. On other machines, you twist the right and left platen knobs counterclockwise. On still others, you have to loosen some screws and remove the shaft of the platen by pulling on the right platen knob. On some Smith-Coronas, you push up the piece on the right of the carriage marked RP (Release Platen), move a little lever, pull out the variable spacing control on the left, and the platen should come out.

After cleaning a platen, if it still feels slick, I apply a thin layer of DOT 3 brake fluid and leave it on for an hour. The brake fluid softens the outermost layer of rubber and will improve the grip of your platen, although it won't change the underlying hardness. Depending on the composition and condition of your rubber, the effect of brake fluid may be major or minor, smelly or not, but it has never ruined one of my platens. Don't type again until the rubber has had a chance to dry out overnight, or else you may leave marks on it.

I've mentioned that it's a good idea to use one or two sheets of backing paper behind the sheet you're typing on if your platen is hard. This will soften the blows a bit and may create nicer work.

Amateur ways of putting a new, softer layer over an existing platen include stretching a bicycle inner tube over it or applying heat-shrink tubing (turn the platen while holding it six inches over a gas burner, or use a heat gun—a hairdryer isn't hot enough). The limitations of these techniques are that the new sheath may be irregular or soft and fragile, and the increased diameter of the platen may also cause some problems.

If you want a proper new platen, a complete replacement, you're the kind of customer that made Ames Supply Co. a successful business for 110 years; this company invented platen-recovering techniques and kept at it until 2012. The need is now met in the US by J. J. Short Associates in Macedon, NY. In Europe there are other experts who do the job. See "Basic Typewriter Restoration" on The Classic Typewriter Page for more information. Experts also recover feed rollers, but I suggest trying some of the techniques below first.

SQUASHED FEED ROLLERS:

Feed rollers have often become deformed over the years, causing problems with feeding the paper. (Don't want your nice rollers to get squashed? Always store your typewriter with the paper release open.)

Replacing the feed rollers often requires removing the platen first. The feed rollers are usually held in a metal paper pan; they may lift right out, or you may have to remove a C-clip or bend the housing apart a bit.

Cut the old rubber off the rollers with a sharp knife. There are various replacement solutions, including pencil grips, latex tubing, automotive tubing, and heat-shrink tubing.

If you can't get the rollers out of their housing or can't get the old rubber off, try wrapping electrical tape or duct tape around them, and/or shaving down the angled portions of the rubber. It is also possible to build up the flattened surface with glue of the right consistency and then file the hardened glue down to a cylindrical shape.

REPLACEMENT PARTS: Collectors and repairmen keep parts machines around to cannibalize. The insurgent network stands ready to help—and when you see a junky five-dollar typewriter at a yard sale, keep in mind that it could be a wonderful source of springs, screws, and more. You may be able to adapt a spring or another piece from a completely different device to work on your typewriter. You can also try making pieces from Instamorph moldable plastic or with a 3D printer.

The intricacies of typewriter construction and repair may be intimidating at first, but you've got lots of time to get to know your writing machine inside and out. Meanwhile, it's eager to do some writing, and so are you. What can you write? Literally anything—but our next chapter will provide some ideas.

Fine-tuning an Olympia SM

The most obvious place to make adjustments on an Olympia is the touch regulator on De Luxe machines. You may also be able to adjust the ease of shifting by tightening two springs in the rear upper corners of the body.

Touch regulator

Shift adjustment

The rubber bushings on fifties Olympia SMs can soften or even melt over time, leading to friction between the carriage and the body. They're located on the bottom of the typewriter, between the body and the panel that holds the feet. The bushings can be replaced with some rubber grommets or other rubber pieces.

The typewriter is designed to have a quiet carriage return, but there's often an annoying little rasp when you return the carriage. Assuming that everything is clean, the problem may be caused by the weakening of a spring (A) that you can find in the middle rear area of the bottom of the machine. Replace this spring or cut off a loop or two to make it tighter (but not too tight).

You may also want a more responsive spacebar. This can be achieved by using pliers to form part B, which connects the spacebar to the escapement, into a tighter angle.

Interlude #4

We strike a blow for coherence against disintegration.

Scientists say juggling e-mail, phone calls and other incoming information can change how people think and behave. They say our ability to focus is being undermined by bursts of information. . . . The stimulation provokes excitement. . . . In its absence, people feel bored. . . . These urges can inflict nicks and cuts on creativity and deep thought, interrupting work and family life. While many people say multitasking makes them more productive, research shows otherwise. Heavy multitaskers actually have more trouble focusing and shutting out irrelevant information, scientists say, and they experience more stress. And scientists are discovering that even after the multitasking ends, fractured thinking and lack of focus persist.

—*The New York Times,* 2010

One of the major problems for writers is that the machine we use to write is connected to the biggest engine of distraction ever invented. One can always disconnect, of course . . . but I think something more elegant as well as radical is needed.

What I'm thinking of is some purely mechanical device, that took the basic QWERTY keyboard with shift and return keys and so on, but with each key attached to an arrangement of levers connected to a physical representation of the given letter or punctuation mark. These in turn would strike through some ink-delivery system—perhaps, though I'm reaching a bit here, a sort of tape of cloth mounted on reels—onto separate sheets of paper, fed through some kind of rubber roller (similar to that on a printer) one by one. The return key would have to be replaced by a manual device, to literally "return" the roller at the end of each line. Tedious, but most writers could do with more exercise anyway. . . .

Someone more patient, less easily distracted, and more mechanically savvy than myself would have to develop such a device, and maybe already has—for all I know, the patent may be gathering dust. Now, its time has come. There's a huge gap in the market for it.

I tell you, someone's going to make an absolute fortune from this.

—*science fiction writer Ken MacLeod*

We're adrift in a sea of information—not just the information that we have right before us, but the infinity that awaits a single click or swipe. Our responsibilities, our social life, our curiosity make it difficult to focus on one task. And our dirty little secret is that we don't want to. We'd rather be interrupted, because concentration is hard, and interruption feels busy and exciting. We let the messages come in, the links and videos and images flow freely. We flick from one to the next, multitasking without doing any task excellently, skimming through life. Our very existence suffers from attention deficit disorder.

Your typewriter is built to do just one thing: type. Every part of the machine is designed to make good typing possible. When you first sit down at a typewriter, you're likely to miss the stimulation and surprise that are so common in the digital world. You may get fidgety and find it hard to stay seated.

But stick with it. When there's nothing else to do, you will do a single thing: write. And when you stay with your train of thought, adding to the text as it takes shape on the paper, you'll rediscover the experience of depth.

Then you'll meet a very interesting person indeed: yourself.

5. 'Writers at Work

"What are you going to do with *that*?"

Expect to hear that fair but unimaginative question from friends and family when you tell them about your new purchase. There are plenty of answers. In fact, a typewriter is as inexhaustible as language itself. Still, you yourself may be looking for some typing ideas.

It helps to look at some models who have pioneered the countercultural practice of twenty-first-century typewriting—people who have shown the rest of us typists the way forward. We met a few of the more innovative of these individuals in Chapter One. In this chapter we'll look at some broader trends in typewriting today—writers using 'writers in ways that have repeatedly proven to be both practical and enjoyable in our times.

VISIONS AND BRAINSTORMS

No question: It's harder to change your words when you're typewriting than when you're word processing. Typewriters do have backspace keys, but most of them have no delete keys. Correcting Selectrics will lift a character right off the page, but who wants to go back and do that for a whole sentence or paragraph? Yes, you can cut and paste a typescript: Go at it with scissors and tape. But there aren't too many of us who look forward to that. For the uninitiated, these obvious points brand the typewriter revolution as a doomed, quixotic quest right away—case closed.

It's true, corrections aren't easy—just as your typewriter can't advise you on spelling, grammar, format, or who won the Best Supporting Actor Oscar in 1968. But can these limitations be advantages? Can less be more?

The first possible reaction to the absence of a delete key is to think out sentences carefully in your mind before committing them to paper. That can be excellent practice in memory, conceptual ability, and concentration. You may be shocked to discover how short the computer has made your attention span, how hard it has made it for you to keep a complex thought in view. The typewriter is a personal trainer for your mind, pushing you to become more focused.

In this way, the typewriter makes you more decisive. "With the typewriter you commit to the story," says Liz Cooke, who chose to feature typewriters in the opening event of National Youth Arts Week in Sault Ste. Marie, Ontario. "Whatever you're typing is out there in the universe and there's no taking it back."

Singer Marian Call says, "On my computer, I'm nervous; I talk too much, I weaken my language by overqualifying and hedging in my logic from every possible angle. I try to write very safely, which means I mostly write very badly. But when I'm short on room and my words can't be deleted, I'm much bolder. There's something really empowering about seeing your words physically stamped into paper. There's strength in the motion."

As Anthony Rocco puts it, "A typewriter requires certainty: You have to be certain about the way you're going to put it down, what you're going to

say. You can throw gobbledygook at a computer and then go back and get it perfect. That doesn't build up confidence; there's a level of confidence that comes with using a typewriter."

Seattleite Lauren Ziemski recounts her own aha moment. She'd been collecting typewriters for some time, but was using a laptop to try to write a memoir, with little success.

I wrote with this terrible anxiety and this fear that I wasn't going to get all the details down, so I crammed the pieces *full* of backstory. They were bloated. I didn't see ever getting to a place where less was more. I was discouraged, to say the least.

On a lark one day, I pulled out one of my machines. I plugged away at my normal clip, but I soon started to notice something happening to both my brain and my body. I had eased into this meditative state. There was something about the rhythm in hitting those keys that was keeping pace with the way my brain was generating thoughts. I suddenly felt like everything I wanted to say was going to get said—nothing was going to get left out. I was relaxed. My breathing slowed down. My heart rate was slower. I realized then that what I had been doing with writing my memoir was trying to keep pace with thirty-some years of billions of stories, all fighting their way out of my fingertips and onto a laptop. I was anxious when I wrote. I never felt like what I was writing was what I intended to say. The words felt like a hundred people trying to squeeze out of a revolving door at once. Bones were getting broken.

Typing on the typewriter generated this sense in me that every story would have its turn. There was time enough for everything, the machine seemed to be saying. You will get *all* of your stories down, and they will be the truth as you know it, and there will be no fluff, it seemed to be saying. There will be no fluff because it is *hard work,* literally, to get those words down. You have to fight the keys down. You can't erase. So you think just a half second more before committing to typing. Just those few extra milliseconds of thought—knowing I couldn't erase and that I would have to press hard—gave me some breathing room. And in that space, that tiny space, I was able to focus and clear out what did *not* need to be said. It was like I was conserving energy. I realized I did *not* do that when I used the laptop, where I could erase whole lines, get sloppy, etc. In short, I was in a Flow state. And it was glorious.

So typewriting can develop a strong, affirmative consciousness that fearlessly holds a vision in mind and puts it on the page.

But the difficulty of changing a typescript can also have what seems to be the opposite effect: You let go. You stop caring about certainty; you stop editing yourself, stop second-guessing yourself, and simply write—mistakes and all. Start typing, keep typing, and don't look back. You may get into a trance state, where you don't reread what you've typed at all. If you're a touch typist, you may even close your eyes and commune with the keys by feel and sound, letting the language pour out.

Robert Neuwirth describes such an altered state:

For me personally, typewriters represent freedom. I wrote the first drafts of both my books on typewriters. The best writing I do is when I disappear, and all that there is are two hands typing, and the words are flowing out of a place that is, in a sense, outside of consciousness. With a typewriter, writing is a physical act. There's something about the activity of typing

on a manual typewriter, and the noise involved—the smack of
the typebar on the paper, the bell dinging, the way the carriage
return smashes back against the margin stop—that pulls me
out of my own self-consciousness. Self-consciousness can
have a tendency to make writing stilted. Using a typewriter is
like an exercise in automatic writing. For me it's liberating.

A key phrase here is "first draft." Chances are excellent that you'll eventually find ways to improve on your initial wording, but by letting your inner writer break free from your inner critic, you can steer clear of writer's block. The point of this quality time between you and the machine is to find the flow of words and thoughts. There'll be plenty of time later for finer wordsmithing and research, using whatever combination of handwriting, typewriter, and computer you prefer.

Typewriters are excellent idea incubators. When it's time to brainstorm—to chase an idea and see where it leads you—a typewriter is a perfect tool. I rarely repeat the results of a brainstorm verbatim when it's time to transform it into a more formal, self-aware piece of writing. The typewriting has served as a breeding ground for ideas which I'll consult later on, but which I may find better ways of expressing. Without that initial brainstorm, though, my writing might well be dead: correct, well-formed, but lacking a fresh insight that only the typewriter can provide. (And sometimes brainstorms come pretty close to just right—like my description of brainstorming, which took shape on a 1948 Remington Rand portable.)

We've seen that using a typewriter can have two apparently contradictory effects: It can increase your powers of consciousness, and it can make you less self-conscious. In fact, these two effects can work together. As your vision of what you want to say becomes bolder and clearer, you feel less need to fix what you've just written. You stop worrying about your writing— you just write. You're confident that the brainstorm will take you where you know you need to go.

You and your machine are one. It moves when you do. It writes when you think. It waits patiently and responds at once—a 'writer at work.

OVER THE RIBBON Max Rudiari

FICTION BY TYPEWRITER

As sportswriter Red Smith put it, there's nothing to writing. "You simply sit down at the typewriter, open your veins, and bleed." (A similar quote is often attributed to Hemingway, but that's unlikely—he liked to *stand* at his typewriter.)

The cold steel of the typewriter fused with the writer's hot blood: The attraction of this idea slumbers or rages in every typewriter lover. We dream of being Writers, punching out stories like the twentieth-century greats.

You won't get any advice from me better than Red Smith's, but I can tell you about a few experiences that typewriting authors have had with their fiction-making machines.

First of all, typewriters focus you on what's essential: your words. Losing what you don't really need may be the greatest gift, even if the loss is involuntary:

> Why do I talk about the benefits of failure? Simply because failure meant a stripping away of the inessential. I stopped pretending to myself that I was anything other than what I was, and began to direct all my energy into finishing the only work that mattered to me. . . . I was set free, because my greatest fear had been realised, and I was still alive, and I still

had a daughter whom I adored, and I had an old typewriter
and a big idea. And so rock bottom became the solid founda-
tion on which I rebuilt my life.

This particular old typewriter served its author very well: It typed the first
volume in the Harry Potter series.

What *isn't* essential to writing fiction? Many would put the Internet on
that list. Yes, it's great for research and communication, but it won't write
literature—in fact, it may lure you away from real writing. That's why Will
Self has been composing his first drafts on a Groma Kolibri or Lettera 22 for
over a decade.

My favourite things are bicycles and typewriters because
they're pure, inert pieces of metal that, when you add
human energy to them, produce relatively high-speed travel
or text. . . . People are deceived into believing that writing on
a computer is faster, but it's not. Using a typewriter is more
disciplined; you don't have the distraction of thinking, "I'll go
online and look up what oven gloves made of fur look like."
I think I felt oppressed by the distractions of digital media
and longed for a certain level of clarity and simplicity that

OVER THE RIBBON Max Rudiari

x "For Whom The Bell Tolls" - Ernest Hemingway

the typewriter afforded. The Internet is of no relevance at
all to the business of writing fiction directly, which is about
expressing certain kinds of verities that are only found
through observation and introspection. It's an incredibly powerful tool and you'd be stupid not to use it, but it's a distraction in the actual business of writing.

Jonathan Franzen agrees. In the eighties, he wrote his first novel, *The
Twenty-Seventh City,* on a Silver Reed typewriter. Although he now uses
a computer, which "makes it easier to find fragments you've written and
then forgotten about," he sees the Internet as a procrastination pit. This
is why, when Franzen got a laptop, he removed the wireless card and
"plugged up the Ethernet hole with superglue." He insists, "It's doubtful
that anyone with an Internet connection at his workplace is writing good
fiction."

Typewriters slow you down a bit and call for a little more effort. That
can make the difference between blurting and writing. Susanna Kaysen,
author of *Girl, Interrupted,* works by typewriter; her editor muses, "Sometimes people who write on computers, you feel like they are just typing.
When you have to type and retype as she does, there's a kind of precision
there."

Gay Talese, who favors a Lettera 22, agrees that less is more: "I want
to be forced to work slowly because I don't want to get too much on paper.
By the end of the morning I might have a page, which I will pin up above
my desk. After lunch, around five o'clock, I'll go back to work for another
hour or so."

But isn't this maddeningly inefficient? Not if you stop judging what you
do in terms of efficiency. The rhythm of typewriting can introduce you to a
whole new experience of time, says Spanish novelist Javier Marías:

> **Q:** Why do you keep using your old typewriter [an Olympia
> Carrera De Luxe]? Is it a phobia of new technologies?
> Superstition?

A: No, I just like writing on paper, taking out the sheet, correcting it by hand, crossing things out, drawing arrows, typing it over again, and doing so as many times as I have to. I'm not in a hurry, I don't have to "save time" when I'm writing. To the contrary: In part, I write in order to lose time.

In case you're wondering, Marías has no problem with productivity. He's published over fifteen volumes of fiction to date.

British novelist Martha Lea also enjoys the process:

I love typewriters for the immediacy of the print on the paper. There is an immediate commitment too, which perhaps has a more lasting impression in your head—words on the screen can be deleted and forgotten so easily. Typewritten manuscripts seem to shout louder than computer printouts. I like that human energy, physical exertion, is tied up in each letter or character made on the typewriter.

Using a typewriter I feel that I am writing in a real space as well. Writing on a computer can be a furtive activity. There can be nothing furtive about the typewriter. But the privacy of the typewritten manuscript is also really important to me. I resent the fact that every single way I have backed up my current project on my laptop is wide open to snooping.

Writer Taylor Harbin testifies to the aftermath of buying a Remington Rand Model 1:

> What happened next? In six months I wrote two books and about half a dozen short stories. None have been published. I'm still working on that. But it's OK, because writing was fun again. I've got five machines now, each one with a unique feel, personality, and story. . . . When I sit down at my desk, I can almost hear my Royal KMM say, "Tell me all about it. Just between us, kid." . . . Even if I have no particular story for that day, I want to write. Computers can function without humans prompting their every move. But a typewriter is purpose-built. Once I've animated it with my own life's energy, I want to keep coming back and see it dance. . . . In a time when people are being pressured more than ever to conform with society's cutting edge, to "get with the times" and "quit clinging to the past," doing something for the sheer pleasure remains one of the best reasons for doing anything at all. It's been almost one full year since I made the switch, and I'm never going back.

Others embracing typewriters today include African-American novelist Tayari Jones and fantasy writer Mary Robinette Kowal.

Most of the authors I've mentioned are "digital immigrants" who grew up without computers. But it's not just the middle-aged who enjoy creating fiction by typewriter. Today, young digital natives are discovering the same pleasures, and spreading the word through online media, as when "SheWrites" says on a YouTube video:

> I want to have something tangible like a typed manuscript on a typewriter, you know, with little notes in the index and the

margins and mistakes that I had to type through. . . . I want to have something I can give to my kids, because at this point in my life, writing my first book is probably my greatest achievement so far. . . . I found this gorgeous little Royal typewriter . . . it's a really fascinating experience . . . the process of putting the paper in, feeding it, and then being able to hold on to the work that you've done . . . is definitely inspirational and fun. . . . It puts you in the moment . . . there are no distractions. . . . When you're typing on the typewriter, that's all there is. It's just you and the typewriter. And for me and the place where I am now in writing, that is amazing, and I love it.

You may even find that typewriters aren't just helping you write your story, but are becoming characters in it. In *Het laatste jaar* (*The Last Year,* 2013), Dutch writer Dirk van Weelden decided to make a series of typewriters the narrators of a story inspired by his own friendship with another author, the late Martin Bril.

THE TYPEWRITER BRIGADE

Time at your typewriter is often an intimate, private experience. But, like SheWrites, you may want to tell others about your experience and hear about theirs. Enter National Novel Writing Month, which has pulled off the trick of turning a solitary, protracted process into a social event with a deadline. The challenge: to complete a novel of at least fifty thousand words during the thirty days of November. This format has made noveling fun, and has brought stories galore into the world. In its first year, 1999, NaNoWriMo had twenty-one participants. In 2013, it had 433,700 around the world.

Are the stories good? Not usually. Are they publishable? Even more rarely. So what's the point? The very experience of telling a story, and the bragging rights: It feels great to say, "I'm a Novelist."

NaNoWriMo embraces hundreds of smaller communities who meet in person and online—including The Typewriter Brigade. Cheryl Lowry, a pioneer typewriting blogger, gets credit for proposing this group in 2007. Ohio writer Devin Thompson, a.k.a. Duffy Moon, describes what a boon the idea was:

Sometime in 2005 I got
obsessed with manual
typewriters. I knew
I just had to have
one. Didn't take long
before I realized that
I really, really liked
typing on the things, and
that typing on a type-
writer felt so much
better, so much
more *natu-
ral* for me,
than typing on
a PC keyboard.
It was just
meant to be, is all I
can say. It felt *right.*

Byron Mark I

I'd been a NaNoWriMo
participant a few times before
my typewriter collecting began, and
I'd even given thought to trying it out on a
typewriter. I needed, however, a poke from the
outside—affirmation from someone else that this wasn't a
crazy idea. Cheryl Lowry provided that affirmation.

That first year, typing my novel on a typewriter, was the
smoothest NaNoWriMo has ever been for me. That *right-
ness* that I felt when typing on an old manual machine had
something to do with it, no doubt. That, and the novelty of
doing something different, something new (to me). But I think
another help was something inherent to working on typewriters: Using a typer forced me to write my novel in a certain way.

First, it kept me on track—paradoxically—because it
severely limited my opportunities for noveling. On a PC,
I could easily sneak in a scene or a chapter while I was at

work—no problem! Not so easy on a typewriter. I had to be completely meticulous in planning out my novel-writing time. There was no little voice in my head saying, "No worries! Goof off, go to bed, read a book—whatever! You can always catch up later, at work!"

Also, there's something inherently rewarding about seeing the page fill up, hearing the bell that ticks off the lines, and seeing the stack of papers piling up.

Californian Mike Clemens, a Typewriter Brigade regular, tells of his own experience with the group:

I finally decided to give NaNoWriMo a try in 2007, deciding literally at the last moment—Halloween night—to commit. First-time Wrimos will tell you that it's pretty smooth sailing for the first week or two, and then you hit rough patches. I'd had really no experience writing fiction at all, and was far too concerned about making it "right" to just let myself go. My characters didn't behave the way they were supposed to behave. The dialogue was flat, stilted, miserable stuff. Scenes laid on the page like beached whales.

Of course the laptop, being connected, gave me plenty of outlets to procrastinate, and the forums on the NaNo boards are destination number one for the self-pitying Wrimo stuck in a self-imposed word count hell. I trawled through them, and came across what I consider the Fateful Post: someone by the nickname "Duffy Moon" saying that he was going to try NaNo on a typewriter, because *Hey Why Not.*

Were there angels singing? I don't remember singing per se, but I do remember thinking This Duffy Person Is a Genius. During my laptop drudgery, I did notice that some of my most productive bursts came when I shut off the Wi-Fi, filled the screen with the editor, turned off the spell- and grammar-checks, and just wrote. I had glimpsed NaNoNirvana for a few fleeting lines, and here someone has figured out how to do it *and* eliminate the temptation to go back and edit, or worse yet, excise what you'd just written. A typewriter! That's what I needed!

The typewriter will never enable your bad habits. If you aren't writing, it's not the machine's fault. You can type by sunlight or candlelight or flashlight, and all you need is ink and paper and your hands and your brain. Don't stop, don't correct, don't revise-as-you-go. Just get it down. A typewriter only types one way, from the start of the line to the finish, and there's no magical "undo" button to save you from your own awfulness.

Sometimes I throw my inner editor a bone by typing a note to myself in the manuscript as a tip to future-me that what I just wrote is probably crazy. The note is usually just this: ((no)). When I hit that note, I just mentally rewind to whatever point I like and keep typing. The stunted, aborted branch of whatever idea I had at the time is still there on the page, waiting for the edit. As is often the case, those little cuttings can become a full-fledged idea later, when transplanted to more fertile ground: either elsewhere in the manuscript, or in another work altogether. With the typewriter, it's all safe. It's on paper. On a computer, the temptation is to smooth it out as you go.

Also, from a purely practical sense, there is no sound happier than a line-ending bell when you're typing for word count. Someone once likened it to your own personal word-count cheerleader. "Hooray, you've just finished another line!" Pulling out a page of completed typing is even better. I love watching the papers stack up over the course of the month. You feel like you've really written something when you're hefting a two- or three-hundred-page stack of paper around.

The Brigade forum is very lively before the event, and as new people stumble by and find us. Typically there's some silliness going on that keeps the topic active. There's certainly a sense that we're a small nugget of extra-weirdness in this whole massive weird experience. We also get a lot of new faces each year, kids mostly. "Omigosh I just found my mom's old typewriter and I totally want to use it this November." We're a pretty loose group as a whole, of course, and membership is intention-based: If you even intend to write a novel in the general vicinity of a typewriter, you're a Brigadier.

My own experience as a Brigadier in 2010 bears out these points. I'd never managed to write much fiction on a computer. I'd once put out twenty-five pages of a would-be novel on a typewriter before discouragement set in. But when I belonged to a whole community of insurgents who were cheering each other on, I felt fortified enough to keep going. Tapping away in my basement late at night—mostly on my Royal KMM—I found a story and ran with it until I reached the finish line: fifty thousand words in a month.

Since then, I've typed some shorter pieces during National Novel Writing Month. Having finally earned the title Novelist, I no longer feel the need for a particular word count, but I still enjoy the sense of camaraderie as I know that others are also plugging away at their typewriters in November. I usually scan my typescript and publish it on my blog; others prefer to keep theirs private. The Typewriter Brigade respects both choices and encourages everyone, with impressive results: Collectively, the Brigadiers have been typing two to three million words every November.

POETRY BY TYPEWRITER

Typewriters aren't just good for pounding out novels and stories. They're also perfect for poetry—an art that depends completely on the well-chosen word.

Scholar Peter Simonsen has even argued that the typewriter played an essential role in the history of poetry. "What seems most distinctive and revolutionary about twentieth-century poetry, its free verse and an experimental layout that must be apprehended through the eye, are intimately linked to this new writing technology." Delighted by the "rigidity" of the typewriter, poet Charles Olson enthused in 1950, "For the first time the poet has the stave and bar the musician has had."

The tradition continues in the twenty-first century. Claire Askew of Edinburgh has a beloved collection of some thirty typewriters, and calls them "the ultimate poet's accessory."

> The typewriter is where it all comes together. I don't start working out where the line breaks or stanza breaks are going to go until I type. When it's in the notebook, it's a fluid thing, but once it gets on the typewriter it becomes a poem. Writers tend to be quite obsessive people and my interest in typewriters has, I'm not ashamed to say, become quite obsessive. It's become part of my creative process and I'm stuck with it now. This is how I write.

Texan Chris Brinson is also stuck with typewriters. He publishes his typewritten poems on his blog, *Tales from the Typer.*

> I first started using a typewriter to write poetry sixteen years ago. I saw this shop called "The Typewriter Exchange," and I had just started reading Charles Bukowski recently and he wrote over and over about how he loved using a typewriter. So I went in and bought one. I quickly found that it seemed to triple, maybe even quadruple, my output. I found things in myself that would have never been discovered with just paper/pen or computer.
>
> And then about four years ago, I came up with the idea of typing something, scanning it, and posting it on a blog. I am not sure where the idea popped into my mind. It just seemed

goofy and glorious at the same time to post something so raw and "non-polished."

So, why use the typewriter at all? Simply put, it seems to awaken something in me that *only* can be awakened in that way. Nothing else works. . . . I like the responsiveness of a manual typewriter, like it's a percussive instrument; you can control the volume and the tempo. I get in so much of a good rhythm sometimes that I can see the subdivision of beats (quarter notes, eighth notes) in my head. And beyond that, it's

typewriter therapist

this is the disney-free zone -
the deliverance from email -
the twenty four hour fix it shop -
no garbage in, no garbage out -
keep it simple, stupid -
keep it easy and breezy -
keep it real -
primal screaming allowed -
don't have to keep your problems
on a leash -
running around in the garden of
eden here -
we don't need no stinking badges
or fig leaves holding us down.

christopher m. brinson

just very honest. It's like saying, "Here I am, it's all that I am. Here's the good parts, the mistakes I made, the blemishes, the typos, but it is also the beautiful flow and idea behind each poem."

It's a rebellion against the newspeak-gobbledygook of the abbreviated text message generation. It does a disservice to language to use so many bloody abbreviations—like "ttyl," "brb," or whatever is the digital parlance of the day. Which is really a weird idea, because by day I am an IT guy and have been my whole professional career. But if I could get paid what I get paid now, with health benefits, to sit in front of the local super- market and type poems for people, I would do that instead.

Poetry by typewriter is an ascetic discipline, forcing you to select and com- mit, facing you with lines stripped of superfluity. There's no hiding behind precious penmanship or flashy formatting: Your poem is stamped into the paper and into your mind.

STREET TYPING

Street typing—the kind that Chris Brinson dreams of—takes guts and smarts. Instead of communing with your own mind and your own typewriter at your own pace, you take the machine into the world and offer your writing talents to the public. It's not for everyone, but a good number of typewriter insurgents have pulled off the trick—and some have earned cash while they're at it.

Some street typists, such as Franki Elliott and Christopher Hermelin (whom we met in Chapter One), specialize in short fiction. Hermelin tells his story:

I saw a street poet in San Francisco. I was fascinated and talked to him for a long time. When I write, I write quickly in short bursts, so it made sense to me that I'd be able to

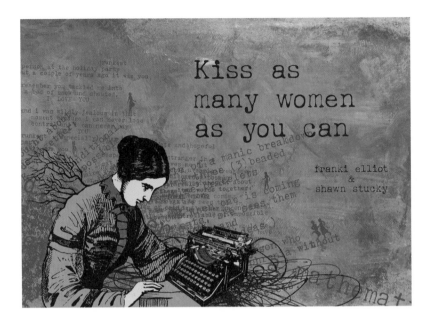

Kiss as
many women
as you can

franki elliot
&
shawn stucky

do it as well. He said, "That's cool. Just don't set up on this street." He was not kidding.

I bought a typewriter the next week, and set up once in San Francisco. It was sort of a disaster. I wrote one story, and the customer came back and said it was awful and asked for their money back. A cellist came over and started yelling at me. We got into an argument that a police officer had to break apart.

I moved to Boston and wanted to try again. I'd used the typewriter for something different at that point: I made and sold stuffed animals, and typed adoption papers with a story about the past life of the animal. This set me up for success; thinking of a giant menagerie of animals gave me a lot of good ideas. The response to stories that are a bit more ridiculous and fun let me understand that it's not about the craft but about the connection between you and the person, and the collaboration, even if it's just fleeting.

Jacqueline Suskin

When I moved to New York, I tried one more time. It was my cousin's idea to go up on the High Line, where there are lots of people—a very beautiful place, and tailor made for this because it's a small path where people have to walk by, in a pretty rich shopping area, so that people have money.

People have asked: Why not bring a computer and e-mail stories to people? I write faster on a computer, but I don't second guess myself on the typewriter. There's no time to. It's immediately permanent, with the ink striking the page, so there's something in it that clicks something in my mind that I just don't have on a computer. The sound of it is not jarring, but surprising: "Is that a *typewriter?*" You don't expect it, so it's like a siren's call.

The act of typing gives people another point of entry

Silvi Alcivar, photo
© Scott R. Kline

because they haven't seen a typewriter in a while, so there's
the intrigue of being able to talk to them about it. People have
something to say. I get a crowd collecting around me, talking
about typewriters and stories.

Other street typists will write a letter for you (as we'll see shortly). But the
most popular genre for street typing is poetry.

As Hermelin's story suggests, the idea of street poetry has often spread
by the power of admiration and imitation: A witness is inspired to give it a
try. The San Francisco Bay Area has become the home of a number of street
poets, thanks largely to the example of Oakland's Zach Houston, who's been
at it since 2005. He describes what he does as "a performance/literature/
business/art piece, composing spontaneous, custom poetry on a manual
typewriter, referred to as 'poemstore.' " In one line of influence, Houston
inspired Jacqueline Suskin (now living in LA with her typewriters of choice, a
Hermes Rocket and a Remington portable No. 3), who inspired Lynn Gentry
(Smith-Corona, Olivetti Lettera 22).

These poets find typewriters essential to what they do. As Suskin says,
"The typewriter does fifty percent of the work—with its unique singing voice
it draws people in. Be it by sheer intrigue or nostalgic interest, the *clack
clack* calls the customers to me. The typewriter possesses some kind of
magic and everyone is charmed by it." And of course, the poets themselves
aren't immune to the charm; just see how Bay Area poet Silvi Alcivar is
devoted to her candy-apple-red sixties Royal.

New Orleans is the home of street poet Kerry Leigh (Hermes 2000).
Billimarie Robinson (pink Royal Quiet De Luxe) has settled in Philadelphia.
In Maine, Holly Morrison (Olympia SM9) sells "custom poems typed fresh"
at a farmer's market along with her organic mushrooms and kale. The
boldest street poets are itinerants, like Abi Mott, with her appropriately
named Remington Travel-Riter, whose experiences on the American road
are documented in the film *A Place of Truth.*

Henry Goldkamp, whom we know from *What the Hell is St. Louis Thinking?*
(Chapter One), got the inspiration for his own street poetry venture—Fresh
Poetry, Ink—in New Orleans. Goldkamp's system involves a file of index

cards with good ideas and words, a dictionary, and notebooks. Like most street poets, he lets his customers decide what his words are worth. Payments have included drinks, backflips, and a check for a thousand dollars.

Another way to repay a street poet is to write a poem in return. This is the concept behind Seph Hamilton's project in Boston, Poetry Exchange. While he types you a poem on his Smith-Corona, you write him one in his notebook. When both of you are done, you read the poems out loud.

> The typewriter attracts people. Every time I go out to exchange there is at least one parent who asks their child, "Do you know what that is?" Some people like to stop and talk about the typewriter, even if they aren't interested in writing poetry. I have had people tell me it looks just like the typewriter they used in college, and some ask if they can type something on it, or if their kids can give it a try.
>
> Another reason why the typewriter means so much to this project is simply that I can't delete. Sometimes people ask if they can exchange a poem they have already written. While I won't say absolutely not, I generally let them know that an unedited poem is really in the spirit of the project. The poetry is never perfect, and many times not even good, but I think it's better that way. What people choose to reveal about themselves with their quickly scrawled lines in my notebook would mean a lot less if they were premeditated. The typewriter is kind of a physical contract that holds me to that same standard. It's a great vehicle for enforcing a commitment to the moment, and to the person standing in front of me, writing in my notebook, just as nervously as I am typing. The typewriter is an equalizer in this way.

Although solo street poets may seem to be lone eccentrics, they are necessarily people who want contact with other people. In fact, they're willing to interact at a level beyond everyday business and pleasantries. It makes sense, then, that street poetry can also be practiced in pairs and groups.

A pioneering, highly successful form of collaborative typewritten poetry was created by Seattle poets Rachel Kessler, Sarah Paul Ocampo, and Sierra Nelson. From 1998 to 2006 they created over five thousand poems on the street and in multiple venues in the US and Europe. They dressed like midcentury secretaries, toted red Olivetti Valentines, and developed a mesmerizing routine: Working with titles that patrons would invent or select from a card catalog, the trio would type away, not saying a word but communicating by ringing bells, honking horns, and blowing whistles; handing off their typescripts to each other, they would eventually produce a three-way poem and stamp it "Typing Explosion Local 898." Their "guerilla poetry construction" was eventually extended to create a stage show, *Dear Diane*, "a symphony for typewriters, dance movement, and spoken word."

The legacy of *Typing Explosion* is evident in the performances of The

Bumbys (Chapter One) and other creative forms of street poetry today. A few examples will suggest the possibilities.

In their Tandem Poetry Tour, Maya Stein and Amy Tingle rode a tandem bike through the heart of the United States, stopping to compose free poems on their typewriters.

In LA, the Melrose Poetry Bureau creates happenings:

> We celebrate direct human interaction and dialogue around art that does not involve any electrical cords, internet, or social media. In an increasingly digital age, the Melrose Poetry Bureau represents a rebellious return to the live and the tangible. Poets and the public meet face to face, shake hands, talk, and the poetry that results is physical ink on paper that exists as evidence of a truly dynamic artistic exchange—even when the electricity goes out. Each installation includes a group of poets sitting at typewriters, all with their own theme. Past themes have included "summer," "underdogs," "movies that never got made," "hipsters anonymous," "love?," "letters from famous dead people," "adventure," and many more. Patrons select the theme that resonates with them and present the poet with some basic information about themselves (favorite color, favorite season, a fantasy, a goal, a dream, etc.); the poet then composes an original work and presents the finished poem (all typed on the manual typewriter) to the patron.

In Austin, Texas, Typewriter Rodeo is a foursome that brings street typing to museums, Maker Faires, and more, stamping every poem with an image of a folding Corona and a lasso. Experience in improv comedy helps, says member Jodi Egerton: "The instrument is playful, the medium is playful, the reactions are playful. . . . The sounds, particularly that ding at the end of a line, bring people right to you. Everyone has a typewriter story, and if they're too young for that, they want to know how in the world a machine with no electricity works."

Melrose Poetry
Bureau

One of the most active teams is Chicago's Poems While You Wait. Their perspectives on typewriters and street poetry are well worth quoting. Here's Liz Hildreth:

> The delete key has essentially destroyed poetry. Because it's taken the risk out of writing. Nobody gets to look dumb or cheesy anymore. Nobody gets to make hilarious mistakes and profound slips. You just back-chip-chip-chip until you can deliver, beyond all argument, a poem by a poet who knows how to write a poem. As a result, we're swimming in poems that "do" a lot but say and feel very little. That's the appeal of Poems While You Wait for me. It makes it impossible to focus on pre-senting oneself as a product. There's no time. There's no digital eraser. There's just sentiment and meaning and forward motion.

David Fruchter, Kari Anne Roy, and Sean Petrie of Typewriter Rodeo

Kathleen Rooney:

> The embodied presence of laboring poets seems key to the pleasure people take in the performance—as does the sheer physicality of our use of vintage manual typewriters: Customers are enchanted by the idea that their poems are one-of-a-kind, suitable-for-framing objects made right in front of them, and not only don't mind but seem charmed by the typos and errors that inevitably creep in because of the speed at which the pieces are typed. . . . It's like the Beni-hana of poetry.

David Landsberger:

> The typewriter, to me, as an instrument, feeds off spontaneity
> and mistakes. It has a rhythm that you feel, you hear, as you
> use it. It's basically a word saxophone.

Finally, Eric Plattner sent me these thoughts in free verse:

> The typewriters themselves, as you well know,
> are immediate attention getters
> at any street-fest, market, library, or even wedding
> we've "performed" at.
> The adults love telling their kids that "this is how we used to do it,"
> and the kids (already tuning their parents out)
> just want to have a go at them.
>
> This is proof to me that, as addictive & enticing as the tools of the
> virtual world may be,
>
> the laptop, the smart phone, the Game Boy
> fail to spark a visceral wonder,
> that the intrinsic human joy in pondering
> "How does that work!"
> is eliminated by the impenetrability of the technology itself.
>
> In short, pressing a typewriter key
> & watching a lever snap up
> & leaving a mark on the page
> is a barrel of monkeys!
>
> From the writer's standpoint
> the permanence of each keystroke
> is counter-intuitively liberating
> in that by erasing the option to erase
> each gesture must be clean & decisive

(like the cut of a samurai's sword)
& the very imperfection of the result
("I could have, should have said that better")
becomes the *life* of the object
(like the tool-marks of a woodworker).

The forced deliberation becomes liberating.

As someone who suffers decision fatigue
when asked what kind of toast I want with my omelette,
I couldn't imagine writing poems on anything *but*
a typewriter.

Something about the mechanical reproduction
of the poem on the page
in the moment
renders the "artifact" more valuable.

We humans are, thankfully, so strange.

There are more writers who offer their typing to the public in Miami,
San Diego, Oklahoma City, Paris, Stuttgart . . . including some widely
acclaimed poets. Marie Howe and Tina Chang, poets laureate of New York
State and Brooklyn, were among those participating in 2014's The Poet Is
In. "Each sat with a typewriter and three-minute egg timer, and invited
passers-by to sit down and talk about an object hidden behind an imagined
secret doorway, or a dream they had had. The poets then banged out verse
inspired by the imagery, and read it out loud to the sitter."

Street typing is one of the most widespread practices in the typewriter
revolution. But if you're inspired, there's plenty of room for more writers who want to try this exciting form of improvised wordcraft. I gave it a
shot myself at a "short-order poetry" event organized by Chase Public, a
community cultural center in Cincinnati. We set up at a music festival and
invited passersby to tell us how they viewed the city. After taking furious
notes on my Kolibri, I had half an hour to draft a poem and type out the

final version. The experience was exhilarating: With no time to waste, I had to focus, listen, and work with the epiphanies and metaphors that fell from people's lips. Poetry was revealed as a vital pursuit that can bring people together.

If you try setting up as a street typist, don't muscle in on another typist's business, and research local laws about busking. (Since 2013, New York City considers street artists "vendors," and allows public performances only in a hundred designated spots.) Think about whether you want any aids, such as index cards or reference books. And there's one more important decision to make: What you will do with your poems. Will you keep a carbon copy of every one? Will you photograph it? Post it online? Or will you just give it away and let it go?

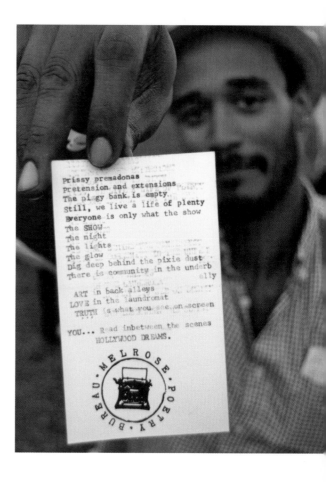

SOCIAL TYPING

Maybe busking by typewriter isn't your thing, but you still feel an impulse to bring your typer out in public—to share it with the world, perhaps to find other typists, or even to recruit new ones. If so, don't be timid. The revolution calls for pride as we publicly reaffirm typewriters as a legitimate tool, flouting the conformism of Laptopistan. And public typing is great for making connections and starting conversations. When I last typed at a chain coffee shop, two other customers approached me separately to tell me how much they enjoyed the sound.

No doubt about it, typewriting in public is a statement. As Robert Neuwirth puts it:

> There's something open about a typewriter. You're not hiding
> the fact that you're writing. People can hear you and see you
> and look over your shoulder (not always the best thing for
> writing well)—and this makes a typewriter a kind of trans-
> parent object. With smart phones, people might be typing or
> photographing you or playing solitaire or saying something
> snarky about you on Twitter. The typewriter's also a bit of
> a performance object: When you start typing in public, you
> announce your presence.

Mark Petersen of Virginia is an inveterate public typist. It started when he
used his little Roytype to write up an assignment in a campus dining hall—a
last-minute resort so that he wouldn't have to choose between having lunch
and finding a printer.

> My friends teased me, but the joke was on them: A cute
> girl from several tables away came over, said she loved the
> typewriter, and left me her phone number. It was at that
> point I began to understand people *like* typewriters.
>
> There is always a bit of a thrill when you open the case.
> How will people react? Is the noise going to bother anyone?
> But it becomes comfortable very quickly for me. I fall into
> a rhythm. I focus on my work. And when someone does
> approach me with the "Why do you use a typewriter?" or the
> innocent, but slightly idiotic "Is that a typewriter?" I am often
> startled out of some writer-trance.
>
> But the interruptions are a fun part. People are friendly,
> and have questions for me or stories they want to tell about
> a typewriter. Sometimes they are writers who want a type-
> writer, or had never considered it but want one now. Most
> importantly, it spreads the word that there are people who

OVER THE RIBBON Max Rudiari

love typewriters still. How many machines have been lost simply because someone assumed they could not be loved or valued?

It is important to the Insurgency that we type publicly. I could name at least five typewriter user/collectors who didn't own a machine until they met me. Getting out there is how we are going to grow, share the passion that we love, and protect many, many machines from lonely neglect or brutal disposal.

As the insurgency spreads, we can expect more typist-friendly hangouts to pop up—places like Ink & Bean, a "coffee saloon and wordshop" in Anaheim, California, that proudly displays a collection of typewriters. Columnist Keith Sharon is a regular:

> The coffee may be good, but in my mind the stars of the place are the typewriters. There are eight of them— Royals, Underwoods, Smith-Coronas—and the plan is to get more. The plans for the whole place, in fact, are big.

Mark Petersen's advice
on public typewriting:

Lighting: Especially in a bar, lighting needs to be considered. Once I find a table I like, I often use the flat palm of my hand (at a similar angle to a sheet of paper in my machine) to see which angle offers the best light as I move around the table.

Comfort: A table is usually better than a booth, which is usually better than a bar stool. An easy way to decide which is best is to sit and pose like you are about to type. Whichever seating allows you to do this with your elbows closest to ninety degrees will work best usually.

Noise: Choose either a place with much other noise (patrons, kitchen, etc.) or a place without hollow echoes. In a good environment with a few other people, you will hardly cause a disruption. You always feel louder than you actually are.

Outlets: If you are in a place where laptops are used, choose a seat far from outlets, so you don't upset the less fortunate people who don't have typewriters and must use a laptop instead.

Interruptions: People <u>will</u> occasionally approach you and ask you about your typewriter. These are opportunities to make a friend or share your passions, be it your machine or your writing or both. Always be kind, never act interrupted, smile. You are representing the typosphere!

Handouts: Have something to give those who approach you. I use a simple business card with my blog and my e-mail address. This makes them feel less like an interruption and provides an invitation for future contact. You never know what opportunities can come from getting your name out there.

Don't be a cheapskate! Buy something--a beer, a cup of coffee, a cookie. Earn a seat and patronize the business.

Generally people don't respond negatively. I have never been thrown out or asked to leave an establishment because of my typewriter. But use common sense and be considerate. Generally a place where you are seated and have a server wouldn't be a good place to type, but delis and coffee shops and burger joints are excellent for it. Chances are good they will recognize you and be glad to see you when you return! Something exciting and interesting like a typewriter mostly appeals to people.

So get out there and have fun!

Writer's workshops, author nights, writing contests, book exchanges, inspirational meetings. . . .

The manager is Janelle Hann. . . . When she's not barista-ing, she's writing scripts for murder mystery dinner events. She uses a 1920s Underwood to type her mystery texts. She calls her typewriter "Atticus" after her favorite literary character, Atticus Finch, of *To Kill a Mockingbird*. . . . Jamie Wood, a marketing director for Ink & Bean, says they're after a "slow-down experience." They want customers to be inspired and finally get started on that novel.

On the other side of the country, in Portland, Maine, writer-friendly tapas bar LFK offers typewriters to its guests, and the design of the bar itself is even inspired by a typewriter. Meanwhile, down in Phoenix, the perfectly named First Draft Book Bar at the Changing Hands bookstore has played host to a type-in; it's typewriter-friendly in both its ambience and its logo.

If you're like me, you can't wait for a place like this to open up in your own neighborhood.

Meanwhile, if you want to hang out with other typists, you may need to

reach out and make some contacts. Inquire in the typosphere (more on that in our next chapter) and find some local insurgents. Organize a type-in (see Chapter One); news and information on type-ins can be found at type-in.org. Hold enough type-ins, and they can become a habit for a social circle—like Michigan's Kalamazoo Typochondriacs, who "get together regularly to toss back a few drinks, type some pages, and make new friends."

Especially if the participants are new to typewriters, things can get chaotic, but very entertainingly so, as Linda M. Au reports from a Pennsylvania type-in:

> Hugh can't figure out how to release the carriage on his
> typewriter, and there are cries of "Release the Carriage!"
> from all corners of the room. . . . Someone else tries to

find the "on" button on hers. (Okay, that was me.) Turns out a manual typewriter doesn't have an "on" button. How very retro.

Shouts emanate from the gallery once we start the typing proper.

"Where is my apostrophe key?"

"Why isn't there a 'one' key?"

"What is this key that says 'MAR REL' on it?"

"No exclamation point! No exclamation point!" . . .

That last paragraph has taken me twenty minutes to type, but this time it isn't the typewriter's fault. Hugh and Val have launched into a recreation of the last scene of *It's a Wonderful Life,* complete with all the characters' voices. . . . Nate's contraption . . . has a button that says "Magic Column" on it. I begin to wonder if we should allow typewriters that have magic keys on them. Hell, I don't even have a *tab* key, let alone a magic key. . . .

I sit here wondering how prolific writers of old ever churned out all those pages when it feels like a gym workout to get twelve words down at any respectable rate of speed. And now, having brought my productivity down to a mere two fingers, I find I have to look at the keys to make sure I hit the right ones at least ten percent of the time.

But I'm also starting to see the sheets of finished paper coming off the platens, being placed lovingly on the table around me. All facedown, of course, because we're all trying to hide the rampant typos spilling off every page. . . .

Every so often, patrons from the main room drink enough coffee to brave wandering back here where the cacophony is erupting. They tentatively ask the question everyone else is thinking but is too frightened to ask us (since we all look like idiots back here and nobody wants to challenge the inner logic of an idiot on a mission): "What are you guys doing back here?" . . . followed by a stunned utterance of, "Are those typewriters?"

One group actively promoting social typewriting is The Carriage Return, in Seattle. It was started by Lauren Ziemski, whose typewriting epiphany we read at the start of this chapter. Her experience of Typewriter Flow inspired her to try an "experiment in pop-up community":

> I wanted to share that feeling with the world. I announced that I was going to bring all my typewriters to a place where others could slow down and experience that same Flow. I also wanted to experiment with environment. I had only ever typed indoors. I wondered what the experience would be like—how that "expansive" feeling in time and space would increase—if we could type outdoors. So I rounded up a bunch of folks and we brought, unannounced, the machines into one park after another. We never did advertise, opting instead to simply have our participants "happen upon us." The idea was to get away from sticking yet *one more thing* on your to-do list, your day planner, etc. and to just let the night take you where it wanted.
>
> The general public's reaction was amazing. They loved it. They, too, were grateful for the experience. They typed love notes and confessions, and rants, and one guy typed a song he'd set to "The Star Spangled Banner."
>
> A couple huddled around the Underwood while their wedding photographer took their engagement pictures. A small family gathered to tinker with the hundred-year-old Oliver Printype 7. "One key at a time," a father said to his small children. "Can I write an angry letter?" a woman asked. I assured her she could. Pictures were taken. A young couple composed love letters to each other. A man climbed a hill and sat at a machine for hours. He needed to catch up on his letter writing, he said.
>
> The sun set, the moon rose, and still a man in a corner of the park hammered away. A story had filled him. It needed to be let out. He typed by moonlight. Eventually we hauled the last machine to the car and said goodnight.

If you have a collection of typewriters, consider sharing them with the world. Bring them out at a neighborhood event or take them to the park. The insurgency spreads when we share the experience of typing.

Ziemski's next project, Ribbon and Rhyme, was just as successful:

> A few months later, the Seattle Public Library contacted me. The librarian wanted to partner up for National Poetry Month. It was lovely. People had the same reaction they'd had in the parks: delight over seeing something so old still working, nostalgia, and there was soooo much gratitude. Kids of all ages took to the machines. There was a surprising lack of jadedness to the whole thing. No one felt he or she was too old/experienced/cool for it.
>
> We had two teenagers cranking out mini-stories on our machines, featuring a character named after a typewriter manufacturer, and replete with hand-drawn illustrations. We had a lovely gentleman stop by and stay the whole three hours to work on the *first* poem he'd *ever* written in his life.
>
> At one point in the day, I stepped outside the room we were all in just to listen. And what I heard was so very satisfying. The librarians even commented on the soothing effect of that sound. And there it was, in the span of a few hours, the whole reason the Carriage Return was launched in the first place: That slowed-down pace of creativity, that soundtrack to our imaginations mimicking our own heartbeats.
>
> This has always been a genuine offer to the public of the experience of being a kid again, to indulge that reckless abandon to create, to give yourself permission, just for a while, to not be distracted, and to do *nothing* but create on a single-purpose machine.

But there can be an aftermath to creation: correspondence. Typists at the park were invited to give their texts to Ziemski and her friends. Some time later, an envelope arrived in each participant's mailbox, bearing someone else's typescript. This brings us to one of the best uses of typewriters today.

THE TYPEWRITTEN LETTER

Letter, n.

*a communication inscribed on a piece of
paper that is wrapped in another piece of
paper (an "envelope") and physically hand-
delivered to its recipient. Every such delivery costs money, and is typically paid for in
the form of small, printed pieces of paper
("stamps") that one purchases at a "post
office." Letters typically take days to reach
their destination, and the author may not get
a reply for a week or more.*

Written communication has never been more popular, but brevity and speed
are its hallmarks. Teenagers often send thousands of texts a month, and
have been known to text each other even when they're sitting side by side.
For the SMS generation, e-mail is too slow and often too wordy, inviting
the fatal reaction "tl;dr" (too long; didn't read). Why on earth, then, would
anyone mail a *letter* today?

As we know from Universal Babel Service and Project 88 (Chapter One), typewriter insurgents have answered that question. Let's look closer.

For quick and practical information exchange, you should definitely send a text. But texting is a kind of conversation, usually a shallow one, instead of an extended rumination. These conversations also often coexist with other activities, so that the person on each end is multitasking and paying little serious attention to the exchange. E-mail, too, tends toward the brief, practical, and superficial. Do you ever pour your heart out in an e-mail? (If so, don't! You never know who's reading them.)

But if you write a letter, either by hand or by typewriter, you can take the time to compose an extended, intimate communication. You can develop some thoughts and feelings in depth in a message that gives both you and your lucky addressee something to chew on during the week or so between exchanges. Letters invite reflection, concentration, and careful articulation.

Then again, a letter can be fun and entertaining. It can just be a silly postcard. But even the shortest and most frivolous paper communication shows that you went to some trouble. That's why the paper greeting card industry still exists: If you sent me a card through the mail, I know right away that you care.

No, you don't have the time to mail a typewritten letter every day to each of your 752 Facebook "friends." But that will make the letter that you do send all the more meaningful. When efficiency isn't the last word, you're willing to sacrifice quantity for quality.

A letter celebrates the very act of communicating. You know that the paper you receive was held in the writer's hands, that she physically put the ink on the paper, that she licked the envelope. And none but the two of you need know anything about its contents. It's like passing notes while the teacher's back is turned. In this case, Teacher is the Internet, whose appetite for storing and analyzing your communications knows no bounds. A letter is one small corner of human expression that still resists surveillance.

Now, why correspond by *typewriter*?

First of all, it's fun. If you like typing, a letter is a nice opportunity to use your machine, experiment with layout, or show off a typeface.

Typewriting used to be considered cold and inhuman, but now it has become quirky and distinctive. The once "impersonal" typewriter is now a tool for discovering one's own and others' personalities. Tom Hanks, a dedicated postal correspondent, writes that "no one throws away typewritten letters, because they are pieces of graphic art with a singularity equal to your fingerprints, for no two manual typewriters print precisely the same."

The artistic qualities of typewriting itself can, of course, be supplemented by drawings, stickers, rubber stamps, photos, or whatever other decorations you want to add.

Previous technologies have expanded communication. But the last round may be contracting it. The eloquence of letters has turned into the unnuanced spareness of texts; the intimacy of phone conversations has turned into the missed signals of mobile phone chat. I think of that lost world, the way we lived before these new networking technologies, as having two poles: solitude and communion. The new chatter puts us somewhere in between, assuaging fears of being alone without risking real connection. It is a shallow between two deep zones, a safe spot between the dangers of contact with ourselves, with others.

--Rebecca Solnit

Scene from a
snail mail social

And don't underestimate the angry typewritten letter—the kind that
slams the slugs against the paper, punches holes in the ribbon, and leaves
your fingers feeling like you've just given someone a good smack in the jaw.
Yank it out of the machine, shove it in an envelope—and mail it to yourself.
When it arrives, you can decide whether it's fit to be sent on to its target, or
(nine times out of ten) belongs in the shredder.

Aside from letters you send to yourself, the epistolary art requires
partners, and it isn't hard to find them. Postcrossing is an online project
that lets you accumulate postcards from pen pals (or typer pals) around the
world. You can ramp up your postal pursuits in February for InCoWriMo—
International Correspondence Writing Month. Mail art is a popular pursuit
that brings people together at events such as San Francisco's Ex Postal

Facto conference. The Letter Writers Alliance, with nearly four thousand members, promotes the practice and hosts Letter Writing Socials, complete with stationery, stamps, and typewriters.

Alliance cofounder Donovan Beeson of Chicago is "sort of obsessed with typewriters," and she's not the only letter writer who is; just look to Singapore. Far from the great typewriter manufacturing centers of the past, this city-state seems an unlikely place for the insurgency, but it may have the highest concentration of typewriter collectors in the world—mostly young women. Over a dozen of them participate in a letter-writing club that keeps their machines clacking. They select interesting stationery and send each other decorated notes.

Meanwhile, in Victoria, British Columbia, at a stationery-store-plus called The Regional Assembly of Text, customers can rent a typewriter workstation for five dollars an hour, including stationery, envelopes, and rubber stamps. Owners Brandy Fedoruk and Rebecca Ann Dolen, who own thirty-five typewriters, also host a monthly letter-writing club. They encourage participants to create "tangible" communication that honestly shows its "endearing" flaws.

Are there takers for these events? Definitely. At Amherst College, a letter-writing social complete with quills, sealing wax, and—of course—typewriters attracted 350 students. The typewriters proved so popular that the campus game room now has a couple available for checkout; their mechanical music can be heard on many afternoons.

Carolee Gilligan Wheeler knows all about the letter-writing movement. She cohosts "snail mail socials" in San Francisco and is the co-author of *Good Mail Day: A Primer for Making Eye-Popping Postal Art.*

> The reason I enjoy writing letters is that it forces me to be generative rather than reactive. While e-mails can be all business, writing a letter is more like imagining a conversation. There is a silent back-and-forth with the reader that has to take place—otherwise it's just a laundry list of things the writer has done and seen. I am constantly trying to improve the letters that I write to be more about the conversation and less about the bare conveying of information.

Because of that, it's really difficult to write a letter if you're not able to concentrate. I have a smart phone and a short attention span just like most other people, but as soon as I sit down to write a letter, I am forced to rein in my peripheral vision. I like practicing that kind of attention.

Typewriters take that slowing-down an extra step. I like to write with a fountain pen, but when I haul out the typewriter, that's like telling my brain I really mean business.

When Annie Yu and I host our Snail Mail Socials (I call them "typewriter parties"), we always wind up interacting with people who know what a typewriter is but have never actually touched one. Aside from not understanding how to line-advance ("there is no 'enter' key; you do it with this lever here"—"whooaaaaa!"), the number one question I get from people is how to make an exclamation mark. I tell them that people in the past were way less effusive. I also really enjoy how delicate people are with these behemoths. Little kids will gleefully pound on them, but adults frequently don't hit the keys hard enough. They don't realize what a workout it is. There are always a lot of comments about the silent strength of *Mad Men*-era secretaries.

The Art of Letters

I'm also really fond of the fact that the typewriter rein-
forces something I used to teach in my bookbinding classes:
You have to learn to deal with mistakes. There's no delete on
these old manuals. I don't allow correction fluid. You have to
accept the mistake and move on!

As you can see, hosting a letter-writing event is a great way for typewriter
insurgents to share the pleasure of their machines and gain new recruits for
our cause.

You might even consider putting your typewriter to work typing letters
for others. Universal Babel Service follows the method of taking dictation. In
England, Rob Bowker runs Type-O-Matic: You send him digital text through
a web page, and he turns it into an unforgettable typewritten letter, mailed
to the recipient of your choice.

Or you can do the creative writing yourself, like Wisconsin's Anja Notanja
Sieger, a.k.a. "La Prosette," who composes quirky, poetic letters on demand
on her Smith-Corona. Her categories: "Poetry, Love Letter, Insult Letter,
Letter of Recommendation, Short Story, Letter from a Pet, Other." Letters
from pets are particularly popular.

In LA, Jennifer Hofer takes to the street with her Lettera 22 to honor the
Latin American tradition of the *escritorio público,* or public writing service.
Her prices: two dollars for a letter, three dollars for a love letter, five dollars
for an illicit love letter.

A final word of practical advice: If you receive a lot of letters, or otherwise accumulate paper documents, you may miss the ease of searching and
finding things on your computer. When it's just your eyes and brain searching for a piece of paper, some patience and extra organization are required.
Visit an office supply store and check out some of the old-fashioned ways to
manage information, such as index cards and Rolodexes. My favorite way to
store letters is an alphabetized accordion file folder.

Three hundred reporters could be seen
at a single glance, making clattering
sounds with their fingertips on the
metal keyboards of bell-ringing
typewriters, their facial expressions
alternating between frustration
and satisfaction, all within view
of everyone else, and all calling
aloud to copyboys whenever they
wanted their completed stories to be
rushed to an editor. Journalism was
then performed with resonance and
impartible vivacity, whereas it was
now the work of walled-in scriveners
delivering stories to their editors
with the click of a mouse.

--Gay Talese

To the surprise of Times [of London]
journalists, a tall speaker on a stand
has been erected in the newsroom to
pump out typewriter sounds, to increase
energy levels and help reporters to hit
deadlines. The audio begins with the
gentle patter of a single typewriter and
slowly builds to a crescendo, with the
keys of ranks of machines hammering down
as the paper's print edition is due to
go to press.

--The Independent, 2014

THE INSURGENT REPORTER

Ah, the classic newsroom. We've enjoyed it in screwball comedies of the thirties, or we glimpse it in memoirs. A far cry from quiet computers in cubicles—or from the more contemporary news world, where writers anywhere on the planet send stories from their laptops, tablets, or phones to news sites or blogs.

Modern journalists, amateur or professional, undeniably need computers in order to research and meet deadlines. Aside from experiments in retro soundscapes, is there still any room in the realm of news and nonfiction for the antiquated contraption we love?

Yes—if you are working on a more extended piece that you have the luxury of writing carefully. A rugged little portable can work anywhere; it can help you focus your thoughts and make sense of your observations; and it will inspire you, for typewriters remain potent symbols of the investigative spirit, free speech, and courageous journalism.

Maybe the typewriter is at its best these days far from a packed newsroom, out where electricity and Wi-Fi are luxuries, such as the underpopulated areas of the United States that Chris Killian loves to travel in a VW van.

> I take the off road, the turn-off that you will never go down . . .
> I find the people progress has left behind—the mad ones who
> lurch forth yelps and screams from their guts and aim them
> at the star sky, the ones who smell and keep on smelling
> because they wear their work, the ones who have the least
> but give the most. . . . So give me the wild, the misinterpreted,
> the throwaways. Give
> me the gaunt and the
> misshapen and the odd.

Leroy Scofield, Faith, South Dakota; photo by Chris Killian

Killian's blog, *Types of America*, publishes his typewritten reports from places such as rural Nevada and a Sioux reservation. Both his van and his connection to typewriters date back to 1984:

> I lost my mom when I was ten; she got brain cancer when I was five. On October 15, 1984, she typed me a letter explaining her hopes and dreams and desires for her only child's life. I received the letter when I was

twenty-one. Listening to my mother's words through this typewritten page was incredibly moving. This is how I was baptized with the blessings of typewriters.

I don't think I'll ever go back to principally creating on a computer. A typewriter feels like I'm actually working: Your fingers get tired, your arms get tired, you have to use physical strength to create what you're building. I come from a family of bricklayers, and it feels like I'm building something with my hands, as my family did in a different way.

I have an Olympia SM3. It's always there. I know all of its quirks. I know what it feels like when you get into a flow, you're typing extremely fast, and the machine is just coming alive. You crawl inside a creative bubble, where what is boiling in your brain is actually being created right in front of you.

Having the typewriter around has been an icebreaker. Folks get that look on their face: They're drawn to it, they want to touch it, they want to write with it. It's an awakening of sorts. I was out in Lone Pine, California, the summer of 2013. I was having some coffee in my van, I had the door open, I was typing a story up, and this woman in her mid-sixties named Mary Winchester was having her morning walk. She heard the clicking of the keys; that's what drew her over to me, and we started talking. She's from Salinas, California, which is where John Steinbeck was from. She was good friends with one of Steinbeck's best friends, who happened to be in Steinbeck's home the day he figured out how to end *The Grapes of Wrath*. He was in his writing nook and shouted out, "I figured out how to end it!"

Journalism is always going to be about telling stories. I don't care how many hits or unique views you have, it's always about stories, and using the typewriter lends itself to telling good stories. There's just a simple grace to it, and any good story is simple.

As Killian says, a typewriter can be a very effective way to invite sources to talk to you. Public typing can draw welcome attention and start conversations with locals. They may even want to type out their stories themselves. Robert Neuwirth reports a small example: "In Edinburgh we left two typewriters out in our hotel room with paper in them and a short note thanking the hotel staff for cleaning our room. The man and woman who worked that floor actually wrote back to us."

In the right situation, a typewriter becomes a distinctive tool for observation and research. The Bumbys (Chapter One) are essentially anonymous roving reporters who write mini-articles about people's appearance for the people themselves. In a more elaborate system, Dirk van Weelden creates "typewriter portraits"—impressionistic typewritten interviews. Working on a little Groma Kolibri, van Weelden asks unpredictable questions and absorbs the answers before selectively and creatively recording the highlights. Sometimes he works with artist Jan Rothuizen, who sketches visual-verbal records of the interviews.

Van Weelden has even created a typewriter portrait on stage, interviewing a volunteer from the audience:

> After six minutes [of questions] I started typing. The crowd was on the edge of their seats: A video camera zoomed in on the paper as the typeslugs hit it; the image was beamed onto a huge cinema screen. I melted a few of [the interviewee's] stories into one dreamlike scene of a little boy on a sunny island. People reacted to the appearance of words and images they remembered from the short interview. Afterwards many people expressed how they liked the suspense, the compact power of words being physically formed in the moment.

Van Weelden observes, "The typewriter portrait is a demanding genre. It requires considerable improvisational skills. The fact you are staring your subject in the face, while he or she waits for you to be finished, ups the stakes."

Dirk van Weelden's rules
for typewriter portraits

- Visit the person you want to portray in their own
  environment. Do not only use what they say, but also
  how they sound, how they look and move, and what can
  be observed (seen, heard, smelled) in their place of
  work, home, etc.

- Don't talk about the typewriter. If your subject does,
  be very selective in using quotes. The typewriter is a
  tool, like a camera. The portrait is about them, not
  you and the typewriter.

- Set a time limit. I usually say it will take thirty
  minutes.

- Prepare a list of about ten questions that tune into
  the subject's life and work (you don't have to know
  much about them) but are meant to surprise them, catch
  them off balance without making them feel
  threatened. Example: I asked Sudeep, born in
  India, an HR manager of a consultancy firm,
  if he liked the idea of the afterlife
  being an eternal cricket match.
  Exclude questions about general
  abstractions (love, ideals,
  art, justice, passion, God,
  etc.) Focus on specifics like
  the role of horses, hamsters,
  being under water, olive oil,

or silk in their lives. I
have a standard question: Is
there a real or imaginary
island that has a special
meaning for you? Or: Do
you or did you collect
anything?

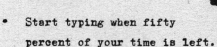

- Start typing when fifty
  percent of your time is left.

- Use carbon paper so you can give your subject a hard
  copy immediately. And file a copy.

- Limit the typewriter portrait to a single sheet of
  paper. It is like a verbal Polaroid, a snapshot of a
  first impression, instantaneously produced.

- Play with margins, spacing, skipping lines, columns,
  to give some rhythm and visual appeal to your
  portrait. Unlock the spacing setting and move the
  platen with one hand, while typing with the other.
  Make a wave out of a sentence, for example, or let
  the letters rain down. In the typewriter portrait of a
  particularly shy person, I typed around an empty spot.
  I have used a blue ribbon, pink paper, etc.

- Do not try to be exhaustive and use all the answers.
  The key is selection and linking it to details seen,
  observed, heard. As time is short, focus on one
  idea or image. With Sudeep it was the sandy island
  he remembered as his happy spot as a child at his
  grandmother's house near the beach. Work around this
  focus point, improvise a form of coherence. Not only
  is time short, there are only about 350 words on a
  page, max.

- When you start typing, make sure your subject stays put. It keeps the pressure up, emphasizes the "operation."

- Should you use pen or pencil to make notes? I didn't, it never occurred to me, maybe because it feels like cheating. It is more exciting, more difficult, more magical to write directly onto the typewriter and compose as if improvising on a musical instrument.

- Close your eyes when you try to form the sentence in your head before typing. Visualize the words as typewritten; it will prevent typos.

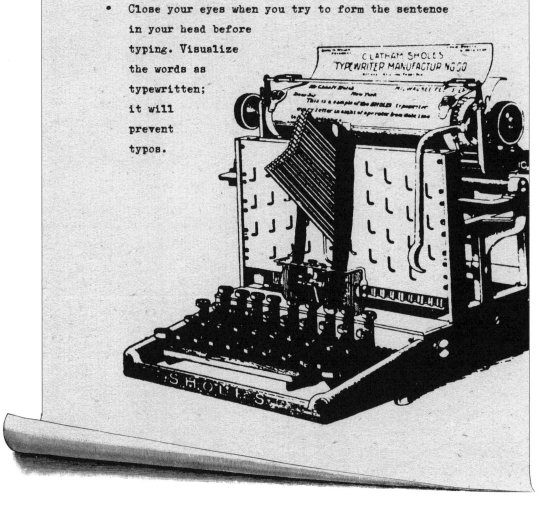

Artist Stacy Elaine Dacheux takes a gentler approach in her typewritten "future portraits":

I am scared of and interested in confrontation—how we talk to each other nonverbally and where our minds go based on first impressions and certain visceral judgments. . . . How will my muse feel about my power to document him or her? How long will I allow them to sit before I feel uneasy about my power to document? . . . What do I admire? How can I push past these personal biases and try to get to the heart or dream of the subject? . . .

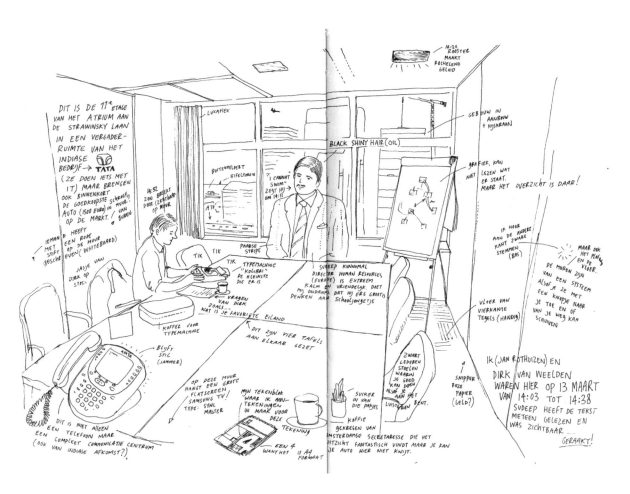

I use the following materials to create each portrait: typewriter, personalized stamp, blue twine, archival ink, newsprint, 4″ x 4″ paper with matching envelopes, pen, pencil, glue stick, scissors, square stencil, ruler, thesaurus. . . . I place a small square of paper into the typewriter and wait for inspiration. Sometimes the subjects speak to me and sometimes they do not. . . . The typewriter is always lingering between us, governing us. . . . When the subject's body shifts into a posture that reflects [a] feeling of warmth or comfort, I know it's time to type. . . . After I have typed the subject's future in the small square of paper, I paste it on a larger one. I outline another square around the paper, to give the appearance of a matted frame, then I seal it in an envelope and wrap twine around it like a gift. I present the portrait to the subject, hug him or her, and say thank you.

You can also create a typewriter portrait of a place. Travel writing by typewriter is feasible and fun. While most visitors are just thrusting a smartphone at what's in front of them—which, research suggests, may actually interfere with the formation of their own, personal memories—you are reflecting on your experiences with well-chosen words, distilling life into a typescript with the help of your trusty mechanical companion. Whether you take out your ultraportable on the spot to tap out some observations, or return to the hotel room where your machine awaits, the typewriter stands ready.

What's more, typewriters can give a unique shape and content to your adventures. In New York, I visited Gramercy Typewriter and watched as the experts there healed machines owned by established writers and curious twentysomethings. In Arlington, Massachusetts, I sought out Cambridge Typewriter, where Tom Furrier works and blogs about life in a typewriter shop. In Paris, I looked for the bar *La machine à écrire* (defunct, sadly) and went on a typewriter photo safari at a flea market. In London, I investigated shops that sell typers in the bohemian Shoreditch neighborhood and enjoyed three type-ins with like-minded souls.

As an insurgent, you belong to an international alliance of intelligent individualists—people who genuinely care about words, and about alternative ways of living and thinking. Look them up when you travel. You can make contact in advance online, and arrange to hold a type-in or simply to meet for a drink and a chat. It's a fine way to get to know a very diverse group of people who are united by their appreciation for writing machines. Without the typewriter connection, I would never have met a printer-poet-artist in London who showed me an Arabic Optima that he found on the sidewalks of Alexandria, and told me about his meetings with William S. Burroughs. When in New Haven I visited America's oldest working typewriter repairman, Manson Whitlock, a few months before his death at age ninety-six, and savored square donuts with a local portable typewriter enthusiast.

By the way, taking a portable onto a plane is no problem, although you may get some questions, smiles, and reminiscences when you go through security. I've often typed in airports, and have gotten into friendly conversations. But don't use your Skyriter in the sky: A plane cabin is a confined place with a captive audience who are already having something less than the best time of their lives, and who may very well be annoyed by the tapping. The one time I tried it, I got a "Hey buddy, can you turn that down?" Let's keep the revolution appealing, not obnoxious.

It's easy to share or publish your reporting, if you choose, with the help of digital technology. You can simply retype on a computer, you can scan or photograph your typescript, or you can use one of the other computer-typewriter interfaces that we'll explore in the next chapter.

PUBLISHING BY TYPEWRITER

Then again, you can publish your typewritten work without computers at all. In a time when so much publishing is instantaneous, free, and global, it has lost much of its significance. Making words public is so easy that it doesn't mean a lot. Publishing by typewriter takes effort, craft, and dedication; it reaches a smaller audience, but may have a greater impact.

How do you do it?

The world of zines offers one answer. Zines have roots in the fanzines that sprang up with pulp fiction, in the samizdat publications that defied Communist authorities during the Cold War, in the underground psyche-delic publications of the sixties, and in the punk culture of the seventies and beyond. Creators of zines have complete control over their content, which may be whimsical, revolutionary, disjointed, or obsessive. Anything goes, including word processing and desktop publishing software, but the typical zine aesthetic breaks free from the slick layouts that computers hand us ready-made, embracing literal cut-and-paste techniques and filling the page freely with drawings, collages, handwriting—and, often enough, type-writing. The raw, amateur quality of most zines is part of their appeal.

The true zine is reproduced on paper; if it's digitized, it becomes a different beast. Early zines were mimeographed, but authors typically turned to photocopiers when that technology spread. Some zine creators avoid all mechanical reproduction; they create one-of-a-kind pieces or laboriously create multiple copies by hand, in a distant echo of medie-val manuscripts. Whatever the means used, a zine is rarely published in editions of more than a thousand, or even a hundred, copies. Profit, obviously, is not the point.

Zines reached a peak of popularity just before the explosion of the Internet, but they persist today as an alternative, nondigital movement, very appropriate to the typewriter revolution. Case in point: I Am Typewriter, a 2011 zine festival sponsored by The Sticky Institute, an art organization that exhibits in an underground walkway in Melbourne. Defiantly celebrating "the triumph of continued usefulness," I Am Typewriter featured sixty tables stocked with typewriters and zines, including titles such as *The Top Eleven*

Things to Do with a Typewriter Ribbon, Just My Typewriter (featuring typewriters made of felt, cheese, and light), *Olivetti episode one,* and *qwerty pop.* "The love affair between zinemakers and typewriters . . . will not be crushed by time," declared The Sticky Institute—and it's true.

Other typewritten publications can't be called zines, but they share zinesters' interests in creating a unique object that uses a typewriter as a personal printing press. Snarky Cards, for instance, is a line of raunchy, disarming messages created by Alisa Starr, who hawks them in bars and online. Each is individually painted and typed. To date, she's sold some sixty thousand of them. Or there's Rob Bowker's text, carefully typed on both sides of a sheet of paper that can be cut and folded into a sixteen-page microbook. Its topic: instructions on how to type a microbook.

Meghan Forbes and her collaborators, Hannah McMurray and Ian Davis, have taken typewriter publishing to a new level with *Harlequin Creature*. Every issue is published in an edition of one hundred copies; fifty are individually typewritten, and another fifty are carbon copies. The journal is hand bound, and in addition to typewritten text includes art and sheet music—but no content that has to be reproduced with the intervention of digital technology or photocopiers. Contributions have come from around the world; contributors are encouraged to participate in the production of the journal, which is typed by dozens of volunteers at "typing bees" in various locations and sold in various American cities and in Berlin.

How did this begin? Forbes writes:

> Because I wanted to create a physical journal, not just something to be downloaded as a PDF, I felt that the cheapest and most original way to do this would be to use a typewriter to produce each copy. I quickly saw the fallacy in that. The first issue was a nightmare to type up (far too many words) and because of the high quality of materials used, it was far more costly to produce the thirty copies in that issue than had we used a cheap printing service. But I was struck immediately by how strongly people responded to the typed contents, and developed a kind of theory of the typewriter during the process of putting out that first issue. Namely, that by bringing together a variety of people to type each issue, and having each person sign the copy they typed, volunteer typists are in essence taking authorship for the copy they type. It is most often the hand of someone whose work is not included in the journal, who perhaps has no experience writing, that transcribes and thereby reinterprets the original manuscript.

Hence the typing bee: a unique event that's social, creative, and low pressure (since typos are celebrated as part of the nature of the journal).

> Typing bees are a fun, communal experience, in which friends and friends of friends of *Harlequin Creature* come together

around a collection of old and aging typewriters, to bang out the beautiful content of this entirely handmade journal. Without our writers, there would be nothing to type, but without our typists, there would be no creature. Snacks and songs are thrown in for good measure, along with a thank you take-home treat.

From Harlequin Creature's manifesto

we are caught in a web where the digital tools we
use daily to remain viable collect our information.
sell some of it to the government. and hoard the
rest of it for themselves.
   we are aware that we live inextricably within
this system and season.
   but we maintain that our stolen metadata does not
define us. and that the safest place to put our words
is on a piece of paper. so we seek to find a place on
the periphery. where we scream our throats hoarse
and call to you to meet us there. so that the margins
may become a new center.
   what does our Revolution look like?
   it is one that embraces the outsider and under-
served.
   it does not sell the written word for a pittance
and art to only the highest bidder.
   it embraces so-called obsolete technologies as
perhaps our greatest allies in generating analogue
content that cannot be immediately absorbed.
chopped up into sound bites. and redistributed
without our knowledge.

Harlequin Creature is not just an artistic experience, but an act of insurgency: Forbes sees typewriting as "a way to circumvent the way information is shared, mutilated, and manipulated on the Internet." The group's manifesto is a defiant vision of a better world—including typewriters.

Zines and *Harlequin Creature* embrace imperfection, taking it as a mark of individuality. But it's also possible to use typewriters to create publications that look every bit as careful and professional as digital creations, yet are instantly recognizable as something from another world. Blurry, misaligned, misspelled text is frowned upon in this approach; the goal is to produce correct and elegant typing. For this, one needs a sophisticated typewriter with features such as a film ribbon, proportional spacing, or margin justification. The most readily available proportional typewriter is the IBM Executive, but it will not justify automatically (you have to do some math) and each machine has just one typeface. The ultimate typewriter for producing print-ready copy is the Coxhead Varityper DSJ, a device descended from the Hammond that features interchangeable, proportional typefaces and justifying capacity. (The scarce IBM Selectric Composer has similar features but is less reliable.)

In Arizona, Fred Woodworth uses Varitypers in combination with offset printing and solar power to publish his incisive, idiosyncratic journals *The Match!* and *The Mystery and Adventure Series Review.* Woodworth adopted the Varityper early on and has proudly kept using it for decades, spurning digital devices for reasons he explains quite clearly. As the world around him has shifted to the digital, Woodworth's expert imprinting of ink on paper has become a statement of its own—an affirmation of individualism and craft.

If you enjoy publishing on paper, consider joining the American Amateur Press Association. It's been around since 1936 as a haven for home journalists, a sort of predigital blogosphere. You get a mailing each month of a "bundle" of some members' creations—everything from word-processed, photocopied mini-newsletters to beautifully letterpressed works of art. Writing about personal experiences is welcome; religion and politics are discouraged.

Publishing with a Varityper

by Fred Woodworth

AT VARIOUS TIMES my work encompasses just about every aspect
of the written word: correspondence, editing, writing, publishing, and even printing. Typewriters—and in particular a
certain very versatile machine—have fulfilled all my needs
in these various lines for a lifetime. Since 1969, when I
started publishing a small newspaper, and of course well before that in my college days, it was always important to be
able to generate neat, legible, and attractive copy in formal
letter-shapes. Lithographic printing required a "camera-
ready" page layout known as a pasteup or mechanical, and for
this even greater formality was demanded, but most ways of
producing such copy were terribly expensive.

One way of generating formal galleys of type was to have
them set up at a Linotype shop and proofs run, the proofs
afterward being pasted up into page form for photographic
platemaking. Here the detour into letterpress prior to actual offset printing was an inefficiency compounded by high
union rates, while use of a phototypesetting service meant
paying for someone's investment in a $50,000 apparatus that
was on the blink half the time. However, there was, I found,
another alternative, which involved a kind of typewriter.

The machine was known as a Varityper, or Coxhead DSJ (the
letters stood for "differential spacing and justifying", and
signified a kind of typewriter-composer that had been developed by the Ralph C. Coxhead Corporation from the late 1800s
Hammond typewriter). For less than the cost of having some
gouging and often censorship-prone shop set up an issue, the
small publisher could buy the typesetting typewriter and a
bunch of fonts (there were hundreds), and achieve instant independence. This is what I did, and I found that I liked
these machines very much.

As years passed there was considerable urging from various quarters to scrap the "obsolete" typewriter and shift
to one or another of dozens of computer systems, most of
which, at least through the 1970s, '80s, and a lot of the
'90s, delivered rather poor typographic results. In addition
they were plagued by crashes and other strange behavior that
seriously hampered or outright destroyed a number of small
periodicals, and as long as I had something reliable, which

by now I'd learned to adjust and maintain, I couldn't see any need to follow the herd. I could use the typewriter for letters, and I could turn on the justifier for straight right-hand margins.

My correspondence still looked good, and now it had an extra quality that kept it from looking like everybody else's. Anything I wrote for publication stayed right on the page in front of me and couldn't possibly vanish accidentally; and for the final formality of publication type itself, I had only to throw another switch and cut in the differential spacing mechanism: Now I had full typesetting at my fingertips, complete with *italics* and hundreds of different fonts, each of them distinctive and clearly not run-of-the-mill computerized copy.

No censorship, no "crashing", no "upgrades", and essentially no expense. At all. Just use and convenience, year after year, decade after decade.

From my standpoint there's a lot wrong with the whole computer/internet syndrome today. At one time activities carried out in the course of a day involved dozens, perhaps hundreds, of disparate operations: playing a record, taking a picture, paying a bill, conferring with an associate or friend, seeing a movie, writing a letter, going to a library or bookstore, doing homework, setting up a dental appointment, reading a newspaper, writing a comment for publication in the paper...

To do all these things, you went a lot of places, moved about, functioned diversely in and all over your town or city. More and more today, though, all of that human scope is being compressed down and moved in and out of your home on a couple of small wires or a fiberoptic cable. How much easier this is for someone to watch or control!

They don't have to hunt around, go to bank, bookstore, library, school, trashcan—they just have to access a little box.

Since I don't like this direction of society, I want to criticize it, but it seems to me that a certain dimension of credibility is compromised when someone is forced to use this very digital technology to make such criticisms. It's as if to admit that though you may be unhappy with matters, you are in the same pen as the rest of the herd.

That's why I don't intend to stop using this typewriter—not now, tomorrow, or ever. I intend to keep typing because it suits me, it's a technology that was there when I needed it, is still here today, and I can use it in every sense, instead of being used *by* it.

KIDS AT THE KEYS

Northside is not your typically bland neighborhood in Cincinnati, Ohio. The grunge is thick on some of the nineteenth-century storefronts, while the houses around the corner may be pristine or dilapidated, expansive or minimal. An abundance of bars, two record stores, and hole-in-the-wall restaurants with vegan options are visited by patrons of all ages, races, orientations, and classes. The norm in Northside is to deviate from the norm.

It was the perfect place to sell typewriters, I figured. I could hardly open a typewriter shop myself, but the owner of Shake It Records was willing to display a Smith-Corona and Royal that I'd found at the thrift store and cleaned up. I just wanted to see whether they'd find owners. If you love vinyl, you could love a typewriter, right?

It took over a year for those two machines to disappear. Hardly a successful experiment in spreading the insurgency.

But in fall 2012 I was walking down Hamilton Avenue and spotted a big Royal FP in a storefront. I peered through the window and saw a thirties Remie Scout on a bookshelf. What was this place? It called itself WordPlay Cincy, and its logo was a stubby pencil with rocket fins. Inside, I found comfy couches, old furniture, kids at tables, and a wiry, determined woman named Libby Hunter.

Hunter conceived the idea for a children's literacy center after a run-in with rock-throwing kids. Wouldn't reading and writing give children something better to do? While working as a realtor and raising three sons, Hunter renovated an old commercial space, raised funds and enthusiasm, and managed to make WordPlay a reality.

The Royal was a donation that was an unexpected hit with the kids who started to come in for tutoring. Other typewriters began to make their way to WordPlay, including a 1911 Underwood No. 5. When I walked in, Hunter had just been wondering whether to invest some of the nonprofit's funds in professional typewriter repair, and where to get new ribbons. Naturally, I offered my services.

With some repair and maintenance work from me, and more donations from the typosphere and elsewhere, WordPlay was soon equipped with a dozen typewriters, and the kids were flocking to them. Hunter wrote:

> The kids love them. They are almost magnetic—even the most reluctant writers are drawn to these relatively simple, elegant machines. The very basic, physical task of tapping out a story and not needing to hit the "print" button is somehow mesmerizing for our young writers. Two of our regular after-school kids even tote in their own personal typewriters every week, working on their stories and homework, offering to share their treasured possessions with fellow students, all motivated by that mechanical, tactile, simple process that is so un-computer age and yet so "totally cool" according to our students-in-the-know. . . . Seeing their work unfold right in front of their eyes is almost transformative; the kids are hooked, and seeing their inspiration, so are we.

The tradition of the "Tuesday typing pool" began, where several girls would come in to type side by side. A boy got fascinated with the mechanisms of the typewriters and was eager to learn repair techniques. A growing library of typescripts was generated in this funky, comfy corner of Northside.

On April 11, 2013, Libby Hunter was honored as Cincinnati's first volunteer citizen of the year. The date also marked the grand opening of the Urban Legend Institute—WordPlay's retail store, featuring offbeat objects to stimulate the imagination and support the nonprofit. One of its signature offerings: typewriters. My dream of running a typewriter shop had come true, in a better way than I could have imagined. The shop offers typewriters that I've found and fixed up, as well as cleaning and repair services. I get the fun of hunting and working on typewriters; WordPlay gets the profits; and my wife is grateful that I get to indulge my hobby without stuffing our house with still more writing iron.

Vivian Emmons was one of WordPlay's earliest fans. She's a Tuesday typing pool regular who was already a typist before WordPlay opened. I interviewed Viv when she was ten years old and owned three typewriters:

> I'm always itching to play the piano or type something. I really want to use the typewriter, even when watching TV. I type stories. I just mess around a bit, it depends on what mood I'm in. I might just do gobbledygook, make up a short story randomly off the top of my head, with no real thought.
>
> Seeing everyone's faces when I use it is neat. Someone came over to our house one time and the kid with them was

```
this is a typewriter
it does things like type and be awesome
  -- typed by a child at WordPlay Cincy
```

bored. She was whining and didn't know what to do. I brought down a typewriter. She messed with it and said, "Wow, this is so cool."

I turned in typewritten work for school once. The teacher was fine with it. She knows I'm the typewriter girl in the class.

In the typing pool, we do journaling about our day for a few minutes. Then we finish the writing prompt from the week before and start on a new one. Sometimes we have some extra time and just talk. Sometimes it gets wacky.

I can fix small problems, like flicking the keys down when they're stuck, figuring out a paper jam, or something.

There are more things you can do with a computer. The typewriter, all it does is type. Sometimes that can be distracting too, though, because it's just so cool.

Typewriters are one of the coolest things you can have, because they're just what they are.

WordPlay Cincy is modeled on the 826 concept, pioneered by novelist Dave Eggers at 826 Valencia in San Francisco—a stimulating kids' writing center combined with a whimsical retail store. 826s are active in eight US cities, and several have experimented with typewriters.

Typewriters are also a fixture at Poets House, a literary center in New York City where the "screenless computers" in the children's room are "a huge favorite." Mike Romanos of Poets House reports:

> We had a couple of founder [US Poet Laureate] Stanley Kunitz's old typewriters; we refurbished them and put them into the children's room. The room is a hands-on area with old things to get kids' imagination going. Typewriters, we found, were really good at getting kids interested in learning something new and tactile. They give the kids something to focus on while composing. The sound, the bell, hitting the keys, pressing the letter to the page—it solidifies their experience and makes it fun. The kids are

I am from the words on the paper, I am what is
on the paper, and no one can tear the paper that
I am on.
    I am from my own heart, the place that all the
ideas come from that power the machine that I am.
    I am from what I want, I am the ink of the
ribbon in the old typewriter, but no one can use
all of it.
    I am from all the books that I will write in
the future.

                              --Vivian Emmons

really focused on making the poem look good and come
out on the page—doing different versions, putting words in
different places, on different levels.

It's more than just a fad. When we set up our typewriters at street fairs, we had long lines of people waiting to
take a turn.

So what makes typewriters so fascinating to kids?

Most children have never seen one before. To them, a typewriter isn't
"retro"—it's brand new. But more importantly, kids like typewriters because
things that stimulate and enlighten you are fun—and kids can feel the benefits. Let's consider them.

First, a typewriter gives kids an understanding of mechanics that can
only be simulated imperfectly on a screen. They can see and feel the workings of the machine. They can grasp the cause and effect; they can make
things happen immediately in a physical object and feel the pushback of the
object on their own body. For instance, they love to press the type against
their fingertips and experience the imprint of a letter on their skin.

Lauren Ziemski describes kids' experience at Carriage Return events: "Nearly every single [child] I spent time with was curious and eager to learn what this button did, what that button did, what she/he needed to do to make the paper advance. . . . After a few halting stabs at the keys, they were eventually cranking out stories, or just experimenting with the way the linkage worked."

In addition, typewriters stimulate kids' curiosity and excitement about language. A typewriter can supercharge the desire to learn the alphabet, to spell, and then to write increasingly complex things.

As single-purpose machines, typewriters also combat distraction. Surely it's no coincidence that the digital age suffers from rampant attention deficit—and in some cases, turning away from the computer is a great help. A reader of Robert Messenger's typewriter blog reports:

> My twelve-year-old son, with mild ADHD, has been using [a Royal HH] to complete all kinds of school "worksheets"—his

teachers are delighted to see his work come in typed. . . . The actual quality of his composition is far better when he types than when he uses a computer *or* writes longhand. Somehow I think the *clickety-clack* and the return carriage lever keep his hands busier so that his mind can work better!

High-school teacher Tad Smith told me:

I have a student with ADHD in one of my classes who currently has a pretty low F as a result of missing assignments and general inattention. Over the last two days, we've been working on a personal narrative in the class. My student asked me if he could try out my typewriter just to see how it worked. I obliged. He spent the next two days more focused than I've ever seen him. He usually needs to be up and moving, but he sat at his desk, intently typing away. He typed two or three pages of narrative, and was really amazed when he finished. He told me that he really had to concentrate on everything that he was typing, and that he realized that the distractions of the computer simply weren't there as he was typing. He wants to know if he can keep using the typewriter for other assignments. I told him that he absolutely could.

These experiences echo the Classroom Typewriter Project, the brainchild of Phoenix high-school English teacher Ryan Adney. His imagination piqued by a rusty machine in the school library, Adney got a hunch that "the lowly and forgotten typewriter had a few tricks left to teach us" and decided to bring some typewriters into the classroom, requesting donations from around the country. He invited his students to try them, and tracked the results through observation, tests, and surveys. After just a week, eighty-six percent of typewriter users strongly agreed that they enjoyed the machines, and sixty-four percent felt their writing was improving. After administering some spelling tests, Adney found that among the poor spellers who managed to improve their skills, two-thirds were typewriter users. Experience over several years has only confirmed Adney's view that the benefits of typewriters are significant.

> What started for me with a couple of typewriters in the classroom and a slightly nutty notion became something far more interesting and unique and powerful. . . . It blossomed into something that ultimately proved that nondigital writing, analog writing, could really be a profound and powerful tool for improving students' awareness of the written word.

Adney encourages teachers to "steal" his idea, and similar projects have popped up in other states and countries. Brad Coulter's first-grade classroom in Kirkland, Washington is equipped with a typewriter for every student: the machines "range from thirty-five to ninety-five years in age, and in general they work as well now as the day they were made. The room sounds like an old newsroom with the kids clacking away." Out of sixteen students in the class, six of them asked their parents for typewriters for Christmas.

Maybe typewriters will become a fixture in Language Arts classes around the world. If you have some spare typewriters, you might ask some local teachers whether they'd like them for their classrooms.

From Geneva to Mexico City, teenagers like Adney's students are on the hunt for typewriters. In fact, teens are probably the largest group of new typewriter users today. Some may have been inspired by their childhood reading of the Kit Kittredge books, where a girl living in Cincinnati during the Depression types a family newspaper on her Royal portable. Others may be thrilled by the machine (another Royal) used by Charlie, the angsty main character in *The Perks of Being a Wallflower.* Or they may be motivated by the insurgent spirit of nonconformism. When everyone around you is obsessed with social (or antisocial) media and thumbing out text messages by the score, what better way to find yourself than to sit down at a typewriter? Here's one sixteen-year-old's typed reaction:

> BRING THESE BACK! This is amazing. Freeing. Freeing me from technology and from my age. From time. From the mon-

ster of phones and static and people walking in the wrong
direction because their nose is glued to a damn screen. I am
going to get one of these things and I am bringin' the typewriter back. Thank you.

In college, where digital devices in the classroom are constant invitations to
distraction (and cheating), young people also often react positively to typewriters. One of philosophy professor Martin Rice's students, after trying a
Royal 5 as old as her great-grandfather, said, "This typewriter is fascinating,
I love it. It's so much better than my computer. I actually have to focus on
what I'm writing. I have to access my mental dictionary."

So let's say a kid gets a typewriter. What to do with it?

Answers are throughout this chapter and this book, around the world,
and in the child's imagination. Usually the typewriter itself is stimulus
enough. As Monda Fason writes, "If you want to grow a writer, give her a
working typewriter, some fresh ribbon, and a generous stack of paper. Then

stand back and give her room, because it takes a lot of unbothered space to try out a new voice. Over and over and over again."

Still, here are a few proven ideas, in case a kid wants some:

- Create a newspaper or zine about the family, friends, school, neighborhood, dinosaurs, or Disney World.

- Have a letter-writing party with friends.

- Time travel with typewriters: Go back a century and type a report on your experience (a concept used by *Harlequin Creature* in workshops for kids in Detroit, New York, and elsewhere)

- Collaborative tales: Several typewriters have several stories going at once. Writers rotate, adding a few sentences at a time to each story.

- Write to seniors: twelve-year-old Californian Catherine Stevens and her friends took the initiative to type letters to

The very young insurgent's library

- <u>Click, Clack, Moo: Cows That Type</u>
  by Doreen Cronin

- <u>As Fast as Words Could Fly</u>
  by Pamela Tuck

- <u>The Lonely Typewriter</u>
  by Peter Ackerman

- <u>Meet Kit: An American Girl, 1934</u>
  by Valerie Tripp

- <u>Hermelin, the Detective Mouse</u>
  by Mini Grey

residents of a local retirement home, bringing delighted
letters in return.

- Type homework, guaranteeing that the teacher will give the
writing the attention it deserves—and will ask curious questions to boot.

Now, the sight of young children tapping away seems bizarre to some.
Shouldn't they have access to "technology" (meaning digital technology)? Don't they need to interact with computers in order to learn
effectively and be prepared for the modern world? Let's take a moment
to question these assumptions.

When kids are entranced by the Internet, are they learning deeply,
or just skimming superficially? Typically, they're flitting through endless
images, facts, factoids, gossip, memes, misinformation, and chatter—not
to mention what they might encounter in the way of more sinister predators
and temptations. If you have a basis in real life—years of experience dealing
with flesh-and-blood human beings in the material world—then you may
have the judgment necessary to encounter this online material. Kids don't.

Kids (and adults) who read and take notes on paper are likely to focus
better and remember their work better than those who do everything
digitally. *Scientific American* reports, "Whether they realize it or not, many
people approach computers and tablets with a state of mind less conducive
to learning than the one they bring to paper." Let's have children learn to
print on paper, write cursive on paper, and type on paper. Digital expertise
can come later.

But what about their professional skills? This is a red herring. Their minds
and fingers will still be nimble at eighteen or twenty-two, if they need to
develop computer skills at that point. And the hardware and software will
certainly evolve between now and then, so any particular abilities they
develop right now will be irrelevant—except for one: typing on the QWERTY
keyboard invented by Christopher Sholes around 1870, which I confidently
predict will still be a primary means of human-computer interaction in 2070.

Trying to keep digital technology out of your kids' lives is like sticking
your thumb in a crumbling dike. But even Steve Jobs put strict limits on
his children's screen time. And if you can pull it off, there would be nothing

I can't be the only parent feeling whiplashed by the pace
of technological changes, the manner in which every
conceivable wonder--not just the diversions but also the
curriculums and cures, the assembled beauty and wisdom of
the ages--has migrated inside our portable machines. Is it
really possible to hand kids these magical devices without
somehow dimming their sense of wonder at the world beyond
the screen? . . . The reason people turn to screens hasn't
changed much over the years. They remain mirrors that
reflect a species in retreat from the burdens of modern
consciousness, from boredom and isolation and helplessness.
It's natural for children to seek out a powerful tool
to banish these feelings. But the only reliable antidote to
such burdens, based on my own experience, is not immersion
in brighter and mightier screens but the capacity to slow
our minds and pay sustained attention to the world around
us. This is how all of us--whether
artists or scientists or
kindergartners--find beauty and
meaning in the unceasing rush of
experience. It's how we develop
empathy for other people,
and the humility
to accept our
failures and keep
struggling.

--Steve Almond

at all wrong with raising your children, at least until age ten or so, in a completely nondigital environment. They can visit real places, make their own music, play sports, read books, and type. What could be healthier?

What sort of typewriter is best for a child? With so many full-featured adult typewriters out there at reasonable prices, there's no need to limit yourself to machines originally intended for kids. Lots of the brands featured in Chapter Three will work great for children. One caveat is that younger kids can be confused by machines with automatic margin systems; they tend to activate them by mistake and get stuck within narrow margins, without a clue as to how to escape. Electric typewriters are also inappropriate for small children.

If you want a very simple typewriter for a young child, you might look into two stripped-down Depression machines, the Rem-Rand Bantam and Royal Signet. There are a couple of versions of the Signet, with and without lowercase letters. The Bantam types only in capitals, and has colored keys that teach correct fingering. These minimal machines are solid, well-built little units.

Ryan Adney finds that Brother portables and mid-century Royal standards have stood up best to the rigors of a high-school classroom.

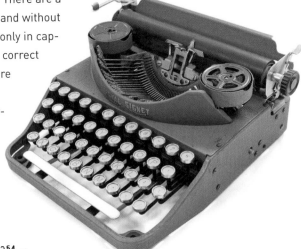

He also likes fifties Remington portables, and warns that the linkages on Smith-Corona midsize portables can disconnect under the stress of excitable young fingers.

Toy typewriters are a world of their own, with a wide variety of designs that charm many collectors. The simplest are index typewriters, where you turn a dial or slide an indicator to select a letter. The more complicated ones have keyboards, usually with three rows and two shifts. Unfortunately, there's no brand of toy typewriter that I can recommend for regular use by kids. These are cheap machines, often of low quality and low user satisfaction. They are slow, messy, difficult, or all of the above.

ODD JOBS

There are many more situations where typewriters make great tools. Let's close this chapter with a quick, partial list.

- Type captions for scrapbooks and photo albums.

- Type thank yous and other social notes when you want to make an impression.

- A typewriter makes a great ledger for visitors to your business, hostelry, or home—or a family message board when guests aren't around.

- Typewriters have become popular as wedding guest books. Set up a typewriter (or many) at your wedding, inviting guests to emboss their thoughts and good wishes on your stationery.

- Typewriting is romantic even on an ordinary Thursday. Leave little typewritten notes for your loved one.

- Arthur Springer, of Eugene, Oregon, brings a little Hermes Rocket with him as he travels from coffeehouse to coffeehouse, fixing espresso machines. He types up his invoices and bills on the Rocket, calling it more reliable than toting around a computer and printer.

- I use typewriters to write checks. The checks are legible, the recipient is tickled. And no, I won't "go green." Paying my bills by postal mail, instead of online, makes me more mindful of my expenses, and typing the checks makes bill paying (just slightly) fun.

- Tom Hanks keeps score at baseball games with a typewriter.

- Keep a typewriter in the kitchen. (Choose a cheap one that you wouldn't mind getting some cooking grease on.) It can type up your shopping list, ideas for meals, or those bright ideas that come to you while you're cooking or snacking.

- Businesses and organizations need ideas too, and what better way to generate them than by brainstorming on a typewriter? Put one on your desk and turn to it when you're reflecting on what just happened, or what you need to prepare for a meeting.

- Install a typewriter in a public place at work, and invite your coworkers to use it. The Olympia SG3 that I set up as a public typewriter in my office building soon accumulated jokes, poems, laments, and expressions of gratitude.

- You'll still run across paper forms to be filled out, envelopes to be typed, and labels to be lettered. Wherever paper is in use, typewriters are useful.

Some of the typing we've considered in this chapter happens purely on paper; some of it can be enhanced by computers, in a happy symbiosis. In the next chapter we'll look at some ways in which the typewriter revolution is creating hybrid forms of expression that straddle the digital and typewritten worlds.

Interlude #5

We affirm the written word and written thought against multimedia, multitasking, and the meme.

How does thinking at the computer differ from thinking with paper and pencil or thinking at the typewriter? The computer doesn't merely place another tool at your fingertips. It builds a whole new environment, an information environment in which the mind breathes a different atmosphere. The computing atmosphere belongs to an information-rich world—which soon becomes an information-polluted world.

—Michael Heim

Richard Dawkins invented the term "meme" in 1976 to mean a symbolic or cultural unit that reproduces like an evolving organism. Now "meme" has become a meme: It itself has "gone viral." We use it all the time to mean an idea, joke, image, or turn of phrase that spreads like the flu. Of course, the Internet increases the probability of a pandemic.

A meme is catchy: People imitate it or build on it. But we usually can't say why. We want to repeat it and pass it on, but we don't want to dwell on it. The typical meme grabs our attention, but doesn't hold it.

Now consider a typical communication experience of the twenty-first century. "News" shows feature multiple scrolling information streams, glittering animation, chattering personalities, and frequent

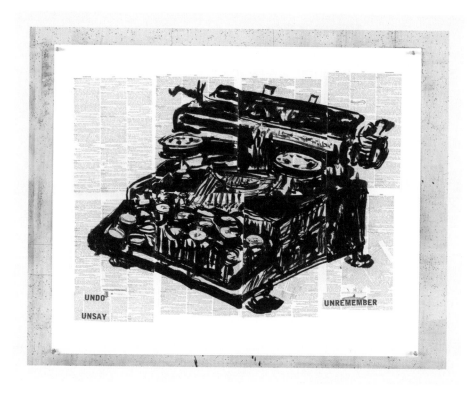

William Kentridge, Undo Unsay Unremember

interruption by manic advertisements. In business and education, PowerPoints give us chopped-up language juxtaposed with graphics. At the movies, we get wide-screen, three-dimensional profusions of virtual disasters. These experiences train a fire hose of memes on our minds to see what will infect us. In defense, the mind develops a thick, nonstick coat. Nothing makes a deep impression anymore.

To fight information pollution, you need to be selective. Ruthlessly cut your consumption of memes, and let your eyes and ears take a rest. It's not that there aren't wonderful audiovisual experiences out there, but you'll enjoy them all the more if you take them in small doses and aren't rushing on to the next thing.

Working at the typewriter cuts out all the chatter and focuses you on the page. It's an ascetic practice, a discipline based on the conviction that less is more. The typewriter brings you face to face with your own naked words. Sit. Wait. Let your brain stop buzzing and hopping. Then, from the blank page, a thought will bloom.

6. Enter the Typosphere

It bears repeating: The typewriter revolution is not an antidigital movement. We just have our priorities straight: the physical over the digital, the real over representation. That leaves room for creative collaboration between the two realms.

As Anthony Rocco says:

> Let's have a dialogue. There doesn't have to be a line in the sand between old and new technology. How do they both actually coexist? What can they learn from each other? Many digital people want their time in the sun, they want to get rid of the old and not have to remember how we got here; but people will blink, three generations will have gone by, and no one will

remember what it was that people actually did. It's important to have the two things support each other, to have these experiences happen at the same time. Because of this, many things we hadn't considered or thought were possible can happen now. It's important to come into the present and see how everything is coexisting, rather than shoehorning the past.

For typospherian Miguel Ángel Chávez Silva of Mexico City,

the charm of typewriters and typecasts, besides their materiality and individuality, is that they build a bridge between two very different eras, two different worldviews and contexts: the world of immediacy, of instant rewards, of efficiency and precision, and the world of craftsmanship, durability, and permanence.

So what's a typospherian? And what's a typecast?

The typosphere, in the narrow sense, is the world of typewriter-related blogs, a small subset of the blogosphere. These blogs may discuss the technical or cultural history of typewriters, their design, or their repair—or they may not be so much about typewriters as about the thoughts and experiences of people who love to type.

In 2005, writer Paul Lagasse started posting scanned typescripts on his blog *Sotto Voce,* convinced that "paper has an important place on the Web." He came up with a clever term for the practice: typecasting. Since that day, typecasting has been adopted by grade-schoolers and retirees, artists and programmers, journalists and screenwriters. Typecasting is a common practice in the typosphere, but it isn't universal, and it's also found elsewhere.

In this chapter we'll start with blogging and then adopt an expanded definition of things typospherical: the realm of all typewriter-computer interactions, from the silly to the sublime. We'll explore how we can carve out a typewritten space within the digital, but not of it; how digital creations can approximate typewriting; and how typewriters can be modified to have digital capacities.

A LIGHTNING TOUR OF THE TYPOSPHERE

The typosphere started to coalesce with Cheryl Lowry's blog *Strikethru*, founded in 2007. Lowry announced that she'd "become enamored with manual typewriters and the general resurrection of predigital forms of communication online—drawings, old film, typewritten or handwritten personal documents, tangible things that seem to be disappearing from everyday

The typosphere is a
curious world peopled
by exotic species.
Through reams of earnest prose, meticulous
description, and simmering
imagery, we try to share
the wonder at the inherent
impossibility of these
machines. How on earth can
a lump of iron and an inky
rag conjure not only meaning
but articulate and coherent thought? Muse, altar, confessional, psychoanalyst, talisman, icon, time machine. Whoever
said that typewriters just did one thing well was wrong. If
you hit a problem, turn to your typewriter--it will never
fail you. All the answers you might ever seek are available
beneath its keytops. Sometime in the real world, just as in
the typosphere, typewriters will be prescribed along with
other, less effective pharmaceuticals.

--Rob Bowker,
as typecast on his blog, Typewriter Heaven

life." Her goal was to help "this old stuff make a comeback on the web." Lowry succeeded, and even edited two issues of *Silent Type: A Retrotech Journal,* a magazine of typewriting and art, published on paper, created by typospherians. She now has a job at the digital-physical frontier—working for Facebook's Analog Research Lab (seriously).

Monda Fason's blog *Fresh Ribbon* was another inspiration to many. Born of her growing "addiction to typewriters," the blog was "a place to talk about typewriter love and writing the way it should be done—without electronic editing-as-you-create and spell check."

Ryan Adney calls the typosphere today "an anarchic collective." Typospherians live in many countries and type in several languages (although English predominates). They might write about intimate fears and hopes, memories, jokes, beer reviews, or, of course, their latest typewriter acquisitions and discoveries. All backgrounds, professions, and passions are welcome. What brings the typosphere together is simply our love of typewriting and our desire to share with the world.

Naturally, blogs come and go with their authors' enthusiasms. To date, some of the most durable blogs in the typosphere have included *ozTypewriter* by journalist and Australian Typewriter Museum creator Robert Messenger; *Type OH!* by cyclist and positive thinker Gerald Thompson; *The Filthy Platen* by Australian Scott Kernaghan; and *Joe Van Cleave's Blog,* from a New Mexico photographer and grandfather. My own blog bears the same title as this book. Messenger's *ozTypewriter* takes the cake for content: Its thousands of pages, with their eclectic wealth of observations, have been viewed well over a million times.

As we follow each other's blogs, topics, trends, and traditions crop up, but we're glad to explain them to newbies. For instance, the typosphere has been celebrating World Typewriter Day on June 23, the anniversary of a landmark patent by Christopher Sholes. This just means that we ramp it up a bit and come up with something special to mark the day—maybe recording a video, typing a message for the occasion, or taking a typewriter on a picnic. For a while the typosphere was experimenting with typing on surfaces such as tin foil, leaves, and crayon-coated paper. And when a typospherian refers to a BAROP, that's a Big-Ass Roll of Paper—a continuous scroll, as used by Jack Kerouac to type *On the Road.*

Where do you find these blogs? A good start is Welcome to the Typo-sphere, a collaborative site with announcements and information of interest to all typospherians and a comprehensive blogroll (blog list). Most blogs have their own blogrolls to explore.

If you'd like to start your own blog, look into the available platforms. The most popular platforms in the typosphere are Wordpress and Blogger (owned by Google). Both are free. Take some time to experiment with your background, header, design, and page elements to create an accessible and attractive visual experience.

When typecasting, I find that it works best to type in a column about half the width of a regular sheet of paper. The typewritten text is best reproduced by a flatbed scanner, although careful photography can also work. An image about five hundred to six hundred pixels wide works well on the screen.

When you're ready to type to the world, visit Welcome to the Typosphere and click on "What is the Typosphere?" for instructions on getting added to the blogroll.

Of course, the Internet offers all kinds of further resources for typewriter admirers, users, and collectors, some of which I mentioned in Chapter Two.

One starting point could be my site The Classic Typewriter Page, which has been around since 1995 and includes a long list of links.

Two Yahoo! groups, TYPEWRIT-ERS and The Portable Typewriter Forum, offer searchable archives of over a decade of discussions.

The Typewriter Database, founded by Dirk Schumann and developed by Arizona typospherian Ted Munk, includes serial number data on many makes, allowing you to date your machine, with thousands of photos that serve as helpful visual references. You can sign up as a "typewriter hunter" to post photos

Some of my favorite
blog names from the
typosphere

- <u>x over it</u>

- <u>b4ksp4ce</u>

- <u>clickthing</u>

- <u>natslaptaps</u>

- <u>writelephant</u>

- <u>Manual Entry</u>

- <u>I dream lo-tech</u>

- <u>Retro Tech Geneva</u>

- <u>A Machine for the End of the World</u>

- <u>To Type, Shoot Straight, and Speak the Truth . . .</u>

yourself, comment on photos from others, download documents, and consult typewriter patents.

The Facebook groups Antique Typewriter Collectors and Antique Type-writer Classifieds are fun places to buy and sell machines, share images, and chat about collecting, repair, and the joys of the typosphere.

Other online forums include the bulletin board *Typewriter Talk* and the "typewriters" subreddit on Reddit.

THE RHETORIC OF TYPECASTING

Whether or not they call it typecasting, many have discovered that online digital images of typewritten text have a certain mysterious power. On social media, typists upload their poems and thoughts, and eagerly read each other's typing. The most successful typecasting poets have enviable audiences: Christopher Poindexter, for instance, is followed by over two hundred thousand readers on Instagram.

A very simple example of typecasting is a Tumblr blog called *Typewriter Music*. Readers submit their favorite lyrics, which get typewritten by a certain Elisabeth, scanned, and then posted online. That's it—no melodies, no words that you can't already easily find in digital form—but every entry gets liked and reblogged by a cadre of fans, who keep submitting more lyrics. Typewriting simply adds magic.

The medium is the message, or at least it gives the message its distinctive punch. How does typecasting—this odd, hybrid medium—address its readers, even before they start reading?

First of all, it immediately says, "I care about my writing." When you take the trouble to use a typewriter, scan or photograph the typing, and upload it, you're saying that the writing process matters to you. You're showing a kind of craftsmanship that has earned your readers' attention. Digital writing may involve just as much care, but we can't tell. For all we know, the text was copied and pasted in a few seconds.

Typecasting shows up on the Internet, but isn't contained in it. You create a unique material object, an imprinted piece of paper (I keep mine in little portfolios). Your readers can glimpse that object through a digital reproduction, but they can't touch the paper, hear it rustle, or smell the ink. The typecast reminds them that the digital isn't everything, that there is a reality beyond it. Of course, this is also true of any digital photos and recordings of physical things. But nondigital *text* draws attention to itself through its contrast to digital text, which consists of pure symbols stripped of matter.

Typecasting shows the individuality and fallibility of the machine and the person who created it. There are the quirks of your particular typewriter, the unique effects of your typing style, and often typos that haven't been fixed or can't completely be concealed. There's a truth, sometimes a less than flattering one, that's conveyed in a typecast but concealed in a spell-checked, grammar-checked, automatically formatted digital text. As Yancy Smith puts it, "The typewriter makes concepts into an actual, tangible product that carries with it, through mistakes and anomalies, the event in which it was made." A typescript's marks of createdness give it a powerful appeal that still carries through when it's represented in pixels.

The materiality and uniqueness of typewriting send the message: "raw, unfiltered, genuine." That's a message that advertisers would kill for—which is why you can spot "typewriter text" in commercial messages every day. But of course, when it becomes a way to sell something, the genuineness of typewriting becomes ungenuine—and in fact, almost always, the "typed" words in ads are the product of a computer using a pseudo-typewriter font. (Does every *e* look just the same as every other *e*? It's digital.) On a personal site, though, when you typecast with a real typewriter, the message of genuineness is much more convincing.

"Raw" goes with "rugged" and "rebellious." You're snubbing efficiency and conformity by creating a typecast; you're challenging the digital domain by making it display a nondigital text. Whatever your typescript may say, simply by uploading it you've joined the insurgency.

GADGETRY

Can there be a writing device that combines the best of the digital and mechanical realms? So far, the USB Typewriter comes closest: a classic manual typewriter, still perfectly capable of typing, that can also serve as a digital keyboard thanks to its sensors and circuitry. Just plug it into a computer or iPad and watch the text appear on screen as you type. The system is available for a variety of popular twentieth-century typewriters.

USB Typewriter is the creation of maker Jack Zylkin of Philadelphia. The way he describes his brainchild makes it clear that it was conceived in the spirit of the insurgency.

> As an engineer, I have a special appreciation for the genius behind technologies like film cameras, bicycles, locks, acoustic instruments, and typewriters, which perform impressively complicated tasks with elegant mechanisms

instead of circuitry. Each typewriter is a miracle—not just the design, but the assembly. I've always thought that antique typewriters are much more similar in design to grand pianos than they are to modern computer keyboards. The designers of these classic typewriters were not just concerned with aesthetics and performance, but the feeling and experience as well.

The USB Typewriter project sets those gorgeous, brilliantly designed typewriters side by side with modern, totally generic, plastic computer keyboards, and hopefully asks people to reflect on what has been lost in the transition. I created the USB Typewriter as a sort of critique of the disposable, thoughtless,

and ultimately forgettable way we fling communication out into the electronic ether nowadays. A lot of folks miss the days when getting a handwritten or hand-typed letter was a very special experience, and those letters could be saved in a special place and looked back upon, like Van Gogh's letters to Gauguin. I am not sure what will happen to the tens of thousands of e-mails currently in my inbox twenty years from now—whether it will be possible to sort through them in retrospect to separate the important ones from the trivial.

Besides the quantity over quality problem, the computer screens themselves represent a threat to honest and truly thoughtful communication. It is often so hard to resist the infinite sources of distraction on a computer, since it is not a single-purpose writing device like a typewriter is, but it has evolved to be a be-all end-all boredom fighting machine. Even the phone is no longer just a phone. With the USB Typewriter, I hope to get typewriters back on people's writing desks, so they can make a conscious choice about when they want to jack into their computer and when they want to keep their mind clear of distraction. I made the USB typewriter so writers can use the paper instead of a screen and stay in an "unconnected" headspace, without sacrificing the ability to use a computer when they need to.

The majority of people who own USB Typewriters use them regularly in their daily lives. I have had customers who use the USB Typewriter because they still have never felt comfortable with computer keyboards even after transitioning to the computer years ago. I also have customers who use the typewriter in their personal writing practice already and begrudge having to switch over to a computer to do most other things. I have even provided USB Typewriters to legally blind customers, and those with vision problems that prevent them from looking at a backlit computer screen for long periods of time. Feeling the tactile response of a typewriter

keyboard and being able to focus on the crisp ink on paper
allows them to write more easily than on a conventional
computer setup.

And then there are my diehard customers, like Larry
McMurtry, who refuse to use anything other than a typewriter
to make their work, but don't want to miss out on the world of
possibilities a computer provides.

Zylkin's creation has been a great success, getting plenty of media attention
and fans. In addition to laboriously assembling USB Typewriters himself,
he's made affordable do-it-yourself kits available, and, in the sharing spirit of

Scanning a typescript

Digitizing a typewritten text doesn't have to mean retyping
the whole thing. Thanks to the standardized nature of
typewritten characters, they can be handled fairly well
by optical character recognition software
(OCR). Many photocopiers now double as
high-volume, high-speed scanners that
can e-mail you a JPEG or PDF or write
it to your flash drive. Free or cheap
OCR applications will then yield
digital text. It's guaranteed to
have errors, but you can
correct them as you
proofread and revise.

makerdom, his design is open-source. In addition to some two thousand USB Typewriters and kits that Zylkin has sold, thousands of people have created their own versions of the project, or adapted it to create games and art. "One maker expanded on my kit to produce a version of the RPG video game *Zork* that could be played entirely on a typewriter, without a computer screen at all."

Don't get a USB typewriter if you want something that will work just like a conventional computer keyboard; as Zylkin says, using one requires conscious attention. To get some characters and functions, you'll need to push a button on an electronic panel while tapping a key. The return of the typewriter carriage may have no relation to the end of a line on the screen. If the contacts aren't right or there's trouble with your typing technique, the screen output may miss a character you typed, or type it twice. (On my USB Olympia SM3, increasing the key tension a bit improved accuracy.)

The main question, though, is: Who's the master? Is the computer the boss, with the typewriter acting solely as an input slave? Or is the typewriter in charge, with the computer playing the faithful copyist? Both arrangements can fit your needs. My own preference (as you might predict) is to give the typewriter the upper hand: I can type something on paper while the computer obediently creates a digital text that I can keep as a record or edit. I recommend dimming your screen to eliminate the temptation to glance at the digital input; you can always fuss with it later.

Connecting a USB Typewriter to a tablet makes a lot of sense, since the rich tactile experience of a typewriter is definitely superior to typing on an image of a three-row keyboard on a tablet's featureless surface—a process that forces you to look at your fingers instead of focusing on what you are writing, all the while making sure that the autocorrect software isn't putting words in your mouth.

The USB Typewriter isn't the only device that tries to meld the experience of typewriting with the convenience of a tablet. It has a tongue-in-cheek but beautiful rival in Austin Yang's one-of-a-kind

iTypewriter

iTypewriter, a mechanical keyboard that holds your iPad and activates typebar-like levers with rubber tips that tap on the screen.

A more practical approach is Brian Min's Qwerkyriter, which imitates a black portable typewriter from the Depression years. It has clicky, metal-rimmed keys and a mock platen and carriage return lever; it connects to a computer or tablet. Min's dream of mass producing his brainchild came true thanks to a successful crowdfunding campaign in 2014.

Other digital-mechanical hybrids seem to come from parallel universes, such as the Electri-Clerk, created by Andrew Leman in 2002 for a game of

Cthulhu Lives. It's an ominous-looking combination of a 1930s Underwood and a 1988 Macintosh.

For Station to Station—a month-long rolling art happening aboard a train—the design team Fake Love constructed the Twitter Typewriter: an early-twentieth-century Underwood that sends messages through Twitter, complete with a Nixie tube display that counts down the characters available for your tweet. Meanwhile, at the Toronto Mini Maker Faire, Michael Schwanzer proudly displayed his Remington 12 that he had modified to type any tweets sent with the

Smartyping

An ultraportable typewriter and a smartphone can make a great team. Enjoy swift writing on a big, four-row keyboard with tactile and auditory feedback. Then just snap a picture of your typing and attach it to an e-mail or text. People will be impressed (believe me) and you'll have a handy paper record of your communication. With a Twitter or blogging app, you can also tweet or typecast by smartphone.

Sichtbare Schrift
Enorme Schreibschnelligkeit!!
11 Buchstaben per Secunde!!

STOEWER

Richard Nagy working on The Nagy Magical-Movable-Type
Pixello-Dynamotronic Computational Engine

fair's hashtag. In theory, one of these venerable typewriters can now activate the other over the Internet.

Steampunk craftsmen have created gorgeous alt-Victorian contraptions that blend typewriters and computers. These creations make computing exciting again by reimagining it as an element in a world of adventure, mystery, and exploration. Prominent constructors of typewriter-computer hybrids include Bruce Rosenbaum and the late Richard "Datamancer" Nagy. Their devices are elaborate monuments to the marriage of the mechanical and digital.

One of the most eye-catching steampunk creations is *Wozniak's Conundrum*, which we saw in Chapter One—a marriage of a Mac from the nineties and a Remington 7 from the nineties (1890s, that is). Artist Steve La Riccia had never heard of steampunk when he created his first interactive contraption in 2010, a television assemblage

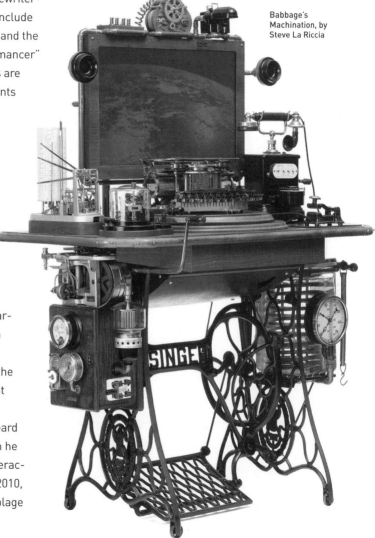

Babbage's Machination, by Steve La Riccia

he called *Farnsworth's Dilemma. Wozniak's Conundrum* followed the next year to great acclaim, and he has now embraced the steampunk movement, offering his services as Steamworks R&D Labs. A more recent La Riccia creation, *Babbage's Machination,* incorporates a Hammond No. 2, connected to a computer by a cleverly adapted USB Typewriter kit. (For *Wozniak's Conundrum,* he designed his own interface.)

If you have the know-how to try constructing a typewriter-computer hybrid, I suggest that, like La Riccia, you experiment with a typewriter whose design is firmly rooted in the nineteenth century, such as a Hammond, Oliver, or Blickensderfer. It will definitely draw attention. And if you can do it without harming the typewriter or degrading its function—a trick pulled off by La Riccia in *Babbage's Machination*—you get extra points.

DIGITAL SIMULATIONS

In summer 2013, billboards around the world promoted the iPad—by comparing it to a typewriter. The tablet was shown serving as an e-reader (featuring Camus's *The Stranger*), a camera (with a picture of a classic Olympus), and a writing machine—using the app miTypewriter. Created by Teru-

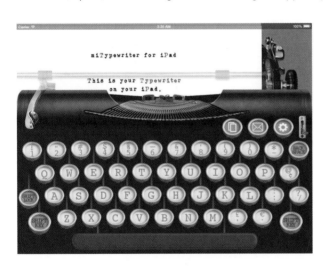

aki Onoda and roughly inspired by a prewar Remington portable, miTypewriter fills the screen with a simulated typewriter and a sheet of "paper" where you can create documents. You can watch tiny typebars move, the ribbon goes up and down, the carriage advances, and there are sound effects.

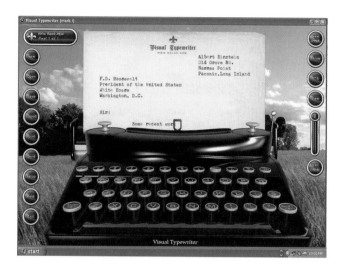

In 2014, typewriter enthusiast Tom Hanks introduced his own version of a touchscreen typewriter—actually, three of them. The Hanx Writer app can take the form of the Prime Select, the 707, or the Golden Touch. "You can rely on a DELETE key to correct your typos, or turn that off. Be bold and fearless!" For a while, the Hanx Writer reigned as the App Store's most popular download.

Naturally, pecking at a slab of glass is never going to be as satisfying as using the real thing, but simulations are fun, and they're another healthy sign that there's something about the typewriting experience that intrigues and entertains people.

To get closer to that experience on a computer you can try Visual Typewriter, a shareware Windows program created by Ithai Levi in 2004. It puts a simulated Remington noiseless portable on your PC screen, with a choice of stationery, beautiful natural backgrounds, and of course, the clicks and dings that we love.

Hemingwrite

The Amazing Type-Writer is an iPhone app that takes a different approach. It doesn't bother to look like a typewriter on screen, but it produces text that could easily be mistaken for a genuine typecast by randomly changing the inkiness of its misaligned letters. The result is a little document that looks like it was created with all the imperfections of an old manual typewriter and a novice typist. You can't delete, but you can easily move the typing point to any point on the "card" that you're creating. This lets you superimpose characters and experiment with all sorts of graphic effects. Your resulting work of concrete poetry or word art can then be shared in a gallery hosted by the developer. You can browse through the gallery to see what's on the mind of other anonymous users; you often find emotional confessions and poetry. You can then "request a mimeograph" of others' cards, adding to them as you wish and posting the modified cards in the gallery again. This form of "typing" is a unique social experience.

If you want a digital "typewriter" that's more than an app, consider the Hemingwrite. It doesn't actually print on paper, so I would not call it a typewriter, but it does catch some of the magic typewriter buzz. It's a word processor with a clicky keyboard and a retro look, designed only for writing.

Yet another way to imitate a typewriter is to install "typewriter" fonts on your computer, for use with any application. There are hundreds of them, many available for free download. As I've said, a typewriter font can never have the impact of real typewriting, but it still has some magic—because, if the mainspring of a typewriter is its heart, its typeface is its soul.

Even as a kid, I was fascinated by the typeface of my Remington Noise-less Portable Model Seven. I liked typing it, copying it by hand, and noticing its little imperfections, such as the missing right foot on its lowercase *m*. That disabled *m* has now appeared on blogs, games, books, packaging, and ad campaigns—because I turned it into a digital font and shared the soul of my typewriter with the world. I've now created over a dozen typewriter fonts that I give away on The Classic Typewriter Page, and I didn't need to know anything about font design to do it.

Here's how. First, find a website that offers to make a font from your handwriting (there are several). The system works via a template that you print, write on, then scan and upload to the site. Of course, the template will work with typing just as well as with handwriting. You can either type directly on the printed template, or use an image editing program to work with a high-resolution scan of your typewriter's typing and paste it into the digital template. Extra characters can be created through some image manipulation. The results won't look just like real typing, but it's a kick to see the soul of your typewriter manifested on a screen.

Ultimately, for all the pleasures of typecasting, simulated typing, and online fellowship, the soul of a typewriter is housed in its very physical body, which leaves physical marks on physical paper. Let's remind ourselves of this reality and then return, in our next chapter, to the typewriter itself as a material object—an object that invites modification.

Interlude #6

We choose the real over representation, the physical over the digital.

The machine is unforgiving. It is reality bled on paper. The punch of the key must be deliberate. Mistakes are indelible. Real action can't be recalled, only regretted. Typing is as real as blood on the evening news and as unavoidable. The virtual is ephemeral, a fog until it's printed. Even then the paper is only painted, not punched. Typing, like reality, hurts. It bruises the paper. When the letter is received, one knows an effort was made, that the writer had to sweat, that he had to meet the real, that he cared.

—*Martin A. Rice, Jr.*

What a special thrill there is to designing and inhabiting a digital environment: It gives us a taste of godhood.

You can create a world and its laws. You can intervene in events, cut things up and rearrange them, distort them, delete them, and undelete them. You can live a second life and third life simultaneously with your first, lose a life and get a new one, redo what you've done, create an avatar and experience the possibilities and excitement of the masquerade.

The only problem is that none of it is real. We know this, for all the talk about virtual reality; we know that in the end, we're pushing around pixels and digits. Yes, our behavior online some-times has huge consequences in the real

world—but there *is* a real world, and it isn't made of malleable information. It's made of objects, forces, and laws, most of which we didn't create and can't control; events that we can't undo; and flesh-and-blood humans, each of whom is going to die.

The digital Paradigm tempts us to forget all this—it seduces us with a fantasy of existence as a game, with a dream of perfect, "seamless" competence. But giving in to this fantasy means losing your real self in a kaleidoscope of selfies.

You can renounce the whole digital world, although it's becoming ever harder. You can avoid the devices, do as much as you can in the physical world, and live with a clear, hard vision of seamy, incarnate existence.

But for most of us, that's an overly harsh, Luddite reaction to digital dreams. Are games and appearances so evil?

Doesn't the human imagination always break free from the physical, and doesn't it deserve to do so in a digital playground? If we don't have that playground, won't we still explore imaginary representations through nondigital media—including type-writers themselves?

Of course—that's why this line of the Manifesto shouldn't be understood in black-and-white terms. In choosing the real *over* representation, we don't reject symbols and imagination; but we try to keep our priorities straight. We'd rather be real mortals than make-believe gods.

Most insurgents don't swear off the digital altogether—in fact, we like to use computers to share facts, stories, pictures, and typecasts. But we understand that reality comes first. Our sessions at the typewriter keep us grounded in the tangible and actual, even when we're writing the wildest fantasy.

7. Kustom Typers

Aftermarket modification has been a feature of the type-writer world for generations. Some companies specialized in typewriter attachments—everything from tabulators and adders to word counters and rubber key cushions. Professional speed typists might equip their machines with custom carriage return levers or big, fat bells that could be heard over the din of a competition. Typewriter repair shops would advertise their services with little plaques, decals, or shift-key inserts on the machines they serviced. And many old machines used to be professionally "rebuilt" so they'd be good for another couple of decades: Their rubber was replaced, they got a complete tune-up, and they were fin-ished in new, contemporary paint and decals. In short, "the lived typewriter," as anthropologist Peter Weil calls it, inevitably acquired accretions and character over the years.

Today, the concept of remodeling and refurbishing a typewriter has gained new life. People are repainting their machines, decorating them, and coming up with ambitious, innovative ways to "pimp your write."

The idea of permanently altering a typewriter isn't universally admired. Typewriter dealer Greg Fudacz worries, "This trend is dangerous. It's numbing new buyers to the value of an aesthetically original typewriter. Though, I have to be honest, some of the paint jobs and customized machines are wicked cool—plus, these trends are introducing new collectors to the hobby."

Typospherian Scott Kernaghan defends the idea:

> Sure, you'd be foolish to paint a rare or particularly old machine. But it is just paint. The hands that made the typewriter are long gone, but their legacy and history is in the machine, and painting it doesn't change the parts and pieces. The real work in the typewriter is still there.
>
> We don't leave buildings built in the 1800s to rot and deteriorate into the ground. We don't not paint classic cars. The paint that is on your typewriter was usually applied en masse. It hasn't been applied by Leonardo Da Vinci or Rembrandt. It is probably the least valuable part of the typewriter.
>
> I say paint. The typewriter isn't losing history, it's gaining it. Long after you've gone the way of the makers of the typewriter, your presence with the typewriter is still there—just like the original makers of the machine.

As Kernaghan suggests, if your typewriter is an antique (say, pre-1920) or a rarity, spray-painting it purple is an act of vandalism that hides its origins from future generations and lowers its value. Don't do it. Collectors are split on the question of whether an antique should be restored to what it might have looked like when new, or whether it should just be cleaned and polished, keeping its scars and blemishes. I favor a pretty conservative approach myself.

But when you have a Royal or Olympia that was made by the millions, I say the situation is different. You're not destroying the history of a scarce object, you're turning a common object into an individualized work of art.

Why not forge a closer bond between your writing machine and your own personality by giving it a distinctive look?

TYPERS FROM THE PROS

A growing number of typewriter remodelers and restorers are finding customers online, as people seek out eye-catching yet practical writing machines. For instance, in Germany, where the insurgency is less advanced than in the English-speaking world but fine typewriters are plentiful, a growing crop of typewriter dealers includes Filipa Freitas and her Typewriter Workshop in Berlin.

My business started when I realized a couple of things. First, that somehow, out of curiosity, I had become the owner of too many typewriters. Also, I had brought back to life some of my own typewriters, and I realized that it was a pleasurable activity for me, this patient, caring work of restoration. I am mainly an artist (with no commercial purposes), and I have to sustain my main work through jobs which allow me an income as well as some free time (and especially free mental space) to continue my artistic practice. Typewriters fit in my life very well, as they demand from me an almost meditative manual work, which is not at all in competition with my artistic work.

Some dealers are applying their artistic concepts to the typewriters they sell. Matt Dillon, for instance, runs an Etsy shop nicely called stillthemind, where he offered this whimsical fifties Smith-Corona clad in giraffe-print velboa.

Jack Zylkin, creator of the USB Typewriter, gave this Underwood an amazing magenta coat.

> This classic Underwood Model F Typewriter came into my typewriter shop used and abused. The original black paint was scratched and corroded, and the machine needed a good tune-up. Unwilling to let such an incredible piece of equipment go to scrap, I stripped it down to bare bones and repainted the frame with powder-coat, which is a type of baked-on enamel paint that is extremely durable, vibrant, and consistent. (It is the same type of paint that shops use on hot-rodded cars.) The gold-leaf decals were then reapplied, and the machine was painstakingly reassembled and tuned.

Kasbah Mod, headed by Chase S. Gilbert, has amplified the perception of typewriters as objects of desire and works of art. Gilbert says, "Our demographic is young people, around fifteen to forty, that are buying these items as design objects. That's not to say they're not using them but it's not the antique collector type." Gilbert himself is a user: "It's nice to get home and work on a typewriter. It frankly gives me more focus and it gives me a break living in New York and dealing with the non-stop connectivity." The company's customized creations have sold in the upper three figures and include copper-plated machines, glossy pink and red machines, and typers decorated in the style of Keith Haring, Piet Mondrian, and other famous artists. To quote a 2014 wall calendar featuring Kasbah Mod machines, "The manual typewriter is making a comeback. Call them retro, restored, or rejuvenated, what's old is new again."

Many of Kasbah Mod's glossiest, most glamorous machines were modded by Dean Jones of Louisville, Kentucky, an innovative technician who has perfected typewriter plating techniques. His favorite "canvases" are the bulbous Smith-Corona portables of the fifties ("the apex of it all"), and the eBay auctions where he sells them are deliciously verbose. Here are a few excerpts:

> My constant quest in this gig is for The Worthy Machine . . . Upon finding a worthy machine . . . my job is simple (although not necessarily easy)—to bring out that worthiness.
>
> I am a notorious Smith-dandier, and this one's no exception. The main chassis is bright white chrome, not unlike the chrome on your dad's old Ford bumper, although maybe less rusty. The finish is as a mirror, true chrome, electroplated, the real deal. . . .
>
> I've learned, both in my own development and through observation, that writing in type fosters the disciplined thinking valued by, and admired in, the best writers. . . . The villain, posing as your pal, is Mr. Delete Key. How often on a computer first draft have you overwritten yourself? You know you've done it when you reread the piece and wonder where its power went. The power still exists, but it's buried back there in that first crude draft. Unfortunately that's gone now, commingled with some overly doctored version of your mighty original idea, courtesy of your right-pinky man Mr. Deleter. . . . Nobody writes a perfect first draft. The day you accept that is the day you enter the zen of the manual typewriter. It is the most sophisticated *thought* processor created by man. Unlike

anything electronic, you completely animate it. . . . It is the
extension of the only true self-propelled machine, your mind.

Who could resist a custom typewriter after a pitch like that?

Some traditional typewriter shops have also caught on to the trend and
are offering their own write-ready eye candy. I purchased my chrome-plated
Olivetti Studio 44 from Berkeley Typewriter in California; owners Jesse and
Joe Banuelos had it plated in Mexico. The chrome brings out the eccentric
shapes of this hefty portable.

WELCOME TO THE COLORBOX

But maybe you'd like to give your typewriter a makeover yourself, instead of turning to the pros.

The most obvious thing to do is paint it. Why be satisfied with a drab or damaged paint job? Many mid-century typewriters were finished in colors that you may find uninspiring, particularly when combined with the common wrinkle paint: beige, brown, gray, khaki. (What were they thinking?) At your local art supply store, hardware store, or auto shop you can find a wide variety of spray paints that will appeal to your imagination. You'll probably want a primer, at least one color of paint, and a clear coat; all are available as sprays. One normal can of spray paint usually covers one typewriter.

When you've picked out your color scheme, remove the painted panels from your typewriter. Usually they're held on with screws, which you should replace in the frame of the typewriter as soon as you've removed the panels. To remove the panels on the ends of the carriage you'll probably have to take off the platen knobs, which may twist loose or may be held on by small screws on the knobs and/or the platen itself. The paper table may be held on with a spring, a C-clip, or a cotter pin.

Trim (chrome strips, logos, and such) should be removed from the panels if possible. You may need to unbend little tabs or push the pieces out from behind. If you can't remove a piece of trim, wipe some wax on it with the tip of your finger. After the machine is painted, the paint will chip right off the waxed pieces when you gently scratch them.

Prepare the pieces for painting by sanding the old paint, especially any irregular or rusty areas; wash the pieces, using a little detergent if necessary, then rinse and dry them thoroughly. If you want to get maximum adhesion from the new paint, strip off the old paint completely using paint stripper, sandpaper, a wire brush drill attachment, or other methods. The easiest and most effective method is sandblasting, using an enclosed blast cabinet in order to recycle the abrasive and avoid inhaling it.

Spray paint releases noxious fumes, so unless you have a great ventilation system you probably want to paint outdoors—but you also want to avoid getting dust on your wet paint, or having a breeze interfere. I place my pieces in a large cardboard box that's set on its side in my garage. (After many paint jobs, the box has become an artwork in itself. I call it the Colorbox.)

If you're not familiar with spray painting, experiment on objects other than your typewriter to get some practice. Read the instructions on each paint can carefully, especially regarding drying times. Some paints dry in minutes, others take a day; you do not want to put a new coat of paint over a half-dry coat, unless you want the finish to crack like a dry lakebed.

The other danger when spray painting is runs. If the paint goes on too thick, it will pool and drip, creating an ugly mess that is going to require you to start all over again. To avoid runs, hold the spray can about a foot away from the parts, keep it moving constantly in even sweeps across the whole breadth of the object, and apply light layers.

A base of white or gray primer is necessary if you want to ensure that the underlying appearance of the parts doesn't show through the new paint. It isn't necessary if, for example, you're spraying glossy black onto old, dull black. Some metallic paints call for a silver undercoat which you can use instead of the usual primer.

A two-color effect will require masking, if you want clean lines. I personally prefer a fade from one color to the other. A touch of black or silver across the bottom of a piece can create a very attractive effect. For the subtlest and most regular fading you'll want an airbrush and well-developed skills, but if you don't mind a little irregularity, you can simply use a can, swiping a spray of the top color in a quick but steady motion across the base color.

A top layer of clear coat isn't essential; you can simply wax and polish the colored paint to get a nice shine. However, the clear coat does add extra protection and gloss.

Do you want to choose your own color, but also want the high-gloss finish and unusual treatments that only a pro can provide? Try taking your parts to an auto body shop. In my experience, the chain shops aren't interested in little custom jobs like this, but independent shops will probably be happy to do it. I've paid a hundred dollars; you can negotiate your own deal.

Other custom techniques include making decals, stripping the paint to reveal the shiny metal underneath, and even swapping parts between machines.

Let's look at a few examples of custom typewriters, mostly from my own collection.

THE BELLE OF THE INSURGENCY

This machine in revolutionary red likes to go by the nickname The Belle of the Insurgency. She started out as anything but a belle: a moldy, rusty, beige Optima Elite that I ran across in an antique shop and decided to adopt.

The rust was bad. It affected springs and many fine interior pieces which couldn't possibly be reached by steel wool or a wire brush. Nothing short of a bath in Evapo-Rust would do the trick. I removed the body panels and rubber, and immersed her overnight. In the morning, the rust had turned into a sludgy, dark film that could be rinsed and wiped off. After I dried her with a hair dryer and relubricated her carriage, she was back from the brink of death.

The beige panels got treated to white primer, bright red paint, a black fade, and a couple of coats of clear finish. After some serious mechanical

repairs (I had to replace the mainspring) and
reassembly, this ugly East German duck-
ling had become a true belle, lovelier
than any digital device I know.

A peculiarity of this model is a
removable paper support that can be inserted
in a hole in the center top of the carriage.
That hole makes the perfect place for a
carnation.

THE SILVER SURFER

I'd been fantasizing about chrome
plating for a while when it hit me that
I might also get a shiny, silvery effect by
stripping all paint off the metal. I set my sights on
my circa-1960 Hermes 3000, a typewriter with curvaceous
lines that's painted in the distinctive Hermes color of the times.
It's usually dubbed "sea-foam green." I think of it as "anemic lichen" or
"hospital tray." No, I'm not a fan.

Different metals, paints, and surfaces will call for different stripping
materials and techniques. I tried soaking the aluminum ribbon cover in
fingernail polish remover, which worked brilliantly, revealing a smooth and
shiny metal molding underneath. The paint on the steel body didn't respond
to the polish remover at all, so I used elbow grease and sandpaper, leaving
a brushed-steel surface that has its own appeal.

Hermes plastic parts are notorious for getting brittle over time. The plastic spacebar on my 3000 was crumbling away, revealing the underlying metal
support. I decided that the metal bar was more appropriate for the Silver
Surfer anyway, so I removed the rest of the plastic and polished the metal.

Silversurferizing can be a slow (but loving) process. Experiment with
chemicals and abrasive tools. Keep in mind that in order to get the smoothest
possible surface, you want to avoid leaving major scratches. Polishing steel

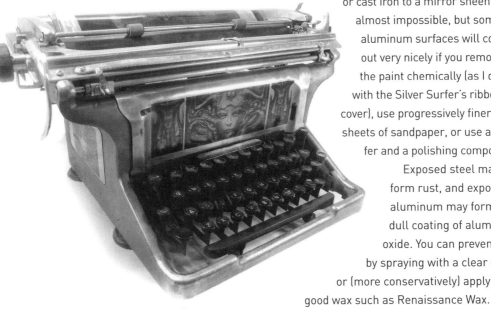

or cast iron to a mirror sheen is almost impossible, but some aluminum surfaces will come out very nicely if you remove the paint chemically (as I did with the Silver Surfer's ribbon cover), use progressively finer sheets of sandpaper, or use a buffer and a polishing compound. Exposed steel may form rust, and exposed aluminum may form a dull coating of aluminum oxide. You can prevent this by spraying with a clear coat or (more conservatively) applying a good wax such as Renaissance Wax. Transparent decals can be applied to the exposed metal for intriguing effects. Robert Messenger has used this technique to overlay H. R. Giger images on a stripped midcentury Underwood, turning it into an eerie biomechanical creature.

THE RETRO-LECTRIC

This 1953 Underwood Electric was a twenty-dollar Craigslist find. Clad in dingy wrinkle paint, adorned with grungy gray plastic keys, and smelling all too much like a cat box, it was in need of a radical makeover. Using a blast cabinet and a buffer, I gave all body panels the Silver Surfer treatment. The plastic keys came off and were replaced by classic metal-ringed, glass-topped keys from a 1930 Underwood portable parts machine. Since the keyboard layouts weren't quite the same, I had to devise some new key legends (the paper inserts that go under the glass), scanning some of the old legends to mix and match characters, and finding an appropriate font to create some legends from scratch. Other parts of the keyboard, such as the space bar, also came from parts machines. A new power cord made the typewriter safer, and the crowning touch was provided by a three-dimensional Underwood logo harvested from yet another parts machine.

The Retro-Lectric now shoots high-powered text around the world from my desktop, grungy no more.

THE PURPLE PROSE PRODUCER

This once-cream-colored Torpedo was another machine from Craigslist. It was fundamentally sound but it was weathered, and definitely needed an exterior refresher. I decided to go all out—to take typewriter pimping to a new extreme and shred the borders of good taste.

The panels got multiple layers of purple paint, sparkle treatment (glitter suspended in clear coat), and regular clear coat. Then the true extreme makeover began:

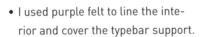

- I used purple felt to line the interior and cover the typebar support.

- Tiny purple dice (made for remote-control model trucks) went on the return lever.

- I designed the "Purple Prose Producer" name on a website that offers custom self-adhesive letters.

- I found a World War II image of Donald Duck riding an aerial torpedo, tweaked it in Photoshop (making the torpedo purple), and turned it into a sticker using an online service.

- The flame stickers and the 3D, chromelike "Turbo" emblem came from an auto shop. What's turbo about the typewriter? Well, I did increase the mainspring's tension a bit and made the spacebar more responsive.

- I had a set of extra-large, round rubber feet that replaced the modest rectangular ones. Uniquely on this typewriter, there are two screw holes toward the front that can be used to move the front feet forward for an extra-stable stance. A little foam rubber under the feet grips the desk and gives this machine a quiet, slightly bouncy response.

- The purple platen was achieved with a suitable color and size of heat-shrink tubing. I turned the platen and tubing above a gas burner and rolled it on a flat kitchen counter until it was nice and smooth.

- The crowning touch: a purple ribbon, of course.

THE TWOLYMPIA

My most ambitious custom typewriter is the result of daydreaming. The basket-shifted Olympia SM9 is by many measures the best portable typewriter ever made, but I prefer the fifties aesthetics of its carriage-shifted predecessors. Then it came to me: Could the mechanics of an SM9 possibly fit into an earlier body, so I could have the best of both worlds?

I couldn't let go of the question until I gave it a try. The answer, as you see, is yes. The body is that of an SM3, but the spacebar rides high and the shift depresses the typebasket. It's a hybrid.

This wasn't a cheap project, since you need two Olympias to create one Twolympia. I also splurged on a professional paint job from an auto body shop. Since I wanted a special typeface too, I held out for an SM9 with Olympia's print-like "Congressional" type, which looks especially nice with a carbon ribbon.

A heart transplant isn't simple surgery, and neither was making the Twolympia. The fit is tight, with about a millimeter of clearance for the typebars, and I had to do some creative tinkering with the screws that attach the body shell to the machine.

To make a Twolympia you need to keep the SM9's nonshifting carriage, but you probably want to replace some of the hardware on it with the fifties hardware. The lever for clearing all tab stops, on the right end of the carriage, is easy to switch. But replacing the carriage return lever is a tougher job that requires using a rotary tool to grind away part of the chromed left carriage end plate.

The SM9's tension adjustment lever (to the left of the keyboard) was also swapped with that of the SM3 (located under the SM3's hood). The tension control and ribbon color control are another very tight fit.

Since the keyset tabulator of the SM9 requires some extra hardware in back, I should have used the body of an SM4, which is designed to accommodate that hardware. However, with a little bending out, the SM3 back panel also worked.

Was all this trouble worth it? I can give an unconditional yes. What could be better than a typewriter that you've built yourself, to your own specifications? This one comes as close as can be to that ideal. It's both handsome and comfortable. It's a keeper.

THE RED DEVIL

Here's a delightful mechanoelectrical project by Piotr Trumpiel of London. Taking a drab Oliver portable, Piotr painted it infernal red and then equipped it with lights that are activated by an eye-catching barrage of switches. My favorite part is the light that shines through the cut-out Oliver name.

FROM WORKHORSE TO COOKIE JAR

An inconspicuous gray office machine becomes an irresistible luxury object when painted ivory with silver or gold accents and appropriate decals. That's the transformation Robert Messenger achieved with a midcentury Royal and Imperial. Here's his account of the process:

> Many standards have solid base sections, with parts welded together. However, to enable servicing of Royals, Imperials and some Underwoods, detachable side panels were built into the base frame. Imperials especially lend themselves to customizing because the carriages are easily removed, along with the keyboard and typebasket section. As well, the top plate under the carriage is detachable. Still, a lot of masking tape is required when priming and repainting, to cover parts (including switches) which are still attached to the main frame.
>
> All parts that can be removed should be cleaned, sanded (to remove flakes and chips), primed and painted separately— notably the carriage end covers, paper plate, and ribbon spools cover. Keeping parts parallel to the ground while repainting achieves the best result. Chromed strips and metal badges can be taken off and cleaned, to be replaced after painting. New decal transfers can be printed, coated, and applied when necessary (using light, gloss or satin colors is advisable if new decals are required). Reassembly should never be a race against time. It's all too easy to damage new

paintwork when putting the machine back together. Do it slowly, with care.

With the gold-painted Royal, I had to use a lot of masking tape on the keyboard, first to spray the gold, then to protect that while spraying white on the front of the main frame. I often use covering cloth in such cases, holding that in place with masking tape. Some parts were hand painted (in such cases it's obviously necessary to get the same shade in spray and can) and gold automobile detailing strip tape was also used.

To print your own decals, use high-resolution scanned images of the originals, if possible, or type the words in a size and font as close to the originals as possible. Take care to measure the originals. Buy decal transfer paper online. Clear (transparent) paper, used for dark type to be applied to light-colored surfaces, works far better than white, which is used to apply light type on dark surfaces. Spray the printed sheet with acrylic paint to protect it. Cut out decal, place it in cold, clean water for ten or fifteen seconds, dry it slightly with paper towel, then apply to machine. Hold in place with paper towel for up to one minute, rubbing gently if necessary to push out any small bubbles.

IN CASE OF REVOLUTION

A typewriter's case is another opportunity for customizing and creativity.

The typical prewar typewriter case is wood covered in black cloth, which is often stamped with a leather-like pattern. Once in a while you'll find a typewriter in a deluxe case, finished in real leather and incorporating all sorts of wonderful compartments for paper, pens, and other tools. Olivetti even offered a Gucci carrying case for its Lettera 32.

The standard black cases will often need a little work. The wood and cloth may need some glue, and corners may need touching up with a black marker or black spray paint. Scrubbing Bubbles works well as a cleaner. If the cloth is wrecked, it can be replaced with black faux-leather shelf liner for a convincing original look—or try other colors and patterns of shelf liner for a custom look. You can also paint a case or decorate it using stencils, stickers, or postcards.

Mark Petersen has replaced a case handle very effectively by the following method: Cut off an appropriate length of a nice leather belt (thrift stores are full of them). Drill holes in the leather and the case, on the outer sides of the brackets that held the old handle. Pass sex nuts through those holes. (Yes, that's what they're called—pairs of nuts, one of which screws into the other.) Use ribbon clamps (available at jewelry-making sections of hobby stores) to put an attractive metal finish on the ends of the leather strap.

An alternative to recovering a case is to remove all traces of the cloth and finish the underlying wood. The results can be very attractive, especially if you have a streamlined fifties Olympia SM case; despite their futuristic look, these cases are wood, painted silver.

What about a whole new case? Look for adaptable boxes and bags of all sorts that might hold a typewriter. An ultraportable can fit into everything from a simple laptop case to an elegant briefcase.

How to Photograph a Typewriter

You'll surely want to share photos of your typewriters--
customized or not--with friends and fellow insurgents. But
taking good pictures of mechanical objects can be harder
than you might expect.

   You want to avoid distracting backgrounds, shadows,
and reflections, while giving viewers a glimpse of the
three-dimensional shape of the machine and its mechanical
complexity. A white backdrop and bright but diffuse
lighting produce the best effects. You can either buy a
photographer's lighting kit or rig up your own. You can
             get good results by placing a typewriter on
             a white continuous surface, such as a wide
             white roll of paper or flexible poster
             board, and photographing the machine in
             indirect sunlight.

                   Your photo is likely to be too dark
             unless you take the light read-
                ing on a relatively dark part
                of the typewriter itself, or
                overexpose slightly. Don't
                use a flash. You may need a
                tripod.
                   Experiment with angles.
                Often the best angle puts
                the right front corner of
                the typewriter closest to
                the camera, giving you a

sense of its overall shape and a good view of the carriage return lever (which is often visually interesting). The closer your camera comes to the typewriter, the more dramatic the foreshortening will be, and some parts may go out of focus. Take lots of pictures and see what happens.

Usually some adjustment with image manipulation software will be helpful to turn the background completely white, get the right color balance, or bring out the details in the shadows.

For my Twolympia, I couldn't resist buying a small wheeled carry-on that has room for the typewriter and is made by . . . Olympia.

Customizing typewriters, like customizing cars, can become an artistic pursuit and a hobby all its own. It's even possible to customize your typeface, using a laser engraving machine to create new acrylic typeslugs that you glue onto the old ones; that's how Jesse England created a "Sincerity Machine" that types in the much-reviled Comic Sans font.

I'm sure that you can come up with possibilities no one else has dreamt of, and adapt techniques from other hobbies to this one. And remember: Like a hot rod, a customized typewriter is not just a thing of beauty—it can take you places. What will you write with *your* artwork?

Remington Noiseless
Portable in a deluxe case

Interlude #7

We choose the durable over the unsustainable.

I once visited a fellow collector whose typewriters reposed in a house, an hour from Barcelona, that has belonged to the same family since before Columbus discovered America. The homestead, the well-worn farm implements, and the fifteenth-century documents on parchment all provide depth and significance to living there.

But the typical twenty-first-century individual moves on to a new place and a new job every few years. We live in buildings that are often newer than our own bodies, drive cars that almost always are, and buy our goods in stores that are the same everywhere: ephemeral outlets for ephemeral things, occasionally dressed up in a designer's stereotype of historical depth. (You may even find an old typewriter on the shelf in a franchise store or restaurant, for "authenticity." But look closely; it may be a recent reproduction, a nonfunctional prop.) Our things, mass-produced so efficiently, are destined for the landfill. We don't repair them, we replace them.

What do you own that is older than you and will outlast you? Certainly not your digital devices; they fail or become obsolete in a few years. As for your digital documents, don't be tricked by the illusion of immortality that's created by easy storage and reproduction. Yes, files can be copied from your old computer to the new one, or kept in the cloud "forever." But we forget to back up, systems fail, and software and hardware evolve. There's a good chance that the current version of your word processor can't read files created by its own earlier versions

twenty years ago. And what about files created thirty or more years ago, stored on floppy disks, tapes, or punched cards? If the storage media have survived, where's the hardware and software that will decipher them? No one is sure about the long-term archival preservation of digital documents.

In contrast, your typewriter may well have been made before your birth, and may well survive to write after your death. My 1937 Remington Noiseless Model Seven, which came into my possession forty years after its manufacture, still types today. It won't be surprising if it still works when it's a century old. My habits and those of its former owners have left marks on it, but haven't worn it out. It endures as a living memento of all the times I've typed on it.

My Remington makes text that is instantly readable and will remain readable. Paper will last for centuries, given good storage conditions and a bit of luck. Your typescripts and your typewriter are lifetime companions, giving your existence a little more weight, a little more depth.

Meanwhile, our defunct computers and smartphones will pile up with millions of their fellows, leaking toxic components. The factories that turn out huge quantities of these devices will continue to demand more materials and more energy. The devices themselves will suck electricity without cease. And our civilization will race on, as quickly as it can, into a future that threatens to be still more insubstantial.

8. Intersections

A typewriter is designed to do just one thing: type.

But at the same time as it puts words on paper, it stimulates the eardrums and delights the eyes. It inspires creative misuse and experiments in other media. In this chapter we'll take a quick tour of how typewriters are intersecting with twenty-first-century art, music, and other areas of life.

TYPEWRITERS IN ART

The line between typewriting and art isn't hard and fast. A typed sheet of paper is already a distinctive arrangement of shapes that appeals to the senses. That's why Derek Beaulieu, who teaches creative writing at the Alberta College of Art + Design, asked his students to write by typewriter, giving them assignments such as: Compose a poem or story on any topic, but you can't use any

letters or numerals—only punctuation marks. "I'm having students
handing in things that they say,
'I'm not really sure if this is writing
or not.' That's what I want to hear,
because if you're not sure, then it
challenges how we read, how we
produce, how we understand."
The young artists in his class are
rising to the occasion, enjoying the
mechanics of their machines and
the visual, tactile qualities of their
typescripts. "They're loving it."

Beaulieu and his students
are rediscovering an enjoyable
challenge that goes back to the
nineteenth century. Ever since
typewriters were introduced,

Kiera Rathbone

users have been intrigued by the new possibilities they offer for putting ink
on paper—not only as text, but also as pictures, which may be original or
may copy existing art or photos. The most basic typewriter art takes the
form of decorations made with repeating combinations of characters, or
simple figures akin to today's emoticons. More complex art might take the
form of a whole sheet of characters, typed in rows and columns, that reveals
a figure when seen as a whole, like some of the more complex ASCII art created on computers. Magazines once published typewriter mystery games,
giving you instructions for creating such an image with your machine but not
telling you what it was supposed to be. In a more sophisticated technique,
a typist can move the platen freely, developing the ability to make a mark
anywhere on the sheet.

Most such creations have been considered a hobby or folk art, or perhaps a form of therapy—since some people with developmental disabilities,
such as cerebral palsy sufferer Paul Smith, have found that typewriter art
gives them the control and the creative outlet they're seeking. But professional artists and writers have also experimented with the typewriter as

One of Gemma
Balfour's Imperials

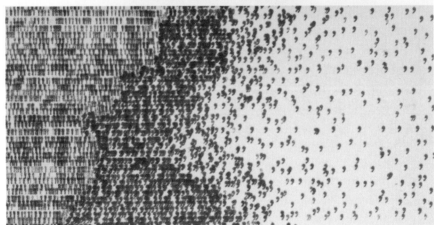

an artist's tool. You can see examples of their creations in *Typewriter Art* by Alan Riddell (London Magazine Editions, 1975), *Typewriter Art: A Modern Anthology* by Barrie Tullett (Laurence King, 2014), and *The Art of Typewriting* by Marvin and Ruth Sackner (Thames & Hudson, 2015).

Traditional typewriter art is about the typed ink on paper, but today the typewriters themselves are increasingly part of the art. Stefano Corazza

sees "typewriters used more and more in art installations as a way to create a bridge between the artist and the audience." As a thing with aesthetic appeal, made to be touched and used, the typewriter is creatively offered by the artist to elicit visitors' own creativity.

This isn't to say that typewritten art on paper is obsolete. In fact, one of the best artists in this genre ever is at work today. Londoner Keira Rathbone can type a scene live, capturing a place or person with fluid motions of the carriage and quick, intuitive stabs of the keys. She likes to type an impression of a concert

at the event itself, or use a typewriter with a non-Latin alphabet
when visiting the country where
that alphabet is used.

Another British artist, Gemma
Balfour, uses a couple of big
Imperials to build up undulating,
semi-abstract shapes inspired by
the Shetland coast and geology.
When you look closely, they consist
of commas, apostrophes, and other
typewritten characters.

Ecuadorian Pablo Gamboa
Santos's *qwerty project* extends over
dozens of sheets that build a flat horizon out of typed characters; his
drawings of people, buildings, and events materialize on that horizon.

Of course, typewriters can also create completely abstract art. Allyson
Strafella uses electric Smith-Coronas and colored carbon paper to build
dense nonrepresentational shapes out of hyphens, colons, or other characters. She loves how "the typewriter pounds the paper": "It transforms
the paper into something else. Sometimes pieces of the drawing have
fallen off because the paper is so tattered and worn." Here's where it gets
meta: Strafella chose favorite shapes from her works and commissioned
machinist Tom Curran to customize a Smith-Corona, with a thirty-six-inch
carriage, that could type all those shapes. Now she's building new forms
out of typed reproductions of her old forms.

Another artist who's fascinated by the repeated action of type on paper is
Tim Youd. He types a whole novel—such as Faulkner's *The Sound and the Fury*
or Bukowski's *Post Office*—on a single sheet of paper with one backing sheet,
reusing the paper again and again, employing the same kind of typewriter
that the author originally used. Youd reads the text out loud as he types it in
public, and likes to type in places that are relevant to the story or the author
(say, at Faulkner's home in Oxford, Mississippi, or in front of the US Post
Office Terminal Annex in LA, where Bukowski worked). He also builds a cardboard, foam, and wood model of the typewriter, which he mounts on a nearby

wall. The typing is not so much about the finished "diptych"—a ragged, ink-soaked rectangle and a battered backing sheet, mounted side by side—as about the performance, which is an artist's unique tribute to a writer.

Youd's project was provoked, in part, by a tourist attraction:

> A couple of years ago I went down to Key West. One of Hemingway's houses is down there; it's beautiful, but unusual in that it's overrun by polydactyl cats. Hemingway's own polydactyl cat was a wonderful Lothario, and they take care of these living descendants of the original cat. There's a cat graveyard, they all have names . . . you have buses of tourists, and the whole experience becomes about the cats. I asked myself: How much Hemingway has been read here, and how recently? I concluded: probably very little.
>
> Using the same make and model of typewriter and going to these places is a reintroduction of the work, and of the dedication to the text, in the most workmanlike fashion that I can come up with. If we're going to appreciate the typewriters the authors wrote on, let's also bring some dedication to what they did, which is write the work. It's a highly devotional performance.

Youd is in the midst of a five-year quest to retype a hundred of his favorite novels. Absurd? Yes, but "all creative endeavors are grounded somewhat in absurdity. The obviously absurd is provoking, in a positive way."

Poet and artist Emmalea Russo came up with a different kind of tribute when she typed Gertrude Stein's *Stanzas in Meditation* and then sewed

Tim Youd,
Philip K. Dick's
"A Scanner Darkly,"
sculpture and 304
pages typed on an
Olympia SG3, 2013

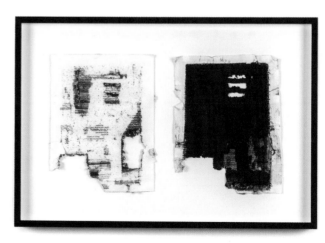

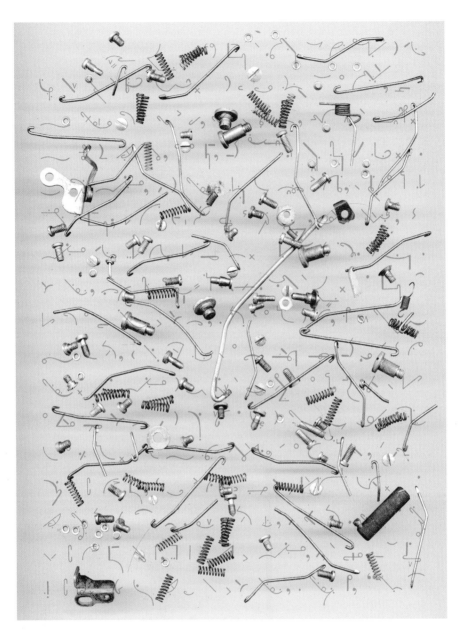

Robert Bean, Parts 8-2 (2006)

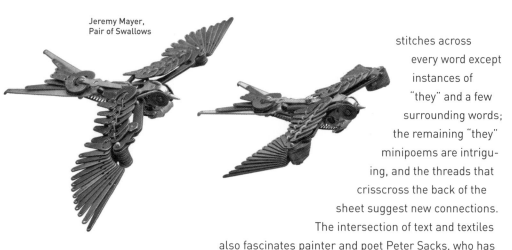

Jeremy Mayer,
Pair of Swallows

stitches across every word except instances of "they" and a few surrounding words; the remaining "they" minipoems are intriguing, and the threads that crisscross the back of the sheet suggest new connections. The intersection of text and textiles also fascinates painter and poet Peter Sacks, who has created striking abstract works that incorporate text typewritten on linen with his big Royal HH. (Don't try this at home unless you want to pick lots of threads out of your typewriter.)

Performance artist Jordan Johnson has developed a new way to type-cast, so to speak. Using presigned sheets attached to helium balloons, he types letters on his Smith-Corona until the balloons carry them off into the unknown. "The helium balloon is a metaphor for the writing. It inflates in the thought process and then it gets exposed to air and it deflates." Jordan has performed at Occupy Houston, among other events.

Canadian artist Robert Bean has explored many aspects of typewriters, from the multilayered effects of hand-corrected typescripts to the battered beauty of typewriter ribbons. He also loves the internal parts of the machines: "The cultural complexity of the apparatus, its design, function, and mechanical precision were conveyed through [the] process of disassembly. The labour that fabricated and implemented the writing machine was also revealed." In this piece, Bean digitally overlays typewriter parts with a shorthand exercise titled *Benevolence* whose hooks and swirls echo the shapes of the springs and links.

Todd McLellan also appreciates the pleasures of disassembly; his book *Things Come Apart* documents the innards of everything from an iPhone to a grand piano, meticulously laid out or floating in space. His photos of disassembled typewriters will make you appreciate the complexity of our beloved machines.

In Oakland, Jeremy Mayer takes those magical pieces and reassembles them into striking sculptures of people and animals, following intuitive and experimental methods. Mayer uses no parts or materials that didn't come from a typewriter, and prefers not to clean or alter the parts. "I like to think that the very DNA of the typist is left on the components." The results are amazingly lifelike, bringing out both the mechanical aspects of living bodies and the biomorphic qualities of typewriters.

Among older typewriters, Olivers are famous for their odd, scarablike bodies. (Check out the freakish Oliver, going by the name "Mujahideen," in the film *Naked Lunch*.) In Spain, industrial designer Octavio Saura has created a series of modified Olivers that blur the line between pimped typewriter and objet d'art, with themes such as love, luck, racing, and robots. At first these machines existed only in cyberspace, as 3D digital models, but creating the models required careful disassembly, observation, and photography of a real Oliver No. 3. Then, Saura found more Olivers and realized his digital visions in the physical world.

Some other typewriters modified by artists include the *Chromatic Typewriter* by painter Tyree Callahan, an Underwood with keys and typeslugs in the colors of the rainbow that looks like it could type an impressionist masterpiece (it can't really, it's just a conceptual piece).

Or there's the *Automatic Typewriter*, designed by Harvey Moon and Alfredo Salazar-Caro, which connects a thirties Remington portable to car door lock actuators, 3D-printed parts, and more in order to type a poem by Abraham Homer again and again and again.

Clack-Clack FACE, designed by Amanda Gelb, Jinyi Fu, and Luna Chen, is a webcam-equipped Royal portable that generates a projected, animated image of your face composed of the characters you're typing.

Another digital hybrid—but not one for the arachnophobic—is the *Life Writer* designed by Laurent Mignonneau and Christa Sommerer:

> When users type text into the keys of the typewriter, the resulting letters appear as projected characters on the normal paper. When users then push the carriage return, the letters on screen transform into small black-and-white artificial life creatures that appear to float on the paper of the typewriter

Octavio Saura, Machine
Revolution Robot

Tim Fite,
his ghost

itself. The creatures are based on genetic algorithms, where text is used as the genetic code that determines the behaviour and movements of the creatures . . . the artificial creatures created by the act of typing can be faster or slower depending on their genetic code and body shape. All of the artificial life creatures also need to eat text in order to stay alive, and when users type a new text the creatures will quickly try to snap up these characters from the paper in order to get energy. Once creatures have eaten enough text, they can also reproduce and have offspring, so eventually the screen can become very full when creatures are fed well. The user can also push the creatures around [with the platen]. She can for example push the creatures back into the machine, which will crush them, or scroll the creatures off the screen altogether, making new place for new creatures.

Sheryl Oring was the cause of cringing among typewriter lovers with *Writer's Block*, her 1999 project that crammed hundreds of prewar typewriters into rusty cages on a Berlin square that was the site of a book burning in 1933. Since then, she's experimented with typewriter-friendlier projects, such as serving as a public typist who offers to write letters and postcards to the president, or organizing a "pool" of eleven typists to record people's memories and feelings in New York City on the tenth anniversary of 9/11.

Rapper and artist Tim Fite took to his typewriter as part of his *I Been Hacked* project, which challenges our digital addictions. He rewarded people who helped fund the project on Kickstarter by "texting" them with typewritten mail. Fite's take on typewriters is all about power:

> For me, I think the number one reason to use a typewriter is how violent they are. You bash the keys to get the word you want. The urgency of ALL CAPS in a text message pales in comparison to the aggressive bite and smudge of heavy typing on paper. I believe that the human/tech relationship is an abusive one, and as our technology becomes more delicate, we lose our physical power over it. As the balance of power swings in favor of technology, we find ourselves offering tender caresses and tickles to our phones and tablets. We become the mistresses of machines rather than their masters.

In addition to all these projects that use real typewriters, of course there are representations of typewriters—typewriters built out of string, wire, wood, or paper; paintings and prints of typewriters (check out the work of Konrad Klapheck and William Kentridge); and photography galore (you can find wonderful typewriter photos on Flickr). One artist fascinated by the shapes of the machines is Carol Wax, who, like Octavio Saura, takes inspiration from Olivers:

Carol Wax,
The Oliver

> In *The Oliver*, minimal manipulation was needed to create a cosmic aura of shadows that bestow a sentient presence to this erstwhile technical wonder. . . . The striated

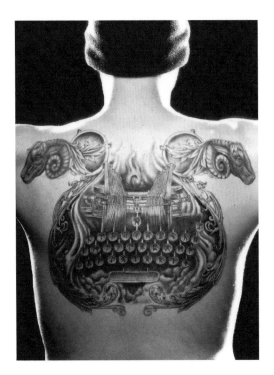

Ryan Oliver,
photo by
Matt Driscoll,
20011

environment—reminiscent of energy fields, meditative imagery, and the Looney Tunes logo seen at the end of Bugs Bunny cartoons—is meant to suggest animation of an object in its emission of an anima-like aura.

I'd be remiss if I didn't mention one artistic medium that fits the rebellious spirit of the insurgency: ink on skin.

Horror filmmaker Ryan Oliver sports a magnificent image on his back that was inked by Omar Gutierrez at Chicago's Revolution Tattoo: yes, it's another Oliver—of course—but this one types runes. Oliver owns several Olivers, includ-ing the No. 3 that was the model for this art; it was a gift that "instantly became my favorite object, and I identified with it." Other details came from ornaments on the Oliver Typewriter Company Building—a Chicago landmark—and period ads for the typewriter. Oliver's next idea: to have a character in one of his films type on an Oliver.

Zac Braun of Brooklyn is a structural engineer by day and artist at night. He's fascinated by "the simple beauty of typewriters, the simple lines, steel casing, and visible mechanisms"—so much so that he chose to have a Corona Four tattooed on his chest.

You can find many more examples of typewriter tattoos online. Why is it a popular theme? We could point to the romantic atmosphere of type-writers, their personal and durable qualities, their delivery of memorable messages and literary quotations. And consider: A tattoo gun is a machine that drives ink, jab by jab, into a soft surface, where deletion is difficult and every mark matters. Sound familiar?

Zac Braun, photo by Jeffrey Kilmer

TYPEWRITERS IN MUSIC

The rhythmic *snick, clack, ding*, and *whoosh* of a typewriter has the power to bring back a vanished world for those who heard it in their youth. It's so twentieth-century that it's included in the online Museum of Endangered Sounds, along with the noise of dialup modems and dot matrix printers. Unlike those cacophonies, though, the sound of a typewriter brings delight. Tom Hanks raves:

> Computer keyboards make a mousy *tappy tap tappy tap* like ones you hear in a Starbucks—work may be getting done but it sounds cozy and small, like knitting needles creating a pair of socks. Everything you type on a typewriter sounds grand, the words forming in mini-explosions of *SHOOK SHOOK SHOOK*.

Typewriter
Tim

That distinctive sound has long intrigued composers. Chances are good that you've heard Leroy Anderson's "The Typewriter" (1950), famously performed by Jerry Lewis.

The parallels between typewriters and musical instruments actually go back deep into the nineteenth century, when some experimental writing machines were built with piano keyboards, and *Scientific American* predicted in 1867 that "the weary process of learning penmanship" would be replaced by "playing on the literary piano."

Typewriter Tim Jordan, as he's known around St. Louis, has been wailing on the literary piano for a couple of decades. In his funk/hip-hop/what-

My top ten twenty-first-century typewriter songs

10. Ergo Phizmiz, "The Dapper Transvestite" (2010)
--uncategorizable

9. Nouvelle Vague, "Dusty Typewriter" (2004)
--alternative

8. Fionn Regan, "The Underwood Typewriter" (2006)
--folk

7. Saturday Looks Good To Me, "Typing" (2003)
--indie pop

6. David Tattersall, "The Typewriter Ribbon" (2009)
--alternative

5. Madison Ray, "Typewriters" (2010)--R&B

4. Tristan Moore, "Typewriter" (2011)--jazz

3. Marian Call, "I'll Still Be a Geek after Nobody Thinks
It's Chic" (2008)--folk

2. Dirtminers, "American Typewriter"
(2007)--punk

1. Alicia Keys,
"Typewriter"
(recorded 1997,
released 2011)--R&B

Marian Call

ever performances, he can get great percussive effects from a Royal Quiet De Luxe or a Japanese ultraportable equipped with a sound pickup. It started with a vision upon his grandfather's death in 1993: "When my grandfather was crossing over to the spirit world, that's what he gave me: He told me to play the typewriter." In a parallel artistic pursuit, Typewriter Tim fuses molten glass with blow-torched typewriters; the results look like living ectoplasm wrestling its way out of a dead writing machine.

Alaskan singer-songwriter Marian Call is a self-described nerd who loves her three typewriters (Madeleine, Neil, and Lily) and uses their clicks, zips, and dings in her brainy songs about astronomy, avocados, and love.

I learned to type on a typewriter in the school library. The library was my happy place: I was typing library cards for new books instead of going to recess. Recess meant cruel children and exclusion. Every book in the library was my friend.

I started using typewriters in my music because I wanted that specific sound. A lot of percussion sounds you simply hear as sounds; others come with signifiers and cultural or historical meanings attached. The typewriter comes with loads of cultural baggage, and I wanted that—the typewriter was a totem for me, a spirit animal. On *Vanilla* I specifically wanted that sound, to take people into a space they had forgotten for a long time. The sound of the typewriter is associated with childhood, with the movies, with history, with literature, with words, with an older moral code—maybe prudishness, but not in a negative way—and it signified all of those perfectly.

    After I finished that first album, someone asked me, "Why don't you play the typewriter in your show?" I said, "That's silly"—and then I realized that's exactly what I wanted to do.

A few typewriters in music videos

- Regina Spektor, "Eet" (2009): Spektor makes music on a Smith-Corona with a customized keyboard.

- Beck, "Black Tambourine" (2004): Beck writes on a Selectric and the typing turns into a video.

- Will.i.am featuring Britney Spears, "Scream and Shout" (2012): A noiseless portable connected to an iPad imitates a USB Typewriter.

- Sander van Doorn featuring Carol Lee, "Love is Darkness" (2011): A blonde types a note to her lover on an Olympia SM.

Today's best-known typewriter music is performed by The Boston Type-writer Orchestra. The ensemble started in 2004 when Tim Devin "envisioned [it] in a bottle of grain alcohol" at Sligo Pub. His girlfriend surprised him at Sligo's by giving him a kids' typewriter. As he tapped along to the music, a waitress asked him to stop. His reply: "It's OK, ma'am, I'm the conductor for the Boston Typewriter Orchestra." The rest is history. While Devin and some other founding members of the group have moved on, others have taken their place, banging on the keys and exploring the percussive possibilities of typebars, bells, and carriages. There's also singing, spoken words, and general silliness. Pieces such as "Entropy Begins at the Office" and "Under-wood Blues" evoke a corporate environment whose hardware may have changed, but whose drudgery is still with us: "Each morning at nine I arrive / I sit in front of my Underwood 5 / I type all day, my fingers hurt / I drink coffee to stay alert / I have the Underwood blues. . . ." A typical BTO perfor-mance starts off with what seems like random tapping but then coalesces into a powerful rhythm, riveting the audience with its sound and its sheer strangeness. The group has performed at clubs, museums, festivals, librar-ies, theaters, and on national TV and radio. They continue to explore the musical possibilities of half a dozen typewriters playing in concert.

Let's hope they keep going as long as the Argentinian group Les Luthiers. For decades they've been using a set of unique instruments, including the *dactilófono*— an Underwood modified to strike aluminum tubes, constructed

D.O.R.T.H.E.

Granville Automatic

by Gerardo Masana and Carlos Iraldi in 1967. Its xylophone-like tones have been heard in Luthiers classics such as "Snow White and the Seven Deadly Sins" and "Truthful Lulu Pulls Thru Zulus." Essentially, the *dactilófono* recreates the Typatune, a musical toy from the forties with a QWERTY keyboard. Unlike many of the unfortunate instruments of Typewriter Tim and the BTO, the *dactilófono* has stayed intact and in tune.

If you happen to find a Typatune, you can experiment with the music of various words and phrases. An electronic version of this concept is D.O.R.T.H.E., The Danish Orchestra of Radios Talking and Hacked Engines. Created by Lasse Munk and Søren Andreasen out of a Consul ultraportable, junkyard electronics, and an Arduino board (makers' favorite microcontroller), D.O.R.T.H.E. emits sounds from a radio, a printer, and other gadgets based on the length of the words you type. The next step, says Munk, would be to create sounds that fit the meaning of words and sentences.

Danes excited by D.O.R.T.H.E. might have been inspired to attend a performance of "Peeled" at the Danish Dance Theatre in 2012:

> With typewriters as the soundscape and a breathtaking light-
> ing design, the choreography creates an intense theatrical
> atmosphere that plays with space, existential scenarios and
> our perception. . . . Itzik challenges the audience to listen to
> their own inner typewriters of interpretation and search for
> the eye's blind spot—the unknown.

"Peeled" is the work of Israeli-born choreographer Itzik Galili, who now
lives in the Netherlands. Just to convince you that he's serious about this
idea, his pas de deux "Mona Lisa" is another piece that unites human
movement with industrial rhythms, including the familiar chatter and *ding*
of a typewriter—"used symbolically for its use as a tool of communication to
underlie the connection between the couple."

Then there are songs about typewriters, typewriters in music videos,
and bands that pay tribute to typewriters—such as Granville Automatic,
a female country duo named after a rare Victorian machine. Vanessa
Olivarez is a typewriter collector, and she and Elizabeth Elkins have posed
with typewriters in the desert. Elizabeth says, "Both of us write on them
frequently. Vanessa has around fifteen of them, and they decorate the
house—whispering old stories at all hours."

Just as in writing and art, typewriters have endless potential in music.

TYPEWRITERS IN FILM AND TV

There's a longstanding association between typewriters and screenwriters, whom Jack Warner of Warner Brothers liked to call "schmucks
with Underwoods." The standard format for a screenplay still calls for a
typewriter-style, monospaced font, because it helps readers estimate the
screen time for a script. Some screenwriters still like to bang out a story
on a mechanical writing machine (Woody Allen has always used an Olympia
SM3). The tradition was honored at the 2014 Academy Awards, where a wall
of dozens of large typewriters formed the backdrop for the presentation of
the Oscars for best original and adapted screenplay.

Some insurgents see parallels between typing on a typewriter and filming on—well, film. Here's Anthony Rocco:

> I was in the last class in NYU film school to actually shoot
> and edit on film; they then made a board decision and con-
> verted everything to digital. They got rid of all their old film
> equipment. The main reason I got a typewriter was that in
> sophomore year of college I took this class where you have
> to edit a film with a razor blade; every distinction you make
> has a physical repercussion that can't be undone. It really
> makes you completely change how you work, not just in a
> conceptual way but the entire aesthetic experience, every-
> thing about it. Digital filmmaking is completely different. It's
> like a word processor: You can type a bunch of junk, toss it
> around, and not necessarily use anything. There is no master
> physical version. Once I started working with film like that, I
> really wanted to work with another tool in another medium,
> almost from an experimental standpoint. Like with a film,
> I'm going to figure out in my mind's eye how I want it to look,
> and the typing is a physical manifestation of it. I'm going to
> let it play out in my brain and then put it down. In film, there
> are sequences that really need the precision that a nonlinear,
> digital editing system has, or an idea I can crumple around
> a few times and it's OK if I make a few mistakes. There are
> other times where there's much more impact to it being a
> one-of-a-kind thing. There's this letter, I typed it, it can't be
> copied, it can't be remade. That is way more meaningful than
> a digital copy that can be cloned a million times. It makes it
> special and magical in a world where not so much is special
> anymore, where magic doesn't happen.

A number of typospherians agree, which is why they pursue film photography. (As devotees of Lomography, which uses the Soviet-invented Lomo camera, like to say, "The future is analog"—a good slogan for our revolution.) Carsten

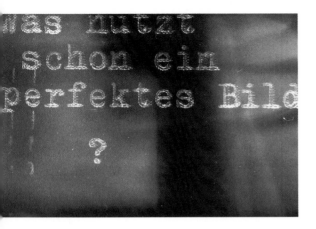

Carsten Schmitt,
What's the use of
a perfect picture?

Schmitt has even fused film and typewriters by typing onto negatives, getting some striking and eerie effects.

However, typewriters generally
intersect with movies and television
today not as part of the production
process, but as elements of the
story and symbols of expression
and imagination. One could develop
some fascinating investigations into
"the history of writing instruments
in the cinema" and ask how "cinema
encodes a changing relationship to
textuality"—which is just what film theorist Kevin Ferguson does on his
often typewritten blog, *Typecast*. Other typospherians simply like to play
the game of "name that typewriter" when they spot one on screen.

For anyone reading this book, two documentaries about typewriting
today are must-sees: *The Typewriter (In the 21st Century)* (dir. Christopher
Lockett, 2012) and a film directed by Doug Nichol (untitled as of this writing).
Lockett's film mainly consists of interviews with a wide range of typewriter
collectors, repairmen, and users. Nichol's film also covers a lot of ground,
but primarily follows three stories: the business of California Typewriter in
Berkeley; Toronto collector Martin Howard and his quest for a Sholes & Glidden; and Jeremy Mayer, who builds sculptures from typewriter parts (such
as the pair of swallows seen in this chapter). I appear in both films, and you
can see me typing the Typewriter Manifesto in Nichol's film.

For this book, I turned the tables and interviewed the directors about the
origin of their projects, their experiences making their films, and their hopes.
Christopher Lockett says:

> I read an article called "Meet The Last Generation of Type-
> writer Repairmen" on Wired.com in May, 2010. It featured
> three San Francisco Bay Area typewriter repair shops,
> talked about the recent resurgence, etc. I thought of the
> typewriter, how every great novel of the twentieth century

was probably written on one, and if the old machine was going gentle into that good night, it deserved a proper send-off. I envisioned the film as a short doc—thirty minutes—three acts.

I knew of a local typewriter repair shop, so [producer] Gary Nicholson and I visited it. And in the spirit of the film, one conversation with a typewriter enthusiast led to more contacts and our first on-camera interviews. We ultimately filmed more than thirty interviews in more than ten US states.

The most unexpected aspect of it was just how many of my personal friends, colleagues, etc. had fond feelings for the machine. Even the ones who griped about how difficult it was to work on one compared to a computer seemed to recall someone or some time that involved a typewriter. It's a subject that almost never comes up in conversation unless I mention, "Oh hey, I directed a film about typewriters and the people who use, love, and repair them. . . ." But when I mention it, the stories come. All ages, too. The machine and the memories and stories it triggers are remarkable.

I hope that the film helps people realize that the typewriter is a wonderful place to unplug. Freeform journaling on a type-writer, moving only ahead, not worrying about spelling, just getting the ideas down on paper—there's nothing else like it.

Doug Nichol says:

In 2008, for some reason I had this desire for an Underwood 5. I don't know why, but I wanted it. I found one and had it in my office, sitting there on the table, but it didn't work. I called up California Typewriter, and met Herb and Carmen Permillion and Ken Alexander. I thought: This would make a good little short film about a family trying to keep a typewriter shop alive in this age. You could tell how much they loved typewriters and believed they were going to stick around and make a comeback. I shot a short film for about six days, then put it away for a couple of years. Then I looked at the footage again . . . Tom Hanks agreed to be interviewed. I thought, this could be more than a short. I started getting more interviews: David McCullough, Sam Shepard, musician John Mayer, and Jeremy Mayer, who loves typewriters but takes them apart and turns them into sculptures. Through Jeremy, I found Martin Howard.

What surprised me about the whole process is how much I've fallen in love with typewriters. This object holds some mystery for me which I've never quite figured out.

There's something driving this thing other than myself. Normally you have a script, an idea, and you go out and shoot that. With this one, I've followed the subject and it's led me places. It's almost like the film is writing itself, and my job is to shepherd that into what it wants to be.

I've started acquiring different typewriters. Now I've got sixty-five taking up a lot of space in my office. I've taken them over to the Permillions and now they're beautiful, all working. I have three I'm actually using a lot, including an Underwood Champion, to write notes and letters.

I hope that typewriters and computers can coexist for those of us who love them and use them. I hope that typewriter shops stay open, that California Typewriter keeps going. There's no reason to get rid of a technology that's really good. As a thing that just takes ideas from your head and gets them down on a piece of paper, the typewriter is great.

To which I can only say: amen.

Two other documentaries give us a glimpse of the lives of street typists. *A Place of Truth* (dir. Barrett Rudich, 2013) follows the adventures of poet Abi Mott, and *The Roving Typist* (dir. Mark Cersosimo, 2014) is a short about Christopher Hermelin.

Typewriters play significant parts in many recent fictional films, including these:

- *The Lives of Others* (dir. Florian Henckel von Donnersmarck, 2006) recreates the East German world of samizdat and surveillance. A little Groma Kolibri proves to be a weapon against totalitarianism in this inspiring film.

- *Atonement* (dir. Joe Wright, 2007): This intense drama gives us a chance to watch a thirteen-year-old girl at a Corona Four and a handsome young man at a Royal 10.

- *Starting Out in the Evening* (dir. Andrew Wagner, 2007) stars Frank Langella as an aging writer. He develops a close relationship with a young woman (Lauren Ambrose), but will it be closer than his connection to his typewriter?

- *Kit Kittredge: An American Girl* (dir. Patricia Rozema, 2008) is based on a series of books and dolls that helped to spark the junior typewriter insurgency. During the Depression, a girl types up a family newspaper.

- *The Adventures of Tintin* (dir. Steven Spielberg, 2011): Tintin collects typewriters. Who knew?

- *The Perks of Being a Wallflower* (dir. Stephen Chbosky, 2012) shows us that a prewar Royal portable is the perfect tool for a teen introvert to write letters to a mysterious friend.

- *Ruby Sparks* (dir. Jonathan Dayton and Valerie Faris, 2012): In a twist on the Pygmalion story, a writer's tool brings one of his characters to life. What device could have such potency? Apparently, an Olympia SM9.

- *Populaire* (dir. Régis Roinsard, 2012) is a fun French film about a young woman's adventures in the world of competitive typing in 1959. (And of course, there's love and sex. The film is French, after all.) Starting with the fetishistic opening shot of a Triumph Perfekt, the typewriters get plenty of attention. Those who like customizing their machines will enjoy the fictional and very pink Japy Populaire (a repainted Japy Style from the sixties).

- *Howl* (dir. Rob Epstein and Jeffrey Friedman, 2010), *On the Road* (dir. Walter Salles, 2012), and *Kill Your Darlings* (dir. John Krokidas, 2013) feature those original hipsters, the beatniks, and their trusty writing machines (Remingtons for Allen Ginsberg and an Underwood for Jack Kerouac). "The typewriter is holy," insisted Ginsberg.

- *The Typist* (dir. Abe Heisler, 2013): A wordless short featuring a guy who loves typewriters and his struggle to find connections with people who are absorbed in their digital devices. I like the part where he tapes a real apple onto the back of his Royal Quiet De Luxe in an attempt to fit in at a laptop-infested café.

Finally, just a few examples of typewriters on TV:

- In *Parks and Recreation,* season three, episode five, Ron Swanson digs an Underwood No. 5 out of the trash, and delights in annoying his coworkers with it.

- On *New Girl* (and "Bein' Quirky," its *Saturday Night Live* parody) Zooey Deschanel's character collects typewriters.

- On *Portlandia,* the oddball Deuce Hotel offers every guest the use of an Underwood.

- And in the last episode of the second season of *House of Cards*, Frank Underwood types a very significant letter on a portable—an Underwood, of course.

TYPEWRITERS IN FASHION

In 2012, Lana Del Rey appeared in *Vogue* posing pensively with a letter at yet another Underwood. At London Fashion Week in February 2013, designer Orla Kiely put on a show where the models worked in a "typing pool" at big Olympias, sporting sixties-style dresses, glasses, and beehives. Could there be any better evidence that typewriters have become cool than their arrival in the fashion world?

Kate Spade's "All Typed Up" bag, a cute red number with a QWERTY keyboard, sells for hundreds of dollars. Wendy Costa Studio offers vinyl handbags shaped like startlingly realistic portable typewriters, designed by Rod Rojas.

Rod Rojas bag

Designer Mary Katrantzou made a big splash with her Fall/Winter 2012 collection—especially a certain dazzling red dress. Typebars fanned out like a necklace; the rectangular shapes of a ribbon cover flanked the typebars like epaulets; and a QWERTZ keyboard spread across the model's chest, with the keys echoed in elaborate folds at the hips. The dress attracted lots of comment, including in the typosphere. A simpler version eventually made its way to the retail market as the "Typo" dress, and since then, typewriter prints have been spotted on other dresses for both women and girls.

Illustration by Naomi Alessandra Schultz

One typospherian, Adwoa Bagalini, a Ghanaian living in Switzerland, admired Katrantzou's creation as well. But the more she looked at it, the more familiar it seemed. Yes, the typewriter on the dress was one that had been in Bagalini's own collection—an Olivetti Lettera 35 that she had painted bright red and featured on her blog, *Retro Tech Geneva.* In a brazen example of online "borrowing," her photo had been appropriated for the dress. Some negotiations with Mary Katrantzou resulted in a promise that

Bagalini would be given her own Typo dress. So you never know: When you customize a typewriter, it may be your ticket to the stratosphere of high fashion.

And then there is the lowest of the low: typewriter-key jewelry. A few years ago, an online poll asked typewriter collectors how they would describe people who cut keys off machines to make rings, bracelets, and the like. The most popular choice was "Not quite subhuman barbarians, but cultural vandals nevertheless, and philistines." Most of us feel it's like killing an elephant for its tusks, or declawing a cat and throwing away the cat. But keychoppers keep chopping, and the jewelry sells. Admittedly, some of the typewriters that get chopped are wrecks that are truly good only for parts; but nice machines and rarities have also been known to fall prey

to this practice. (I have a keychopping survivor in my collection: the only known Pittsburg typewriter labeled "Aztec." Its keys had to be reattached.) Some hope is offered by the availability of good reproduction typewriter keys—and, after all, the persistence of the jewelry is a sign, misguided though it may be, that typewriters have an enduring charm.

Oh, speaking of dubious practices in the fashion world: that Typo dress promised to Adwoa Bagalini? It never showed up.

TYPEWRITERS AND BIKES

Here's an intersection that sounds far-fetched at first—but there's a real affinity between biking and typing, as well as historical connections. Both inventions took off in the 1890s, with a profusion of designs that appealed to people looking for innovative and empowering machines. Several companies, such as Adler and Triumph, manufactured both bicycles and typewriters.

The Anti-Keychopper Manifesto
by Annalese Stradivarius

A typewriter is a grand old machine. It is worth more
than the sum of its parts.
It is like a living thing, spilling words of love, joy,
war, sadness, hate,
chronicling life . . . and death.

WE CELEBRATE IT.

A typewriter, even malfunctioning or nonfunctioning,
is more than just a set of pretty keys or interesting
typeslugs. Our history, our progress, has been recorded
upon these mechanical wonders since their invention
and they are an integral part of our past.
We shall insure they are a part of our future.

WE SHALL TAKE BACK THE MACHINE.

We shall take back these machines from the hands of the
ones who would disfigure them . . .
and from those who already have.
And we shall restore them to their former glory so that
their typebars tap out their song once more --
their song of defiance that flies in the face of
"modern technology" --
a glorious old song for a brave new world.

THE REVOLUTION SHALL BE JOYOUSLY RUNG INTO EXISTENCE
BY A SYMPHONY OF BELLS, THE BEAT POUNDED OUT BY A
MAELSTROM OF TYPESLUGS.

When you're cycling or typewriting, you've put the efficiency obsession behind you and you're working with a machine that's designed to respect your body. It translates your muscle movements into mechanical action and brings you down a path of pavement or words.

An ultraportable makes a great companion on a bike trip; stash it in a pannier or carry it on the back rack. Pause when you want to type a few observations. (No typing while cycling, please!) Add your thoughts to some snapshots and upload them to create a "bikecast," like typospherian Peter Baker, who likes to document his rides around the Seattle-Tacoma area with a Lettera 22, Hermes Rocket, or Smith-Corona Skyriter, and post bikecasts on his blog, *Manual Entry*.

My own bikecasting machine is a fifties Tower Chieftain—the Sears version of the Skyriter—with a stripped top and a body painted brilliant blue. I bungee-mount it to my handlebar pack. The holes in the back of this typewriter's body make perfect places for bungee hooks, and the machine is a rugged little writer, although once my left shift key did pop off on a pebbly road. It's garnered some compliments, as well as some puzzled questions: "Did the bike come with the typewriter like that?"

The greatest act of typewriter-bicycle insurgency so far was devised by poet Maya Stein. To mark her fortieth birthday, Stein embarked on a five-week, thirteen-hundred-mile trek from Massachusetts to Milwaukee by bike, towing an aqua Remington 1040 that she'd found at Amherst Typewriter. She called the project "Type Rider." In the towns and cities where she paused, she set up the Remington with a sign:

Write Yourself Here. Passers-by were invited to type what they wished in response to Stein's open-ended prompt for the day, such as:

No matter what . . .
It wasn't my fault . . .
It comes down to this . . .
Everything changed when . . .

Stein tells her story:

I was twelve and in the thick of sixth grade when my father began an evening ritual with a typewriter in our upstairs hallway. He tapped out the first lines of a short story and invited my older sister and me to contribute some sentences of our own. Over the next two years our collective words took new turns and expanded into a wildly inventive, collaborative literary adventure. . . . Nearly twenty-eight years later . . . I understood what "type rider" was: a way to share this experience of creative collaboration with others. . . .

No matter how many people came to type, or where, or when, I witnessed a transformation occur each time—a drawing inward, a focus, a concentration, an engagement that I hadn't anticipated. It was as if that intimate interaction with the keys—stiff as they were sometimes and so unlike our overly sensitive keypads and touchscreens—gave participants not only direct contact with their words but a more substantial, introspective connection with their stories. . . . The Remington Ten Forty met with the hands of carpenters and ad execs, accountants and schoolteachers, security guards and newspaper reporters, young children and their parents and their parents' parents.

Without a screen to separate or isolate their stories, participants mingled on the page and shared poignant details of their lives, sometimes even lingering afterward to connect further with their fellow typists. . . .

Witnessing strangers bend low to the page, striking the keys with a look of both fierce concentration and deep contentment, I felt . . . something in them coming alive, waking up, being written into being.

Stein documented her tour in words and photos, collecting them into an e-book along with the best typewriting from the people she met along the way.

For "Type Rider II," Stein and her partner Amy Tingle set off on a tandem bike through middle America with two typewriters, writing tandem poetry for those they met ("Give us one word, we'll give you two poems"). They also had a mission to fund Little Free Libraries for small towns. A Little Free Library is a public box where anyone can donate or borrow books—a word-intensive, paper-and-ink, freewheeling initiative that's very much in the spirit of the typewriter revolution.

TYPEWRITERS AND HANDWRITING

The typewriter used to be a rival to handwriting. This upstart that produced quick, impersonal texts was resented by old-school clerks. Typewriters even muscled in on cursive by introducing script typefaces, much to the horror of the defenders of penmanship.

Now, both handwriting and typewriting find themselves on the "wrong" side of history. As digital keyboarding has become the predominant way of producing text, handwriting has declined, to the detriment of our minds. Research shows that hand printing and cursive remain valuable skills that engage the brain.

There's no quarrel between pen and writing machine anymore. Many typewriter lovers also admire calligraphy and fountain pens; we find satisfaction in any skilled production of text on paper. Typecasters produce the occasional "pencast," or use a mix of typing and handwriting to report on their favorite new pen or pencil. The traditional annotated typescript—a first draft that gets marked up in editing—is a dynamic blend of typing and handwriting.

I myself find that different writing tools feel appropriate for different purposes. For my personal journal, lecture notes, and cards to friends and family, I like to use a vanishing-point fountain pen with blue-black ink. For brainstorms, letters, and typecasts, a typewriter is the way to go. For e-mails and footnotes . . . you get the idea.

A lot of what I've said about typewriting in this book could also be said about handwriting: It's a leisurely, ink-and-paper alternative to the dominant Paradigm. A traditional handwriting tool, such as a fine pen, can be just as durable, precious, and personal as a typewriter.

So is it time for a fountain pen revolution? Well, pens never declined as drastically as typewriters did. Fountain pens at all prices are still very popular in Europe, and high-end pens sell all over the world to an active group of connoisseurs and collectors. You might say that pen aficionados aren't the insurgency—they're the establishment (in the best sense of the word). That's why, if you really want to turn heads and rattle some assumptions, a typewriter is the weapon of choice.

Interlude #8

We choose the self-sufficient over the efficient.

Sometime in the 1870s, a skilled Type Writer operator surpassed the speed of an expert penman. At that moment, the manual typewriter became the most efficient way to write. But the manual was eventually outpaced by the electric, which in turn gave way to the word processor. Today, while some of us love to type fast, we don't turn to our typewriters just for the speed.

So why would anyone choose to use something inefficient?

Inefficiency is heating a city with a coal stove in every drafty home. Efficiency is electric heating and insulation.

Inefficiency is a gas guzzler. Efficiency is a hybrid that gets fifty miles per gallon.

In these examples, the efficiencies and inefficiencies are both means to an end.

The only question is how to get the result you want—heat or transportation—as quickly, cheaply, and conveniently as you can. And if that's the only question, there's no doubt that efficiency is better.

But is there a third option, neither efficiency nor inefficiency?

Some things we do aren't means to an end, but ends in themselves. Attending a concert, playing ball with friends, enjoying a glass of wine, reading fiction—we don't do these things for the results. If we slug down the wine or race through the story, we're cheating ourselves of the experience. These activities are neither efficient nor inefficient; they're self-sufficient.

And isn't it the self-sufficient activities that make life worth living?

Writing can be self-sufficient, too. Whether you do it with pen or pencil, by typewriter, or on screen, you can take pleasure in writing as an end in itself. We in the insurgency find that our typewriters focus us on this activity and let us explore language at our own pace. Time spent at the typewriter is time that doesn't need to be justified by its results; it is its own reward.

9. The Typewritten Future

When is a tool dead? When no one perceives it as the best way to do something anymore. The Greeks and Romans often wrote on tablets, hinged panels covered in a layer of wax that could be marked with a stylus and then smoothed out again. In some ancient art, they look shockingly like laptops. They were great solutions at the time, but the Greeks themselves would probably agree that our own tablets do the job better.

Not every old tool dies out, though. Traditional musical instruments haven't been replaced by electronic ones. Bikes haven't been replaced by motorbikes. Not only are all-mechanical watches still in production, but they have cachet.

For a while, the typewriter was fighting for life; it looked like it was going to be the next wax tablet. The insurgency has given it a fresh burst of energy. But does it have a future?

Let's hope so, because the typewriter revolution has something to offer the information age. Our movement isn't nostalgic, much as we love our objects from a bygone world. We insurgents are pointing a way forward to greater focus, creativity, and independence. Typewriters are one way to keep the digital in perspective and keep ourselves free. They remind us that "technology" doesn't have to mean only electronic devices, and the future doesn't have to belong exclusively to the new.

In fact, as a durable record that transcends the needs and pressures of the moment, typewriting is addressed to the future. "Who knows?" says Miguel Ángel Chávez Silva. "Maybe ten, twenty years from now someone will open the case of one of my typewriters and find a typed message in it. Through it, I'll be greeting the future from the past." That someone may even be your future self.

THE FUTURE OF TYPEWRITERS

If the revolution thrives, what will this mean for typewriters themselves? Will we keep relying on old machines that, despite their quality, can't last forever? Would anyone be interested in making new typewriters, either in large quantities for the typing masses or as boutique, artisanal hardware? And what about the most essential go-with: ribbons?

Let's address the ribbon question first. A few manufacturers today still provide ribbons that will work on most typewriters, including a handful of small companies in the US. One of these is Baco Ribbons, near St. Louis, run by Charlene Oesch. Charlene is a second-generation ribbon maker and the only full-time employee of the business she owns. She told me:

> You buy fabric in reels, like you'd buy a bolt, slit into widths from a half inch to four-and-a-half inches. I've got the inking machines in my basement. An inking machine is like a wringer washing machine; it has wheels that pick up ink and throw it onto rollers. You change the rollers for different degrees of inking. The rollers have a shoulder on the edges; they're ten to twelve inches long with a shoul-

der of two inches on each side, and in the middle they're recessed so the fabric can run through. There's hardened steel on the shoulders. They get worn after a while; a machine shop has to put new steel on them. Most of the time they look at me and say, "You want me to do what?" It's down to the millimeter as far as the tolerances go. There are spoolers, loaders, stuffers. . . . The machines should be preserved. They're definitely antiques; no one makes that kind of equipment anymore.

There used to be five different spool and cartridge manufacturers that did the molding process; now there are two or three. The company making the IBM Selectric III cartridges just quit making them, and no one picked up the mold. To get an impression mold made is thirty thousand dollars or so. If there isn't enough demand out there, it's not profitable.

I don't think someone could come in and run my business. It's such a specialty. One machine is run by touch. Some are run by air compressors, some by motors. The touch, the feel, the degree of inking is so specific that no one else could do it. I've seriously thought about videotaping myself doing it so there are some references. It was all in my dad's head, and it's all in my head. Nothing is written down, there's no reference material.

You can't evenly ink fabric on your own. You need specially formulated ink that doesn't dry. Supplies of impression-grade ink are dwindling.

Now I'm really busy. The competition has died; if they don't make a hundred thousand of something, they quit making them. I started to notice a rise in demand a couple of years ago. I don't solicit; I don't go for retail at all. I've had people find me through word of mouth. The ribbons go to law offices, people with forms to fill out, typewriter repairmen . . . lots of interesting people around the US.

Yesterday I sent out two dozen green ribbons. I've got an order right now for Canada. I don't get vacations.

In short, there's rising demand for a product that requires rare, specialized equipment and knowledge. The infrastructure is fragile. Is this a dire situation? Are we about to see typewriting go up in smoke?

I am not pessimistic. Some typists have successfully re-inked ribbons using ink intended for metal stamps. Other improvised solutions will, no doubt, arise when necessary. Although I don't have technical answers, I have confidence in the collective ingenuity of the insurgency. After all, there are people making needles for gramophones—and, as we saw in Chapter Four, our need to recover platens has been met by a company (J. J. Short) that rose to the occasion. New techniques and materials may help us produce ribbons without the specialized machinery that was once made for this purpose.

As our typewriters age, another need is parts. As it stands, most parts have to be scavenged from defunct machines. This is changing with the 3D printing revolution. In Decatur, Georgia, Jim Riegert of Progressive Methods sells some fifteen hundred refurbished electronic typewriters a year. In addition to buying up typewriters from estate sales and auctions, he's acquired a 3D printer to make new parts.

Typospherian Scott Kernaghan has designed a successful printed replacement for his broken Remington Noiseless Portable carriage return lever, experimenting with the shape and design along the way.

Let's imagine some more possibilities. The plastic platen knobs on the Hermes 3000 get notoriously brittle after decades. It just takes one generous collector with a 3D scanner (increasingly affordable and accurate) to create digital instructions that can be followed by any 3D printer (which is also becoming an affordable household item). It no longer takes thirty thousand dollars to create the mold for a ribbon spool or cartridge—just 3D print it. And what about playing with the exterior shell of typewriters? That's what manufacturers did, often keeping the mechanics essentially the same while evolving the exterior of a typewriter from Deco to Space Age to groovy. Now, twenty-first-century designers can create their own fantastic new bodies for Olympias or Olivettis, including fine and complex shapes that are best created with a 3D printer.

In the foreseeable future, every typewriter lover will have free access to a digital library of thousands of parts that can be manufactured at home on demand. Note that different kinds of materials are required for different parts. Some parts need to be very hard and rigid; others must be flexible but durable. 3D printers began by using plastic, but now they can make metal, ceramic, and glass objects as well. Other advanced manufacturing technology for metal parts, such as laser cutters, selective laser sintering, and electrical discharge machining, is now a reality. You can order parts from companies that own such sophisticated equipment; but why not imagine that many of these machines will eventually become as affordable as microwaves or 2D printers? You'll either make your own parts at home, or get them from a fellow insurgent who owns a printer.

So what about printing an entire typewriter? It's not a simple project by any means. As Scott Kernaghan points out, some mechanical parts may need to be manufactured to a tolerance of 0.05mm in order to work well together. But with careful disassembly and expert measurement, perhaps consulting original technical drawings and patents, it is possible to digitize all the distinctive parts of a machine. Won-min Kim has proved it by creating a "working" 3D digital model of a 1938 Remington Remette. Felix Herbst has done the same for Malling-Hansen's writing ball.

In 2015, artist Jeremy Mayer was commissioned to travel to India, disassemble the remaining stock of Godrej typewriters, and form them into

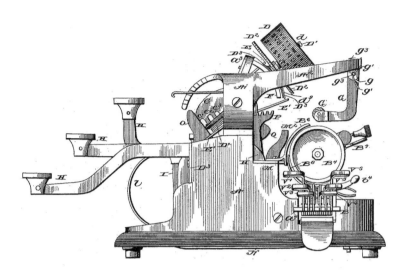

a sculpture symbolizing the new reality of the company: a great lotus that opens its petals every morning. It was a powerful piece of symbolism that might create some melancholy feelings in typewriter lovers—but along the way, Mayer created a library of digital specifications for those parts. The event seems to say that typewriters aren't dead; only the means of production are changing.

Even with new ways to produce parts, human assembly will still be required for a long time to come, but imagine how much fun it might be. I'm envisioning a typerspace where insurgents gather for a make-in. We can either set up an assembly line or work on individual projects. We consult digitized original factory drawings, 3D schematics, and a constantly-evolving wiki where those who've done such projects in other typerspaces around the world share their experiences and questions. Our printers and other machines generate parts that are supplemented with standard screws, springs, and gears. Eventually we turn off the digital equipment, admire our freshly built Crandalls, Blickensderfers, and Alpinas, and enjoy a type-in over coffee or beer.

Incremental improvements can be made along the way, allowing old typewriter designs to mutate and evolve, just as they did in the old days. Ted Munk has mounted an ultraportable on a tripod to create a traveling desk. I'm no engineer, but I've designed the Polt Silencer, a formed piece of spring wire that eliminates the rattly sound of the carriage return on some Smith-Coronas.

And Dean Jones has developed what he calls the Turboplaten:

> This platen represents what I believe platens might have
> evolved to had the manufacture of typewriters continued in
> strength. It's fairly simple to understand (if not so easy to
> make). 1) The black rubber is stripped; 2) the inner metal
> core is cleaned and polished; then 3) sheathed in tight-fitting
> PVC tubing (not to be confused with PVC pipe); and finally
> 4) sanded: a) to obtain a smooth, uniform surface; and b) to
> apply low-level heat by which the tubing bonds to the core
> and achieves a wholly practicable roundness. . . . Turboplaten
> should outlast rubber—that is, not harden with the years.

In the generous spirit of the typewriter revolution and the typosphere, such
ideas will spread.

So far, we've been imagining small-scale, limited-run manufacturing,
pursued as a hobby. Are there any possibilities for mass factory production?

First let's remember that, as we saw in Chapter Two, the typewriter
industry is not yet dead. In 2009, the media buzzed about the manufacture
of "the last typewriter," but the real story was considerably more limited:
Godrej had ceased production of typewriters. This was in fact a landmark,
because this was the last company making manual standards—but it wasn't
the last typewriter maker. In 2012, stories about the last typewriter made
in the UK set Britons reminiscing about their writing machines, but the
Brother plant in Wrexham wasn't the last manufacturer either. Both electronic and manual typewriters are still being made in China.

As of this writing, you can still buy a Chinese-made manual portable. A little factory oddly named Shanghai Weilv puts out carriage- and
basket-shifted machines that have been sold under various names, both
famous (Olympia, Olivetti) and obscure (Classic Typewriter). These are based
on Japanese and Italian mechanical designs, and come in various plastic
body shapes, including a handsome streamlined one. Recent models, which
continue the Royal name, include the Scrittore II and Epoch.

Can this last? I doubt it. Manual typewriter manufacturing is complex and requires a lot of skilled labor, but the profit margin for the Chinese manuals is low. In the US they sell for under two hundred dollars, after shipping from China and distribution by middlemen. (In contrast, a good typewriter often sold in the twentieth century for the equivalent of thousands of dollars in today's money.) The markets for new manual typewriters are shrinking as every spot on the planet gets electrified and digital technology gets ever cheaper.

Most typewriter admirers in developed countries are using the mid-twentieth-century machines that I recommended in Chapter Three, which easily beat the new manuals for precision and durability. The marketers of today's Royals have tried to make a silk purse from a sow's ear by touting their "variable kerning, subtly ghosted letters, and nuanced baseline shifts"—in other words, the erratic and misaligned typing that used to be typical of heavily-used old machines in need of service. This kind of "character" is now found on Chinese typewriters as soon as they roll off the assembly line, due to maximum cost-cutting and minimum quality control.

Electronic typewriters, which are cheaper to produce, are likely to continue for a while. They have niche markets such as prisons and police departments. But we can expect that as business and government continue their transition to digital documents, the electronic typewriters will gather more dust. And even though they may persist for some time, they hold little charm for most creative writers today. Those of us who intentionally adopt typewriters mostly dislike the electronics; there's no satisfying tactile experience, there's a delay between pushing a key and printing a letter, the visibility is hampered by a clear plastic barrier, and the cheapness and lightness of the machine makes it seem like anything but a lifetime companion. Plus, it won't do you much good on a sailing expedition or a hike on the Appalachian Trail.

So what are the prospects for a whole new manual typewriter, one that would match or surpass the high standards set in the twentieth century—a typewriter that would cost plenty and be worth it, a typewriter that would be embraced by enough writers to make it a viable business proposition? As typecaster Teeritz asks, "If you build it, will they come?"

Never dismiss the possibility of reviving a "dead" industry—or a "dead" place. Consider Shinola, which is turning out high-end watches and bicycles in Detroit. Then there are companies that are making supplies for lovers of vinyl records and traditional photography. Anthony Rocco wonders, "Is any company, in a similar way to Polaroid or turntables, going to step up? All the pinball companies shut down at the end of the nineties, but one company, Stern Pinball, saw a market. Will someone create a new generation of typewriters for a very small market?"

These questions have also been on Dirk van Weelden's mind. He calls the concept of a great new manual typewriter The Phoenix Typewriter Project. The Phoenix would harness innovative techniques to create the

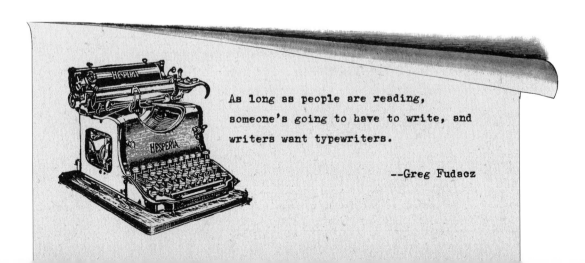

As long as people are reading,
someone's going to have to write, and
writers want typewriters.

--Greg Fudacz

perfect typewriter of the future. "The ultimate combination is that of classical craftsmanship and knowledge of the best that contemporary technology and materials can provide. So where is the portable typewriter of the twenty-first century, designed and built in that spirit?"

What features should the Phoenix have? A "perfect typewriter" poll that I ran on my blog indicated that the machine that would please the most typospherians would be a midsize manual typebar typewriter with features including basket shift, a traditional typeface, a paper bail, and sliding margin stops on top of the carriage—and we'd want it to be easy to disassemble (we're tinkerers). No existing typewriter fit all our preferences, but some favorites, such as the Olympia SM9 and 1950s Smith-Coronas, come close.

However, we could try to be more imaginative—the Phoenix might return to the bold experimentation of the 1890s. How about a machine with a carbon-fiber body that gets an energy boost from a solar panel? Or a compact, manually driven cousin of the IBM Selectric? Some respondents to my poll imagined a shift key for italics, self-inking ribbons, word counters, and a "muse switch" (helpful for those with writer's block). It might take a radical new concept to galvanize wide interest.

In his typewriter-narrated novel *Het laatste jaar*, van Weelden came up with his own concept, which he describes to me as follows:

> A completely manual midsize typewriter (no USB or wireless output) with a typewheel/cylinder (like a Blick) using the latest in light and strong materials and a clever solution with double springs (one to power the escapement, the other to enhance the power of the printing movement). The fine tuning of the mechanical solutions (such as the ink supply) would be solved using the power of digital computing and the newest in robotic metalwork (or ceramics? 3D printing?).
>
> It would be a machine with four different looks or design shells. One (classic thirties) in black or deep blue, shiny, with subtle gold trimmings. Second, a sleeker, more modern matte aluminum look, possibly with leather details. A third

one would be futuristic, techie, with different keys, handle, etc., sporting see-through Perspex panels. The fourth would have a hipster look, homier, rounder shell, faded paint colors, maybe even wooden accents.

The Phoenix Typewriter would be marketed as something in between a high-end fountain pen and a very good modern racing bicycle. Millions of Europeans own and occasionally use these mechanical miracles for recreation without going much faster than twenty-seven kilometers per hour; they own them for their beauty, social outings, mild exercise, and as a fetish to make the owner feel closer to the superstars of bicycle racing.

Estimated price (much like a decent modern racing bike): around twenty-five hundred euros.

Who knows? With lots of support from the typewriter insurgency, an international design competition, and crowdfunding, a brand-new typewriter for the twenty-first century may yet emerge.

THE FUTURE OF TYPEWRITING

But the future doesn't exhaust itself in the technical. The greatest innovations are the cultural and personal transformations in how we use things, perceive, and think—the changes that rewrite our world but that we didn't see coming at all. In the year 2000, a typewriter revolution was hard to imagine; today it's a reality.

As we look forward, we can predict that we'll see more of what the world has already become: a digital domain under automated surveillance, packed with distractions and dependencies. But that's also why I anticipate the growth of the insurgency and other unexpected forms of resistance.

What future does the typewriter revolution envision for world culture? Only an ever-growing network of data that's continually processed, exploited, and applied? Where human beings are only weak participants, assisted by ever more powerful devices that demand their devotion?

No—it's a world where the devices help, enable, and invite, but aren't mistaken for our equals or our masters. A world where each of us feels free to set any device aside and take up his or her own favorite tools—or no tools at all.

It's a world where humans can be sufficient in their finitude—mortal, ignorant animals who can do and express a few things, but who will never know or control the whole. People with a sense of their own place and who they are. People who can esteem their own inventions and achievements without overestimating them.

Graffiti by Pablo Fiasco, London

The spirit of the typewriter revolution is to select and concentrate. Instead of piling up thousands of travel snapshots that you may or may not skim in the future, focus on a few moments that you sketch, commit to memory, and describe intensely with the help of your typewriter. Instead of scanning hundreds of headlines, select an in-depth report—or type one of your own—and get to know reality through the prism of a single, rich story. Instead of entertaining yourself with a disconnected series of clips, delve into a novel—as reader or writer. Instead of spamming all your acquaintances, type a letter to your best friend. We are finite, and when we spread ourselves too thin, our life can't have depth.

What will our relation be to history? We won't see it as a trash heap of the obsolete and superseded, or as a trove of period costumes to be adopted ironically in an endless race to stay just ahead of the fashion wave. We'll understand that past thoughts, ways, and inventions haven't passed—that they are present, alive, just waiting for us to learn from them. They continue to speak to us; they can trouble us, delight us, and make us think again. This is especially true of words and thoughts, but also of some machines. They're not just contraptions, but achievements. They have something to teach us, just as ancient texts do. They can teach us fresh ways of thinking, writing, moving, and relating to the world—new ways of experiencing ourselves and our surroundings.

We imagine a future where individuals and communities can find their own ways to live, where each way, "new" or "old," gets the chance to unfold its distinctive strengths.

Making these points may require some acts of insurgency, staged in places consecrated to digital orthodoxy and corporate homogeneity— wake-up calls from the typewritten revolution.

Imagine a typewriter flash mob.

A guy walks into a Kumquat Computer store, inspects the latest gad- gets, then takes a Lettera 22 out of his bag. He places it on an available surface and starts typing. A few people smirk, point, or whisper. Then, from another corner of the store, comes the sound of more typing. A woman has taken out a Royal Quiet De Luxe and is tapping away. Now there's a third customer with a typewriter. Laughter, puzzlement, and finally a sense of awe and delight come over everyone in the store as they wonder who's going to surprise them next. Someone shoots a video, while the Kumquat staff don't know whether to chase the typists out or pretend that they're in on the joke. One by one, the typists pack up their machines and stroll out, leaving their typescripts behind. The remaining customers pick them up and read: "This location has been infiltrated by the Typewriter Insurgency." Our Manifesto follows.

Down the block, there's the local Laptopistan: a Megabucks coffee shop packed with people absorbed in their screens, silently sipping their lattes. Then the click of typebar against platen starts up . . .

I expect such events to pop up as cells of resistance to the digital Para- digm spontaneously organize—just as knitting "craftivists" have organized acts of "yarnstorming" around the world (I kid you not). Try it in your neck of the woods. I can't wait for the videos to go viral.

But the greatest typewritten transformations are the interior ones, the revolutions that happen one typist at a time. A typewriter is a personal machine, a tool that doesn't make you share anything at all, a tool that invites you to spend time with yourself. By escaping the digital Para-

digm, it serves as a weapon against the state of mind that Rebecca Solnit
describes so well:

> Our lives are a constant swirl of information, of e-mails
> that can be checked on phones, and phones that are
> checked in theatres and bedrooms, for texts and news that
> stream in constantly. There is so much information that
> our ability to focus on any piece of it is interrupted by other
> information, so that we bathe in information but hardly
> absorb or analyze it. . . .
>
> Nearly everyone I know feels that some quality of con-
> centration they once possessed has been destroyed. Reading
> books has become hard; the mind keeps wanting to shift
> from whatever it is paying attention to to pay attention to
> something else. . . . My time does not come in large, focused
> blocks, but in fragments and shards. The fault is my own,
> arguably, but it's yours, too—it's the fault of everyone I know
> who rarely finds herself or himself with uninterrupted hours.
> We're shattered. We're breaking up.
>
> It's hard, now, to be with someone else wholly, uninter-
> ruptedly, and it's hard to be truly alone. The fine art of doing
> nothing in particular, also known as thinking, or musing, or
> introspection, or simply moments of being, was part of what
> happened when you walked from here to there alone, or
> stared out the train window, or contemplated the road, but
> the new technologies have flooded those open spaces. Space
> for free thought is routinely regarded as a void, and filled up
> with sounds and distractions. . . .
>
> The real point about the slow food movement was
> often missed. It wasn't food. It was about doing something
> from scratch, with pleasure, all the way through, in the old
> methodical way we used to do things. That didn't merely
> produce better food; it produced a better relationship to

materials, processes and labor, notably your own, before the spoon reached your mouth. It produced pleasure in production as well as consumption. It made whole what is broken.

Some of the young have taken up gardening and knitting and a host of other things that involve working with their hands, making things from scratch, and often doing things the old way. It is a slow everything movement in need of a manifesto that would explain what vinyl records and homemade bread have in common. We won't overthrow corporations by knitting—but understanding the pleasures of knitting or weeding or making pickles might articulate the value of that world outside electronic chatter and distraction, and inside a more stately sense of time. . . . Perhaps the young will go further and establish rebel camps where they will lead the lives of 1957, if not 1857, when it comes to quality of time and technology. Perhaps. Right now we need to articulate these subtle things, this richer, more expansive quality of time and attention and connection, to hold onto it. Can we? The alternative is grim, with a grimness that would be hard to explain to someone who's distracted.

Typewriting is one of these "subtle things," a small island of attention and care, a meditative practice. Buddhist minister Danny Fisher reflects: "In an increasingly cluttered and dopamine-jolting digital landscape, the absolute simplicity of manual typewriters, and the attention required to use one most effectively, are certainly refreshing reminders of the importance of mindful awareness."

Let's close, then, with three personal experiences that show how the practice of typewriting can serve as a personal revolution that brings us a step closer to mindfulness.

Anthony Rocco recalls:

> I wrote a lot by typewriter in college. I remember the paper I wrote for my poetics class, a meditation on lost photographs that I found at an antique swap meet. It was a one-of-a-kind document, with no reference copy; I didn't edit it, every other

day or so I'd type a page and keep adding to it. I decided, I'm just going to give it away and be completely separated from it, unlike my other papers that sit on my hard drive in some form. But I have a fonder memory of it; I don't remember exactly the words I wrote, but I can close my eyes and physically mock it up in mind's eye and read it that way. I have a much deeper connection with it than if it were on a digital hard drive.

There's this old story about a reporter who goes on a walkabout. An Aboriginal guy goes into this meditation, and the Westerner asks what he's doing. "I'm communicating with my tribe to let them know that I'm three days out." The reporter has a radio to connect with Sydney. The Aborigine says: "You and your society have decided to evolve this ability outside your body. By using your machine you are able to communicate across great distances; you believe this thing can do it. But we have a belief that within our brain you can do greater things." Now we have completely externalized memory. Now we have a machine that holds data, so that it "preserves" it better than we can. If people want to allow the machine and technology to invalidate their body, that's their business, but I'm not going to participate in that. That's why I use and dance with machines

that are more analog. The analog machine gives so much
more back to me. We have more of an unspoken language.

In Los Angeles, artist Stacy Elaine Dacheux had fallen into a habit that
may sound familiar: As soon as she woke up, she'd reach for her device and
check status updates on Facebook. "My past was overwhelming my present state of mind. The past was in my head before the present had time to
happen." Dacheux makes an important point: Social media may seem like
they're all about what's happening now, but what they give us is reports from
the recent past, on people and topics that have interested us in the past. So
Dacheux decided to create a new ritual, her own form of status update. She
would go out in the morning, sit in the center of a little roundabout in her
neighborhood, and type on her Skyriter about "whatever the day provokes."
Then she'd mail her updates on postcards to those who wanted them.

> I am not good at typing on a typewriter—however, I like that
> I am not good at it. The way you play it is like an instrument
> you need to learn . . . like a piano. I wanted to "simulate" an
> online experience at the roundabout—interacting with peo-
> ple and recording my thoughts/experiences as they happen.
> . . . When we post something online, are we drawing atten-
> tion to ourselves or a representative of ourselves? Does our
> typing there create its own presence, and if so, what are we
> looking for? What are we missing out on by being there as
> opposed to being out in our neighborhood doing the same
> thing? This translation is what I was interested in exploring,
> and maybe I was hoping for some type of clarity/epiphany.
> I wanted to engage with people and record my thoughts,
> experiences, and feelings as I might do online, but instead,
> do it in person—trying to connect with actual people who live
> in my neighborhood.
> Typing on a typewriter feels more spontaneous than on
> the computer—you are looking outward into a real breath-
> ing space, and if you aren't doing that, then you are thinking

inward about moments or images to share. It is harder to "go back" and "edit" when typing a thought on a typewriter. You just have to push forward. It feels like letting go or meditative. I am looking less at the lines I type and thinking more about capturing and releasing the moment. There is no screen showcasing my errors to disrupt my train of thought or gaze.

Dacheux rediscovered the present through her typewriter. And in that present, she found new, unmediated social connections: Her neighbors took notice, admired her efforts, made friends with her, and opened their hearts to her. A Vietnam vet says, "I've actually cried in front of her, and I don't do that." For Dacheux, "This was incredible and definitely changed my life."

Finally, a word from playwright and filmmaker Patrick Wang, who reflects on his typecast blog:

Much is owed to this typewriter. The reasons for selecting this tool may have been whimsical or reactionary, but the consequences are solid. The tempo by which thoughts become sentences is unique to the manual typewriter. I find the tempo ideal for gathering and harmonizing many strands of thoughts, for discarding, and for switching direction altogether. Typos feel aligned with the spirit of searching, questioning. This is messy business.

In my first typewriter sessions, I was made aware how many things in my home beep. There is a mighty psychological pull to the beeping sound, so I silence all the sources when I type. Without this quiet I would not be able to make all my small discoveries, like now, realizing how apt it is that we call these beeping things devices, from the Latin root *divis*, divided. At their root they are expert dividers, of our attentions, our understandings, our lives.

So I put the dividers to bed, and there is digital quiet in the house. But then in my mind, all things begin to flash and cry for attention. Enough abandoned memories to trip over, today's passions beginning to smoke. It appears the housework of the soul has gone neglected. There is a chaos demanding a worthy opponent. There is feeling looking for form. God, even without our devices, we were already in pieces. But with time and the spaciousness of solitude, we can pull ourselves together. It is this coming together that forges vital elements of a mature identity.

Finding ourselves amidst clicks and dings, not beeps. Nourishing our powers of memory. Building communities from our reshaped solitudes. Living in the present. Discovering the future.

Let's get typing, insurgents. We've got work to do.

Sources

—

All photographs are by the author unless otherwise credited. Drawings on pages 112 and 305 by the author. *Over the Ribbon* comics by permission of Max Velati. Street art on pages 135, 184, and 361 by permission of WRDSMTH.

INTRODUCTION
Billimarie Robinson: photo by permission of Tom Reifsnyder.
Matt Chojnacki: personal interview.
Fred Woodworth, "Typographical Corner," *The Mystery & Adventure Series Review* 46 (August 2012), 26.
Comrades Unite!: poster by permission of Ted Munk.
"The Revolution Will Be Typewritten": quoted by permission of the Boston Typewriter Orchestra.
Typewriter Insurgency logo designed by Ryan Adney, rubber stamp created by Nick Tauriainen.

CHAPTER ONE: THE INSURGENCY
Mike McGettigan: http://phillytyper.com, accessed February 13, 2014.
1967 type-in: Smith-Corona advertisement, *Life*, November 10, 1967, 89.
Jennifer Rich: Grant Butler, "Old-fashioned Writing Machines Get New Respect on International Typewriter Day," *Oregonian*, June 23, 2013.

The New Typists
Bino Gan: Heather Dubin, "Typewriter Repairman's Job Was Punctuated by Changes," *The Villager*, November 27, 2013.
Richard Clark: personal correspondence.
Jamie and Matt Chojnacki: http://oldforttypewriterco.com/blog/happy-new-years-from-old-fort-typewriter-co/2014/1, accessed February 13, 2014; and personal interview.
Tom Furrier: Gerry Holt, "Five Feasons to Still Use a Typewriter," BBC News Magazine, November 20, 2012, http://www.bbc.co.uk/news/magazine-20410364, accessed February 13, 2014.
Greg Fudacz: Meg Jones, "Vintage Typewriters Enjoy Comeback among Aficionados Who Collect and Write," *Milwaukee Journal Sentinel*, June 23, 2013.
Jeff Hendrie: personal correspondence.

From Steampunks to Burning Men
2 Broke Girls: http://en.wikiquote.org/wiki/2_Broke_Girls, accessed January 1, 2014.

Wozniak's Conundrum: photo by Digital Latte, used by permission of Steve La Riccia, Steamworks R & D Labs.
Mark Hatch, *The Maker Movement Manifesto: Rules for Innovation in the New World of Crafters, Hackers, and Tinkerers* (New York: McGraw-Hill, 2013), 1–2.
Spider: personal correspondence.
Writer's Blocks, © Carol Wax, 2008, color mezzotint engraving, 9 3/4 x 8 3/4 inches, courtesy of the artist, all rights reserved.
Duane Fuhlhage: personal correspondence.
Jack Zylkin: personal correspondence.
Anthony Rocco: personal interview.
Wendell Berry, "Why I Am *Not* Going to Buy a Computer," *New England Review and Bread Loaf Quarterly*, 1987; reprinted in *Harper's*, May 1987.
Danny Fisher: http://www.buddhistpeacefellowship.org/green-machine-for-this-engaged-buddhist-the-manual-typewriter-is-a-practice-thats-time-has-come/, accessed February 13, 2014.
Leyla Acaroglu, "Where Do Old Cellphones Go to Die?" *New York Times,* May 4, 2013.
Factor e Farm: http://opensourceecology.org/, accessed January 1, 2014.
Stefano Corazza: http://www.sunflowerrobots.com/timelovememory, accessed January 8, 2014; and personal correspondence.
Time Love Memory: photo by permission of Stefano Corazza.

The Power of the Letter
John Freeman, *The Tyranny of E-mail: The Four-Thousand-Year Journey to Your Inbox* (New York: Simon & Schuster, 2009), 202–3.
Slow Communication Manifesto: http://babeler.com, accessed January 4, 2014.
Arthur Grau: personal interview.
Universal Babel Service at Burning Man, 2011: photo by permission of the Black Rock Yearbook.
Keith Sharon: http://www.ocregister.com/articles/wrote-499606-letter-typewriter.html, http://www.ocregister.com/articles/jackson-533406-jayne-letter.html, http://www.ocregister.com/articles/letters-540804-write-letter.html, accessed January 6, 2014; and personal correspondence.

Attack of the Typewriters: https://www.facebook.com/
events/454603054608160/, accessed January 6, 2014;
http://attackofthetypewriters.tumblr.com, accessed
February 13, 2014.

Activism, Typewritten
Occupy Portland: Mark Kronquist, message to TYPEWRIT-
ERS group, November 16, 2011, http://groups.yahoo.
com/neo/groups/TYPEWRITERS/conversations/
topics/51563, accessed February 27, 2015.
Occupy Portland: photo by permission of Lanakila Mac-
Naughton.
Robert Neuwirth and Andrea Haenggi: personal correspon-
dence.
Photo of Robert Neuwirth by permission of Axel Dupeux.
Andrea Haenggi (artist, choreographer, performer),
Sense-Collection with a Typewriter, at a rally against
police brutality, Saturday, March, 24, 2014: photo by
Robert Neuwirth.

Typing It like It Is
The Bumbys: http://www.thebumbys.com, https://www.
facebook.com/TheBumbys
accessed January 7, 2014; Ashley Halpern, "Analog
Renaissance," *New York Magazine,* July 3, 2011.
Photo by Billy Leland Downing, used by permission of
Viranda Tantula, producer for the Bumbys.
Mark Sussman: personal correspondence.
Personal interview with Henry Goldkamp.
Erin Williams, "Forget Twitter. In St. Louis, Bare Your Soul
Via Typewriter," NPR, September 5, 2013.
Patrick Clark, "Writer Places Typewriters Around St. Louis
for People to Share Thoughts," Fox 2 St. Louis, July
29, 2013, http://fox2now.com/2013/07/29/writer-
places-typewriters-around-st-louis-for-people-to-
share-their-thoughtsfeelings/, accessed February 23,
2014.
Bram Sable-Smith, "What the Hell Did Henry Goldkamp
Think St. Louis Would Be Thinking?" *St. Louis Beacon*,
September 20, 2013, https://www.stlbeacon.org/#!/
content/32738/henry_goldkamp_wthstl_091213,
accessed June 3, 2014.
Danny Wicentowski, *"What the Hell Is St. Louis Thinking?*
Book Finds Upstart Publisher for November Release,"
Riverfront Times, July 18, 2014.
Photo of Henry Goldkamp by permission of Robert Rohe.
Word on the Street: http://myeverettnews.com/2014/07/18/
typewriters-placed-around-downtown-everett-
interactive-art/, accessed July 18, 2014.

The Romance of Typewriting
Love on the Run: http://porridgepapers.com/new-year-new-
love-on-the-run/, accessed February 15, 2014; Chris
Heady "'Love on the Run' Pairs Amorous Authors with
Antique Typewriters," *Lincoln Journal Star*, February
9, 2014, http://blog.flywheelpress.com/2012/02/love-
on-runsan-mateo-california.html, accessed February
15, 2014; "Love on the Run Delivers Hundreds of
Valentines," KLKN-TV, http://www.klkntv.com/
story/28111084/love-on-the-run-delivers-hundreds-
of-valentines, accessed February 15, 2015.
Photo by permission of Aubrey and Josh Leeker.
Alex Cooney: Eric Hanson, "This Is Iowa: Typewriter Connection," KCCI News, March 10, 2104, http://www.
youtube.com/watch?v=gRMisGO120o, accessed March
11, 2014.
Tyler Knott Gregson: *Chasers of the Light: Poems from
the Typewriter Series* (Perigee, 2014); and personal
correspondence.
Yancy Smith: "The Typewriter People," unpublished
research, quoted by permission of the author.
"Behind the Scenes of 'Typewriter' with Muhammad
Abdullah Syed," http://www.ideasevolved.com/behind-
the-scenes-of-typewriter-with-muhammad-abdullah-
syed/, https://www.facebook.com/typewriterr,
accessed January 12, 2015.
"Yaser Khan—The Mad Typist," http://revolutionflame.
com/2013/11/mad-typist-interview/, https://www.
facebook.com/themadtyp, accessed January 18, 2014.

Digital Detox
Melrose Poetry Bureau: photo courtesy of Kimberly Moreno
National Day of Unplugging: http://NationalDayof
Unplugging.com/, accessed January 28, 2014.
Analog Tuesdays: http://www.robroyseattle.com/upcoming
Events.php, http://www.3030dundaswest.com/
blog/2012/6/18/analog-tuesdays-its-a-good-
thing.html, http://www.3030dundaswest.com/
blog/2012/9/11/analog-tuesdays-typewriters-pinball-
dj-nick-bandit-stichin-a.html, accessed January 18,
2014.
Photo from the 3030 Dundas Street West Facebook page,
used by permission of Jameson Kelly, owner of 3030
Dundas Street West, Toronto.
Anthony Rocco: personal interview.
Freespace: http://freespace.io, accessed January 29, 2014,
http://www.sfgate.com/bayarea/article/Work-play-
Freespace-4690303.php, accessed February 9, 2014.
Camp Grounded: http://campgrounded.org/, accessed Feb-
ruary 9, 2014; Matt Haber, "A Trip to Camp to Break a
Tech Addiction," *New York Times*, July 5, 2013.
Camp Grounded Olivetti: photo by permission of Rusty
Blazenhoff.

Digital Detox: http://thedigitaldetox.org/, accessed February 9, 2014.

Ellen Huet, "Party Begins When Adults Surrender Cell Phones at Unplug SF," *SFGate*, March 9, 2014, http://m.sfgate.com/business/article/Party-begins-when-adults-surrender-cell-phones-at-5302121.php, accessed June 11, 2014.

The Hipster Brouhaha

Ryan Adney: personal correspondence.

Christopher Hermelin: http://www.theawl.com/2013/09/i-was-a-hated-hipster-meme-and-then-it-got-worse, accessed January 1, 2014; and personal interview.

Zachary Schepis: http://gizmodo.com/5990402/starbucks-typewriter-guy-is-here-to-answer-all-your-burning-questions, accessed 14 March 2013.

Interlude #1

Type-out: photo by permission of Piotr Trumpiel.

CHAPTER TWO: THE TYPEWRITTEN PAST

For my knowledge of typewriter history I am indebted to the authors of the books listed at the end of this chapter, to the many contributors to *ETCetera*, and to fellow typewriter collectors, particularly Peter Weil, Robert Messenger, Will Davis, and Frank Notten.

Writing Ball: photo © Uwe H. Breker, Cologne, Germany.

Sholes & Glidden: photo © Uwe H. Breker, Cologne, Germany.

Geoffry Crabthorn (pseudonym of John Howard Clark), "Echoes from the Bush," *South Australian Register*, September 14, 1875. I thank Robert Messenger for this text.

"Busy Day" cigar box label, ca. 1887: Cornelia and Peter Weil typewriter ephemera collection, courtesy of Peter Weil.

Caligraph No. 1: photo © Uwe H. Breker, Cologne, Germany.

Fox typewriter advertisement: *Typewriter Topics: The International Office Equipment Magazine*, January 1918.

Sears stereograph: courtesy of John Lewis.

Carmen Bugan, *Burying the Typewriter: A Memoir* (Minneapolis: Graywolf Press, 2012).

Cahill Electric: photo courtesy of Berthold Kerschbaumer.

Godrej & Boyce: Shine Jacob, "Typewriters About to Become a Page in History," *Business Standard*, April 17, 2011, http://www.business-standard.com/article/beyond-business/typewriters-about-to-become-a-page-in-history-111041700035_1.html, accessed June 9, 2014.

Colin Paterson, "UK's 'Last Typewriter' Produced," BBC, November 20, 2012, http://www.bbc.com/news/uk-20391538, accessed June 9, 2014.

Michael Bloomberg: http://newyork.cbslocal. com/2012/01/30/bloomberg-defends-city-spending-on-typewriters/, accessed January 11, 2014.

Messenger collection: photo by permission of Robert Messenger.

Interlude #2

Manson Whitlock: Michael Birnbaum, "One of America's Last Typewriter Repairmen," *Christian Science Monitor*, April 26, 2007.

Cora Lewis, "Backstage: The Oldest Typewriter Repairman in New Haven," *Yale Daily News*, September 3, 2010.

Oral bards: William Dalrymple, "Homer in India," *The New Yorker*, November 20, 2006

William Kentridge, *Large Typewriter*, 2002. Spitbite, sugar lift on Somerset Satin paper, 77.5 x 94 cm, edition of 40. By permission of William Kentridge Studios.

CHAPTER THREE: CHOOSE YOUR WEAPON

Thanks to Alexander Veselak for his comments on this chapter.

Typewriters for sale at Oblation Papers & Press, Portland, Oregon: photo by permission of Ron Rich.

David McCullough: "A Bit of History About My Typewriter," http://blog.wellreadlife.com/my_weblog/2009/12/david-mcculloughs-ode-to-slow-and-a-tribute-to-the-typewriter.html, accessed February 19, 2014.

Don DeLillo: quoted in Mark L. Sample, "Unseen and Unremarked On: Don DeLillo and the Failure of the Digital Humanities," in *Debates in the Digital Humanities*, ed. Matthew K. Gold (Minneapolis: University of Minnesota Press, 2012), 194. Thanks to Kevin Ferguson for the reference.

Geared and noiseless Remington mechanisms: *Remington Touch Method Typing Instruction Book*, ca. 1940.

Underwood-Olivetti Studio 44: photo by permission of Alan Seaver.

Nick Cave: http://www.last.fm/user/BlackCoffeeDuck/journal/2009/06/20/2t9a2w_nick_cave_-_the_exhibition_(part_5:_typewriter,_computer,_grinderman_&_moustache), accessed March 3, 2014.

Larry McMurtry: quoted in Joseph McBride, *Writing in Pictures: Screenwriting Made (Mostly) Painless* (New York: Vintage, 2012), 193.

Leonard Cohen: quoted in Scott Cohen, *Yakety Yak: Midnight Confessions and Revelations of 37 Rock Stars & Legends* (New York: Simon & Schuster, 1994).

Royal Eldorado: photo by permission of Alan Seaver.

IBM Selectric I: photo by permission of Georg Sommeregger.

Hunter S. Thompson: http://www.theparisreview.org/interviews/619/the-art-of-journalism-no-1-hunter-s-thompson, accessed February 19, 2014.

Hemingwrite: https://www.kickstarter.com/projects/
adamleeb/hemingwrite-a-distraction-free-digital-
typewriter, accessed December 10, 2014.

K-Mart 300: photo by permission of Steve Hirsch.

Close-up of types: "Whisky Zulu," by Dennis van Zuijlekom
on Flickr, Creative Commons Attribution-ShareAlike
2.0 Generic license.

Urban Legend Institute: photo by permission of F. D. Harper.

"Now is the time . . .": Charles E. Weller, *The Early History of
the Typewriter* (La Porte, Indiana: Chase & Shepherd,
1918), 21.

Tom Hanks, "I Am TOM. I Like to TYPE. Hear That?" *New
York Times*, August 3, 2013.

Interlude #3

Edward Snowden: Peter Maass, "How Laura Poitras Helped
Snowden Spill His Secrets," *New York Times*, August
13, 2013.

Chinese picture frames: Deborah Gage, "Virus from China
the Gift that Keeps on Giving," *San Francisco Chronicle*,
February 15, 2008.

Mail scanning: Ron Nixon "U.S. Postal Service Logging All Mail
for Law Enforcement," *New York Times*, July 3, 2013.

Kremlin: http://izvestia.ru/news/553314, accessed February
13, 2014.

Hanslope Park: Ian Cobain, "Foreign Office Hoarding 1m
Historic Files in Secret Archive," *The Guardian*, October 18, 2013.

Rahul Bedi, "Indian High Commission Returns to Typewriters," *The Telegraph*, September 27, 2013.

Philip Oltermann, "Germany 'May Revert to Typewriters' to
Counter Hi-tech Espionage," *The Guardian*, July 15,
2014; Oliver Voss, "NSA-Affäre beflügelt Absatz von
Schreibmaschinen," *Wirtschaftswoche*, July 19, 2014.

Bugging Selectrics: Sharon Maneki, *Learning from the
Enemy: The GUNMAN Project*. Center for Cryptologic
History, National Security Agency, 2009.

Chris Williams, "Snowden to Warn Brits on Xmas Telly:
Your Children Will NEVER Have Privacy," *The Register*, December 24, 2013, http://www.theregister.
co.uk/2013/12/24/snowden_channel_4_christmas_
message/, accessed June 12, 2014.

Man typing at the Burning Man Decompression Party,
San Francisco, 2010: photo by permission of Tristan
Savatier.

CHAPTER FOUR: LEARN IT AS A BROTHER

I thank Tom Furrier of Cambridge Typewriter in Arlington,
Massachusetts, and Alexander Veselak of Mobius Ship
Enterprises in Berlin for advice on this chapter. I also thank
Annie Atkinson, a.k.a. Claire La Secrétaire, for the inspiration provided by her e-book *Typewriter S.O.S.: A DIY Guide
to Common Problems* (2014). Thanks to Jim Pennington for
information on mimeographs.

Brother Opus 889: photo by permission of Alan Seaver.

The Typist's Creed: adapted from Major General William H.
Rupertus, "The Rifleman's Creed" (1941).

Anthony Rocco: personal interview.

Yancy Smith: personal correspondence.

Les Murray: "The Privacy of Typewriters," http://www.
nybooks.com/blogs/gallery/2013/dec/13/privacy-
typewriters/, First published in *Little Star* #5, 2014.

Charlie LeDuff: "The Dan Schneider Interview 9: Charlie
LeDuff," http://www.cosmoetica.com/dsi9.htm,
accessed March 8, 2014.

Albert Tangora, *50 Common Typing Faults and How to Avoid
Them*, Royal Typewriter Co., 1939.

Tips to Typists from Smith-Corona: reproduced by permission
of Smith Corona Corporation.

California Typewriter: photo by permission of Tony Min-
dling.

Ken Alexander: photo by permission of Brian Awehali.

Matthew Shechmeister, "Meet the Last Generation of Typewriter Repairmen," *Wired*, May 31, 2010.

Kinsee Morlan, "Mitchell Vassiliou: The Man That Time For-
got," *San Diego CityBeat*, March 19, 2014, http://www.
sdcitybeat.com/sandiego/article-12817-mitchell-
vassiliou-t.html.

Leigh Raiford: http://cowbird.com/story/10721/Reasons_I_
Love_My_Typewriter/, accessed June 23, 2014.

"Typewriter Doctors" decal: photo by permission of Nick
Beland.

Chester Typewriter, 1004 East Tremont Ave., Bronx, NY,
2002: photo by David Monderer on Flickr, Creative
Commons Attribution-NoDerivs 2.0 Generic license.

Noiseless Model 1: photo by permission of Ed Neuert.

Interlude #4

Matt Richtel, "Attached to Technology and Paying a Price,"
New York Times, June 7, 2010.

Ken McLeod: http://kenmacleod.blogspot.com/2010/08/
filling-much-needed-gap.html, accessed February
14, 2014.

CHAPTER FIVE: 'WRITERS AT WORK

Visions and Brainstorms

Liz Cooke: Brian Kelly, "Typewriters Ring in Arts Week,"
Sault Star, April 28, 2013.

Marian Call: personal interview.
Anthony Rocco: personal interview.
Lauren Ziemski: personal correspondence.
L. A. Marler, *QWERTY Is a Rainbow*, by permission of the
    artist, lamarler.com.
Robert Neuwirth: personal correspondence.

Fiction by Typewriter

Red Smith: Quoted by Walter Winchell in his column, *Nau-
    gatuck Daily News*, April 6, 1949, p. 4. Cited in Quote
    Investigator: http://quoteinvestigator.com/2011/09/14/
    writing-bleed/, accessed March 8, 2014.
J. K. Rowling, "The Fringe Benefits of Failure, and the
    Importance of Imagination," Harvard University com-
    mencement address, 2008, http://harvardmagazine.
    com/2008/06/the-fringe-benefits-failure-the-
    importance-imagination, accessed March 16, 2014.
Will Self: http://www.shortlist.com/cool-stuff/will-selfs-
    long-term-relationship, accessed June 12, 2014.
Carl Wilkinson, "Novelists Are Finding New Ways to
    Break Internet Addiction," *Business Insider*, Sep-
    tember 6, 2012, http://www.businessinsider.com/
    novelists-are-finding-new-ways-to-break-internet-
    addiction-2012-9, accessed May 26, 2014.
Jonathan Franzen: Interview with Jonathan Franzen by Stephen
    J. Burn, *The Paris Review*, Winter 2010, http://www.
    theparisreview.org/interviews/6054/the-art-of-fiction-
    no-207-jonathan-franzen; Jonathan Franzen interview
    on the AV Club, http://www.avclub.com/article/jonathan-
    franzen-44716, accessed March 16, 2014; "Ten Rules for
    Writing Fiction," *The Guardian*, February 19, 2010.
Susanna Kaysen: Matthew Gilbert, "Susanna Kaysen: The
    Chronicler of 'Cambridge,'" *Boston Globe*, March 15, 2014.
Gay Talese: Katie Roiphe, interview with Gay Talese,
    The Paris Review, Summer 2009, http://www.
    theparisreview.org/interviews/5925/the-art-of-
    nonfiction-no-2-gay-talese, accessed March 16, 2014.
Javier Marías: "Chat de Javier Marías con los lectores de El
    País," *El País*, April 11, 2011, http://javiermariasblog.
    wordpress.com/2011/04/11/chat-de-javier-marias-
    con-los-lectores-de-el-pais/, accessed May 26, 2014,
    translated by the author.
Martha Lea: personal correspondence.
Taylor Harbin: personal correspondence.
SheWrites: "How to Write Your First Book on a Vintage
    Typewriter," http://www.youtube.com/watch?v=jY-
    GmdlAbQw, accessed March 16, 2014.

The Typewriter Brigade

Devin Thompson and Michael Clemens: personal corre-
    spondence.

http://typosphere.blogspot.com/2013/12/what-does-rhino-
    say.html, accessed June 11, 2014.

Poetry by Typewriter

Peter Simonsen, "Typewriter Poetry Makes Nothing
    Happen," *Aktuel Forskning. Litteratur, Kultur og
    Medier*, 2010, http://static.sdu.dk/mediafiles/Files/
    Om_SDU/Institutter/Ilkm/ILKM_files/InternetSkrift/
    TeksterInternetskrift/PeterSimonsen.pdf.
Charles Olson, "Projective Verse," in *Selected Writings*, ed.
    Robert Creeley (New York: New Directions, 1966), 22.
Claire Askew: Sean O'Hagan, "Analogue Artists Defying the
    Digital Age," *The Observer*, April 23, 2011, http://www.
    readthismagazine.co.uk/onenightstanzas/?p=1669,
    accessed May 26, 2014.
Chris Brinson: personal correspondence.

Street Typing

Franki Elliott, *Kiss as Many Women as You Can* (Chicago:
    Curbside Splendor Publishing, 2013). Cover illustra-
    tion reproduced by permission of Shawn Stucky.
Christopher Hermelin: personal interview.
Jacqueline Suskin: photo by permission of Shelby Duncan.
Zach Houston: http://zachhouston.com, accessed May 31,
    2014.
Jacqueline Suskin: http://www.yoursubjectyourprice.com,
    accessed May 31, 2014; and personal correspondence.
Photo of Jacqueline Suskin by permission of Shelby Duncan
    and Jacqueline Suskin.
Lynn Gentry: http://www.lynngentryprose.com, accessed
    May 31, 2014.
Silvi Alcivar: http://thepoetrystore.net, accessed May 31,
    2014.
Photo of Silvi Alcivar by permission of Scott R. Kline.
Kerry Leigh: "TRAILER: Baffle Their Minds with Bullsh*t
    Kerry Leigh," http://vimeo.com/36829964, accessed
    May 31, 2014.
Billimarie Robinson: http://www.typewriterpoetry.com,
    accessed May 31, 2014.
Holly Morrison: Beth Quimby, "Pownal Farmer Pounds Out
    Poems at Markets," *Portland Press Herald*, May 30,
    2014.
Abi Mott: http://www.aplaceoftruth.com/, accessed May 31,
    2014.
Henry Goldkamp: Jason Schwartzman, "Poetry for Every
    St. Louisan, One Stanza at a Time," *St. Louis Beacon*,
    November 20, 2012, https://www.stlbeacon.org/#!/
    content/27830/street_poet, accessed February 23,
    2014.
Erin Williams, "With 37 Typewriters Around Town, Poet
    Henry Goldkamp Asks 'What The Hell Is St. Louis

Thinking?'" St. Louis Public Radio, August 20, 2013, http://news.stlpublicradio.org/post/37-typewriters-around-town-poet-henry-goldkamp-asks-what-hell-st-louis-thinking, accessed February 23, 2014.

Seph Hamilton: http://www.poetry-exchange.com, accessed May 31, 2014; and personal correspondence.

Night poetry: photo by permission of Margie Pratt.

Typing Explosion: http://www.typingexplosion.com, accessed May 30, 2014.

Tandem Poetry Tour: https://www.kickstarter.com/projects/MayaStein/type-rider-ii-the-tandem-poetry-tour, accessed May 31, 2014.

Melrose Poetry Bureau: http://www.knudsenproductions.com/artist.php?id=melrosepoetrybureau&aview=bio, accessed February 26, 2015; and personal correspondence with Bobby Gordon.

Photo courtesy of the Melrose Poetry Bureau.

Typewriter Rodeo: Nancy Flores, "Poetry Improv: Typewriter Rodeo Wrangles Personalized Prose," *Austin American-Statesman*, April 12, 2014; and personal correspondence with Sean Petrie.

David Fruchter, Kari Anne Roy, and Sean Petrie of Typewriter Rodeo at the Briscoe Western Art Museum in San Antonio, TX: photo courtesy of Sean Petrie.

Poems While You Wait: http://www.poetryfoundation.org/article/243492, accessed May 30, 2014; http://www.literarychicago.com/word-saxophone/, accessed June 14, 2013; and personal correspondence with Eric Plattner and Kathleen Rooney.

Miami Poetry Collective: http://www.smithmag.net/obsessions/2010/08/04/two-bucks-clik-clak-personalized-poem-the-miami-poetry-collectives-poem-depot/, accessed May 31, 2014.

The Poet Is In: Jennifer Schuessler, "Is Poetry Dead? Not if 45 Official Laureates Are Any Indication," *New York Times*, July 27, 2014.

"Prissy": poem by Ary Katz, photo courtesy of Kimberly Moreno.

Social Typing

Robert Neuwirth: personal correspondence.

Mark Petersen: personal correspondence.

Public Typewriting: Your Right, Your Duty: poster by Ted Munk.

Ink & Bean: Keith Sharon, "Coffee Shop Suggests We 'Slow Down' . . . and Maybe Write," *Orange County Register*, December 30, 2013, http://inkandbeancoffee.com/.

LFK: Bob Keyes, "Typewriters Making a Return," *Maine Sunday Telegram*, February 3, 2013.

First Draft Book Bar: photo by permission of Ryan Adney.

Kalamazoo Typochondriacs: https://www.facebook.com/

KalamazooTypochondriacs; http://archive.org/details/MNLGloriaTypo07-08-13.mpg, accessed December 1, 2013.

Linda M. Au: http://lindamau.wordpress.com/2013/02/23/writers-start-your-platens/, accessed June 12, 2014.

The Carriage Return: http://www.thecarriagereturn.com, accessed May 27, 2014; and personal correspondence with Lauren Ziemski.

Typist on a hill: photo by permission of Stan Rawrysz.

The Typewritten Letter

Rebecca Solnit, "Diary: In the Day of the Postman," *London Review of Books*, August 29, 2013.

Postcard by Fabio Sassi, Bologna, Italy, fabiosassi.foliohd.com.

Snail mail social: photo by permission of Carolee Gilligan Wheeler.

Postcrossing: http://postcrossing.com, accessed March 1, 2015.

International Correspondence Writing Month: http://incowrimo.org/, accessed March 1, 2015.

Letter Writers Alliance: http://16sparrows.typepad.com/letterwritersalliance, accessed May 27, 2014.

Singapore: personal correspondence with Claudia Tan and personal interview with Adriana Chua.

Regional Assembly of Text: Carla Wilson, "Typewriter Notes, Papery Treasures at New Lower Johnson Store," *Times Colonist*, March 15, 2013.

Don Troop, "At Amherst, 'Clack Clack Clack' Drowns Out 'Thump Thump Thump,'" *The Chronicle of Higher Education*, December 4, 2011.

Carolee Gilligan Wheeler: personal correspondence.

L. A. Marler, *The Art of Letters*, by permission of the artist, lamarler.com.

Type-O-Matic: http://www.typeomatic.com/, accessed March 1, 2015.

La Prosette: http://laprosette.com/about/, accessed May 27, 2014.

Jennifer Hofer: Zachary Block, "An Evangelista for Our Times: Jennifer Hofer '94," *Brown Alumni Magazine*, May/June 2004.

The Insurgent Reporter

Gay Talese, *A Writer's Life* (New York: Random House, 2007), 413.

Ian Burrell, "The Times' Newsroom Set to Ring with the Sounds of Typewriters Once More," *The Independent*, August 26, 2014.

Chris Killian: http://typesofamerica.tumblr.com/post/89070347750/with-all-due-respect, http://

typesofamerica.tumblr.com/post/57726125468/leroy-in-faith-south-dakota, accessed June 17, 2014; and personal interview.

Robert Neuwirth: personal interview.

Dirk van Weelden: http://www.dirkvanweelden.net/2009/01/10/typewriter-portrait/, http://www.dirkvanweelden.net/2011/11/26/typewriter-portrait-live/, accessed May 30, 2014; and personal correspondence.

Drawing by Jan Rothuizen reproduced by permission of the artist.

Stacy Elaine Dacheux's future portraits: http://dailyserving.com/2013/02/hashtags-what-is-reflectedwhere-we-meet/, accessed June 11, 2014.

Smartphones and memory: http://www.npr.org/series/314571508/photography-and-memory, accessed June 11, 2014.

Remington in the outback: photo by permission of Scott Kernaghan.

Publishing by Typewriter

Thanks to Annie Atkinson for information on typewriters and zine culture.

I Am Typewriter: http://www.stickyinstitute.com/vault/iat/iamt2.html, accessed May 28, 2014.

Snarky Cards: http://superalisa.com/, https://www.etsy.com/shop/snarkycards/about, accessed May 28, 2014.

Micro-book: http://issuu.com/robbowker/docs/micro-book-type, accessed May 28, 2014.

Harlequin Creature: personal correspondence with Meghan Forbes, http://www.harlequincreature.org, http://20minutegarden.com/2014/02/23/5-things-i-relearned-typing-at-the-harlequin-creature-typing-bee/, accessed May 28, 2014.

Harlequin Creature issues: photo by permission of Sasha Arutyunova.

Fred Woodworth: Personal correspondence.

American Amateur Press Association: http://www.aapainfo.org/drupal/, accessed March 1, 2015.

Kids at the Keys

Boy at a Hermes 3000: photo by permission of Stan Rawrysz.

Libby Hunter: http://wordplaycincy.org/latest-news/2012/10/the-typewriter-guy/, accessed June 12, 2014.

Vivian Emmons: personal interview.

Poets House: http://thevillager.com/2013/11/27/typewriter-repairmans-job-was-punctuated-by-changes/, http://www.poetshouse.org/childrens-room/visit, accessed May 30, 2014; and personal interview with Mike Romanos.

Lauren Ziemski: http://www.thecarriagereturn.com, accessed May 27, 2014.

Type-in, Jr.: poster by Christine Larsen, thelarsenproject.com.

ADHD: personal correspondence with Robert Messenger and Tad Smith.

Magic Margin: http://www.magicmargin.net/2013/06/magic-margin-vlog-episode-1.html, accessed May 30, 2014; and personal correspondence with Ryan Adney.

Brad Coulter: personal correspondence.

Girl typing: photos by Piotr Trumpiel.

Sixteen-year-old's reaction: Maya Stein, Type Rider: Cycling the Great American Poem, ebook, 2014.

Martin Rice: personal interview.

Monda Fason: http://freshribbon.blogspot.com/p/about-me.html, accessed June 1, 2014.

Time travel with typewriters: http://harlequincreature.tumblr.com/, https://www.youtube.com/watch?v=-W_rE61115o. accessed May 30, 2014.

Catherine Stevens: Keith Sharon, "Mail Bonding: Just His Type," Orange County Register, August 19, 2013.

Ferris Jabr, "The Reading Brain in the Digital Age: The Science of Paper versus Screens," Scientific American, April 11, 2013.

Nick Bilton, "Steve Jobs Was a Low-Tech Parent," New York Times, September 10, 2014.

Steve Almond, "My Kids Are Obsessed with Technology, and It's All My Fault," New York Times, June 21, 2013.

Christmas: photo by permission of Sue Richardson.

Ryan Adney: personal correspondence.

Odd Jobs

Arthur Springer: Grant Butler, "Old-fashioned Writing Machines Get New Respect on International Typewriter Day," Oregonian, June 23, 2013.

Tom Hanks, "I Am TOM. I Like to TYPE. Hear That?" New York Times, August 3, 2013.

Interlude #5

Michael Heim, "Logic and Intuition," in The Metaphysics of Virtual Reality (Oxford: Oxford University Press, 1993).

William Kentridge, Undo Unsay Unremember, 2012. Lithograph and collage on book pages with text, 70 x 86 cm, edition of 35. Reproduced by permission of William Kentridge Studios.

CHAPTER SIX: ENTER THE TYPOSPHERE

Anthony Rocco: personal interview.

Miguel Ángel Chávez Silva: http://writingball.blogspot.

com/2012/07/theses-on-typecasting.html#comments, accessed June 1, 2014.

Paul Lagasse: "Tuesday Is Off to a Good Start," *Sotto Voce* blog, September 20, 2005, http://sottovoce.avwrites. com/?p=163, accessed June 1, 2014.

A Lightning Tour of the Typosphere

Cheryl Lowry: http://strikethru.net/2007/07/welcome-to-strikethru/, accessed June 1, 2014.

Monda Fason: http://freshribbon.blogspot.com/2008/03/welcome-to-fresh-ribbon.html, accessed June 1, 2014.

Ryan Adney: personal correspondence.

Rob Bowker: http://typewriterheaven.blogspot. com/2013/10/the-new-colossus.html, accessed June 1, 2014.

Welcome to the Typosphere: http://typosphere.net, accessed March 1, 2015.

The Rhetoric of Typecasting

From Your Typewriter to the World: poster by Ted Munk.

Christopher Poindexter: https://instagram.com/christopherpoindexter/, accessed March 1, 2015.

Typewriter Music: http://typewriter-music.tumblr.com/.

Yancy Smith: "The Typewriter People," unpublished research, quoted by permission of the author.

Gadgetry

Jack Zylkin: http://www.usbtypewriter.com, accessed June 1, 2014; and personal correspondence.

USB Royal: photo by permission of Jack Zylkin.

iTypewriter: http://www.austin-yang.com/, accessed June 2, 2014.

Photo by permission of Austin Yang.

Qwerkyriter: https://www.kickstarter.com/projects/954250822/the-qwerkywriter-typewriter-inspired-mechanical-ke, http://www.qwerkytoys.com, accessed June 4, 2014.

Photo by permission of Brian Min.

Electri-Clerk: http://www.ahleman.com/Props/ElectriClerk. html, accessed June 9, 2014.

Twitter Typewriter: http://www.fakelove.tv/work/levis-station-to-station, accessed June 1, 2014.

Photo by permission of Josh Horowitz, Fake Love.

Tweet-printing typewriter: Kim Nursall, "Toronto Mini Maker Faire, Featuring Robots and 3D Printing, a Family Affair," *Toronto Star*, September 21, 2013.

Richard Nagy: photo by permission of Datamancer Enterprises.

Steve La Riccia: S. La Riccia, *Steamworks R&D Labs* (Blurb,

2014), http://www.steamworksresearchlabs.com, accessed June 2, 2014; and personal correspondence.

Babbage's Machination: photo by Digital Latte, used by permission of Steve La Riccia, Steamworks R & D Labs.

miTypewriter: https://itunes.apple.com/us/app/mitypewriter-for-ipad/id364381386?mt=8, accessed June 2, 2014.

Hanx Writer: Ben Child, "Tom Hanks Typewriter App Tops iTunes Store Chart," *The Guardian*, August 19, 2014.

Visual Typewriter: http://www.nolad.com/vt/, accessed June 2, 2014.

The Amazing Type-Writer: http://typewritten.doormouse. org/, accessed June 2, 2014.

Hemingwrite: http://hemingwrite.com, accessed March 1, 2015.

Interlude #6

Martin A. Rice Jr., "The Type-Writer—An American Icon," *Typewriter Exchange* 25, no. 4 (November 2013), 1099.

Continental typewriter: photo by permission of Georg Sommeregger.

CHAPTER SEVEN: KUSTOM TYPERS

Peter Weil: personal correspondence.

Greg Fudacz: personal correspondence.

Scott Kernaghan: Message to the Portable Typewriter Forum, August 10, 2013, quoted and edited by permission.

Filipa Freitas: personal correspondence.

Giraffe-print Smith-Corona: photo by permission of Matt Dillon.

Magenta Underwood F: photo by permission of Jack Zylkin.

Kasbah Mod: Drew Guarini, "Kasbah Mod Typewriters: Analog Beauty in the Digital Age," Huffington Post, April 25, 2012, http://www.huffingtonpost.com/2012/04/25/kasbah-mod-typewriters_n_1453776.html, accessed June 4, 2014.

Dean Jones: quoted by permission from an eBay auction, June 2013.

Giger Underwood: photo by permission of Robert Messenger.

The Red Devil: photos by permission of Piotr Trumpiel.

Royal and Imperial: photos and text by permission of Robert Messenger.

Mark Petersen on case handles: http://www.totallyyourtype. com/2014/01/new-handles-on-cheap.html, accessed June 4, 2014.

Sincerity Machine: http://jesseengland.net/index.php?/project/sincerity-machine-the-comic-sans-typewriter/.

CHAPTER EIGHT: INTERSECTIONS

Typewriters in Art

Derek Beaulieu: http://www.cbc.ca/news/canada/
calgary/there-is-an-art-to-typewriting-says-acad-
instructor-1.2576550, accessed May 30, 2014.
Paul Smith: http://cerebralpalsy.org/inspiration/artists/
paul-smith/, accessed March 1, 2015.
Stefano Corazza: personal correspondence.
Keira Rathbone: http://www.keirarathbone.com/kr_site/,
accessed June 4, 2014.
Photo of Keira Rathbone by permission of Marc Sethi.
Gemma Balfour: https://www.facebook.com/pages/Gemma-
Balfour-Typewriter-Artist/413222882108014, accessed
June 4, 2014.
Photo by permission of Gemma Balfour.
Pablo Gamboa Santos: http://qwertyproject.blogspot.com/,
accessed June 8, 2014.
Photo by permission of Pablo Gamboa Santos.
Allyson Strafella: Suzanne Snider, interview with Allyson
Strafella, *The Believer*, February 2013, http://www.
allysonstrafella.info, accessed June 5, 2014.
Allyson Strafella, *shield*, 2011, typed marks on carbon paper,
9 x 8 inches; reproduced by permission of the artist.
Tim Youd: personal interview, http://www.timyoud.com,
accessed June 5, 2014.
Photos by permission of Tim Youd.
Emmalea Russo: http://dl.gauss-pdf.com/GPDF096-ER-T.
pdf, accessed June 5, 2014.
Peter Sacks: http://www.petersacks.com, http://
cambridgetypewriter.blogspot.com/2013/03/using-
typewriter-to-make-art.html, accessed June 8, 2014.
Jordan Johnson: http://writeaction.tumblr.com/
post/20961770591/occupy-houston-protestor-jordan-
johnson-types-a.
Danielle Furfaro, "Speak Easy," *The Brooklyn Paper*,
August 30, 2013, http://www.brooklynpaper.com/
stories/36/35/24_marathonspeeches_2013_08_30_
bk.html, accessed June 5, 2014.
Robert Bean: http://www.circuitgallery.com/browse-by/
artist/gallery-artists/robert-bean/, accessed June 5,
2014; and personal correspondence.
Parts 8-2, 2006, reproduced by permission of the artist.
Jeremy Mayer: http://jeremymayer.com/, accessed June 5,
2014; and personal correspondence.
Pair of Swallows: photo by permission of the artist.
Octavio Saura: http://theoctavioart.com/, accessed June 5,
2014; and personal correspondence.
Machine Revolution Robot: photo by permission of the artist.
Chromatic Typewriter: http://tyreecallahan.blogspot.
com/2011/12/introducing-chromatic-typewriter-2012.
html; accessed June 5, 2014.
Automatic Typewriter: http://vimeo.com/63481843,
accessed June 5, 2014
Clack Clack FACE: http://www.engadget.com/2013/12/16/
clack-clack-face/, http://chenqingyuan.
me/?portfolio=clackclackface, accessed June 8, 2014.
Life Writer: http://www.interface.ufg.ac.at/christa-laurent/
WORKS/CONCEPTS/LifeWriterConcept.html, http://
vimeo.com/63735655, accessed June 10, 2014.
Sheryl Oring: http://www.sheryloring.org/, accessed June
5, 2014.
Tim Fite: Eric R. Danton, "Rap Satirist Tim Fite Takes On
Tech," *Wall Street Journal*, October 2, 2014; Ben
Greenman, "Only Disconnect," *New Yorker*, October 6,
2014; and personal correspondence.
his ghost: reproduced by permission of the artist.
Carol Wax: personal correspondence.
The Oliver, © Carol Wax, 2004, Color mezzotint engraving,
Image: 18 x 18 inches, courtesy of the artist, all rights
reserved.
Ryan Oliver: http://www.deathblowproductions.com/DBBio.
html; and personal correspondence.
Photo by permission of Ryan Oliver and Matt Driscoll,
photographer.
Zac Braun: http://www.papermag.com/2009/04/kids_from_
my_travels_zac_braun.php, accessed June 5, 2014;
and personal correspondence.
Photo by permission of Zac Braun and Jeffrey Kilmer,
photographer.
Thanks to Molly Rubin for her insights on typewriters and
tattoos.

Typewriters in Music

Museum of Endangered Sounds: http://mrgory.info/sm/#,
accessed June 6, 2014.
Tom Hanks: "I Am TOM. I Like to TYPE. Hear That?" *New
York Times*, August 3, 2013.
Literary piano: "Type Writing Machine," *Scientific American*,
July 6, 1867, 5.
Top 10 typewriter songs: with help from Ton Sison and
from Thomas Blatchford's *QWERTY Pop* (typewritten
zine compiled for the I Am Typewriter festival, 2011)
along with his playlist at http://www.mixcloud.com/
ttfb/qwerty-pop-a-typewriter-based-compilation/,
accessed June 7, 2014.
Typewriter Tim: Stefene Russell, "King Qwerty: The Return
of Typewriter Tim," *St. Louis Magazine*, August 2006;
Thomas Crone, "Typewriter Tim's Documentary Day:
Massages, Glass-Pouring, and a Gig at the Venice,"

St. Louis Magazine, November 21, 2012; https://www.youtube.com/watch?v=_IdcXh1ht54, https://myspace.com/typejordan, https://www.facebook.com/typejordan, accessed June 6, 2014.

Photo of Typewriter Tim by permission of Tony Favarula.

Marian Call: http://mariancall.com, accessed June 7, 2014; and personal interview.

Photo of Marian Call by permission of Brian Adams, baphotos.com.

Boston Typewriter Orchestra: Mary Curtin, "The Boston Typewriter Orchestra Performs Their Comedic Satirical Repertoire," *Charlestown (MA) Patch*, November 10, 2010.

Sean Hurley, "Boston Orchestra Makes Typewriters Sing," NPR, October 9, 2008, http://www.bostontypewriterorchestra.com/, accessed June 6, 2014.

Les Luthiers: http://www.lesluthiers.org/, https://www.youtube.com/watch?v=FAzYLWlOf0o, accessed June 6, 2014.

D.O.R.T.H.E.: http://www.soundjuggling.com/projects/dorthe, http://www.creativeapplications.net/maxmsp/d-o-r-t-h-e-creating-music-from-thoughts-written-in-the-form-of-words-and-sentences/, accessed June 7, 2014.

Photo of D.O.R.T.H.E. by permission of Lasse Munk.

Itzik Galili: http://www.danskdanseteater.dk/node/228, http://contemporarydancevideos.com/itzik-galili-mona-lisa/, accessed June 7, 2014.

Granville Automatic: http://granvilleautomatic.com, accessed June 7, 2014.

Personal correspondence with Elizabeth Elkins.

Photo by permission of Abby Linne.

Typewriters in Film and TV

Max Wilk, *Schmucks with Underwoods: Conversations with America's Classic Screenwriters* (New York: Applause, 2004).

Anthony Rocco: personal interview.

Carsten Schmitt: http://carstenschmitt.wordpress.com/2013/09/06/phot-o-type-fun-with-typewriters-and-film/, accessed June 8, 2014.

Photo by permission of Carsten Schmitt.

Kevin Ferguson: http://typecast.qwriting.qc.cuny.edu/2012/03/18/written-on-the-scrim/, accessed June 10, 2014.

Christopher Lockett: personal correspondence.

Doug Nichol: personal correspondence.

Bill Morgan, *The Typewriter Is Holy: The Complete, Uncensored History of the Beat Generation* (Berkeley: Counterpoint, 2010).

Typewriters in Fashion

Lana Del Rey: *Vogue Australia*, October 2012.

Orla Kiely: http://blog.krisatomic.com/?p=6507, accessed June 7, 2014.

Rod Rojas bag: http://www.wendycosta.com, accessed June 7, 2014.

Photo by permission of Wendy Costa, Wendy Costa Studio.

Mary Katrantzou typewriter dress: http://nymag.com/thecut/2012/03/typewriter-collector-scores-free-katrantzou-dress.html, http://www.retrotechgeneva.net/2010/12/olivetti-lettera-35-revisited-and.html, http://www.retrotechgeneva.net/2012/03/mary-katrantzous-red-typewriter-dress.html, accessed June 7, 2014; personal correspondence with Adwoa Bagalini.

Illustration of Mary Katrantzou typewriter dress by Naomi Alessandra Schultz, reproduced by permission of the artist.

Key jewelry: Poll results in TYPEWRITERS group, December 11, 2005, https://groups.yahoo.com/neo/groups/TYPEWRITERS/conversations/topics/30306.

"?!" keys: photo by permission of Carsten Schmitt.

The Anti-Keychopper Manifesto: by permission of Jennifer Sexton.

Typewriters and Bikes

Maya Stein, *Type Rider: Cycling the Great American Poem*, ebook, 2014, http://www.mayastein.com/type-rider/, http://www.huffingtonpost.com/maya-stein/typewriter-pilgrimage_b_1940782.html, https://www.kickstarter.com/projects/MayaStein/type-rider-ii-the-tandem-poetry-tour, accessed June 8, 2014.

Photo by permission of Maya Stein.

Typewriters and Handwriting

Maria Konnikova, "What's Lost as Handwriting Fades," *New York Times*, June 2, 2014.

What to do with small notebooks, reproduced by permission of Cheryl Lowry and Iris Carpenter.

Interlude #8
Photo by permission of Amy Miller.

CHAPTER NINE: THE TYPEWRITTEN FUTURE

Miguel Ángel Chávez Silva: http://writingball.blogspot.com/2012/07/theses-on-typecasting.html#comments, accessed June 9, 2014.

The Future of Typewriters

Charlene Oesch: personal interview.

Progressive Methods: Adam Ragusea, "Typewriters, Somehow, Still in Demand," Marketplace Morning Report, November 14, 2013, http://ssl.marketplace.org/topics/business/typewriters-somehow-still-demand, accessed June 9, 2014.

Scott Kernaghan: http://filthyplaten.blogspot.com.au/2012/07/mystery-part-or-six-million-dollar.html, http://filthyplaten.blogspot.com/2014/04/thoughts-on-3d-printing-typewriter.html, accessed June 9, 2014.

Digital Remette: Won-min Kim, "E128 Final Project Type-writer (UC Berkeley, Spring 10')," https://www.youtube.com/watch?v=Ki6CC_Fmg-g, accessed June 9, 2014.

Digital Writing Ball: http://www.malling-hansen.org/the-writing-ball.html, accessed February 15, 2015.

Jeremy Mayer: personal correspondence. US Patent #472,692 by George C. Blickensderfer

Typewriter on a tripod: http://munk.org/typecast/2013/02/15/tripod-mounted-empire-aristocrat-field-typewriter/, accessed June 12, 2014.

Polt Silencer: http://writingball.blogspot.com/2012/04/mystery-revealed-polt-silencer.html, accessed June 9, 2014.

Dean Jones: quoted by permission from an eBay auction, June 2013.

Description of new Royal portables: http://www.hammacher.com/Product/Default.aspx?sku=84295&refsku=82670, accessed June 9, 2014.

"If You Build It, Will They Come?- Could a Modern Type-writer Company Succeed?" The Teeritz Agenda, November 23, 2013, http://teeritz.blogspot.com/2013/11/if-you-build-it-will-they-come-could.html, accessed June 9, 2014.

Anthony Rocco: personal interview.

Greg Fudacz: personal interview.

The Phoenix Typewriter: http://www.dirkvanweelden.net/the-phoenix-typewriter/, accessed June 9, 2014; and personal correspondence with Dirk van Weelden.

Poll: http://writingball.blogspot.com/2014/04/the-perfect-typewriter-results.html, accessed June 9, 2014.

The Future of Typewriting

Graffiti by Pablo Fiasco: "Typewriter Head, Brick Lane," photo by Cory Doctorow on Flickr, Creative Commons Attribution-ShareAlike 2.0 Generic license.

Rebecca Solnit, "Diary: In the Day of the Postman," *London Review of Books*, August 29, 2013.

Danny Fisher: http://www.buddhistpeacefellowship.org/green-machine-for-this-engaged-buddhist-the-manual-typewriter-is-a-practice-thats-time-has-come/, accessed June 3, 2014.

Nick Reynolds, *Self (A Portrait of Will Self)*: photograph by permission of RedHouse Originals.

Anthony Rocco: personal interview.

Stacy Elaine Dacheux: personal interview and correspondence, http://revisingloneliness.com/2013/11/16/the-roundabout/, accessed June 10, 2014.

Nita Lelyveld, "A Writer's Experiment Becomes a Neighborhood Ritual," *Los Angeles Times*, November 28, 2013.

Photo by permission of Stacy Elanie Dacheux and Allan McLeod, photographer.

Patrick Wang: http://monkeyatatypewriter.com/2013/09/22/tomorrowand/, accessed June 10, 2014.

Index

—